ANSWERS
FROM THE
ANCESTRAL
REALMS

ALSO BY SHARON ANNE KLINGLER

Books

Intuition & Beyond

Life with Spirit

The Magic of Gemstones

*Power Words**

*Secrets of Success** (with Sandra Anne Taylor)

Speaking to Spirit Workbook

Card Deck

*The Akashic Tarot** (with Sandra Anne Taylor)

Kits

Advanced Spirit Communication

Drawing on Your Intuition

GemCast: A Gemstone Oracle for Your Future

Speaking to Spirit Workbook (deluxe and seminar editions)

Audio Programs

*Archangels, Higher Realms, Higher Powers**

*Healing Journeys Guided Meditations** (with Sandra Anne Taylor)

*Meditations & Visualizations for Divine Connections**

*Meditations for Speaking to Spirit**

*Openings to Your Spirit Guides**

*Spirit Comes to Life!**

*Meditations to Tap the Powers of Spirit**

*Travel into Your Past Lives**

*Winds of Possibility Meditations**

*Working with the Masters**

*Available from Hay House

Please visit: Hay House USA: www.hayhouse.com®; Hay House Australia:
www.hayhouse.com.au; Hay House UK: www.hayhouse.co.uk;
Hay House India: www.hayhouse.co.in

ANSWERS
FROM THE
ANCESTRAL
REALMS

Get Psychic Help from
·············· Your ··············
Spirit Guides Every Day

Sharon Anne Klingler

HAY HOUSE, INC.
Carlsbad, California • New York City
London • Sydney • New Delhi

Published in the United States by: Hay House, Inc.: www.hayhouse.com®
Published in Australia by: Hay House Australia Pty. Ltd.: www.hayhouse.com.au
Published in the United Kingdom by: Hay House UK, Ltd.: www.hayhouse.co.uk
Published in India by: Hay House Publishers India: www.hayhouse.co.in

Cover design: Shubhani Sarker • *Interior design:* Nick C. Welch

**Cataloging-in-Publication Data
is on file with the Library of Congress**

Tradepaper ISBN: 978-1-4019-6414-6
E-book ISBN: 978-1-4019-6422-1
Audiobook ISBN: 978-1-4019-6537-2

11 10 9 8 7 6 5 4 3 2
1st edition, October 2022

Printed in the United States of America

To our dear friends whose lights will live forever:
Rev. John C. White
Michael Freedman
Linda Smigel
Stephanie Turachak
George Koury

Contents

INTRODUCTION

Your greater consciousness is in constant connection with the consciousness of all others, part of an inseparable and undivided whole. You're in an energetic relationship with every other person on the planet—as well as those who have passed. This book is your guide to turning on your intuitive senses so you can connect with all of the spirits in the ancestral world, including your Higher Self, your loved ones, and all your different ancestral guides.

For myself, growing up as an identical twin was a daily and life-long training in telepathy. There are lots of special connections that happen for siblings no matter where they were born or where they lived. But the experience of being an identical twin carries with it an impact that, I think, only twins can truly understand.

Many extraordinary events happened with my sister and me that could go beyond the description of *otherworldly:* feeling a touch and other physical sensations when nobody was in the room; hearing words and noises when there wasn't a sound; knowing events, thoughts, and feelings when they were happening many miles away. It all came down to a sharing of the minds that occurred spontaneously and—because we really didn't know any better—always seemed completely normal.

My childhood was a gift that helped kick the doors open on other telepathic experiences at a very early age—and for the rest of my life. I started reading Tarot at 14, and that set me on a course to greater intuitive experiences, including becoming a professional reader. But when spirit started coming to my psychic consultations, I realized that these were not just psychic sensations but messages from spirit people.

Many of the spirit folk who first appeared to me were my clients' fathers and grandmothers and other family members in spirit. So I thought, as most people do, that *ancestors* belonged only to family. I soon found out that I was wrong. The word *ancestor* simply means "those who have gone before." And there are many, many different kinds of people who have gone before.

Writers who had already gone to spirit, came to the readings of people who had writing projects. So did architects, musicians, journalists, and all manner of spirit people interested in what my clients were doing. They were not biologically related to my clients, but they were energetically connected to them, having had done those very activities before in their own lives. There were also those who had gone before on their own evolutionary journeys, who came to share their spiritual insight and guidance.

My life has been a wonderful discovery of spirit that I have loved sharing with my clients and students. I have been a professional medium for more than 40 years, and I have taught spirit communication, reincarnation, and all manner of spiritual studies all around the world. Whether I was teaching classes in lovely, little Spiritualist churches in Toronto or Annapolis, or lecturing at Georgetown University or St. James Church on Piccadilly in London, people around the globe have always had a few important things in common: Most people really would like to be able to talk with their spirit ancestors for themselves. Also, they don't realize how many different *kinds* of ancestors there are. Oh, and there's one more thing. A lot of people—even many professional mediums—don't realize how quick and simple so many spirit communication techniques are!

In this book, you will learn who all of your different ancestors are, how you can reach out to them, and how you can get their guidance and messages. Feel free to jump around to the chapter topics that interest you most. All of this is easier than you can imagine! After all, your ancestors are standing right next to you, ready to whisper in your ear. So now that you've opened this book, it's time to open your heart and your inner senses . . . because your ancestors are calling!

CHAPTER 1

THE ANCESTRAL WORLD

Past and Always Present

Descend, and touch, and enter; hear
The wish too strong for words to name;
That in this blindness of the frame
My Ghost may feel that thine is near.

—ALFRED LORD TENNYSON

By the time Tennyson wrote these words in the 1800s, more and more people were looking to connect with spirit. But for many cultures through the ages, it was commonly believed that the door to the ancestral realms only opened on special holidays once or twice a year. Those days may have been a bit scary for some, yet they were celebrations for others. And they were celebrations for spirit, too!

Your ancestors and guides don't want to wait for a special day to come to you. They visit you every day. (And please don't let that concern you; visits from the afterlife can be far less daunting than holidays with living relatives!)

The Afterlife and Ancestors through History

Many people use the terms *ancestral realms* and *the afterlife* interchangeably. That's appropriate because they both point the way to the spirit world where all types of ancestors reside. Most cultures through time and across the globe have believed that their ancestors play an active part in their lives. From Shintoists to Buddhists, from the Celts to the Chinese, from the ancient Romans and Etruscans to the Spiritualists of modern times—all have sought to connect with their ancestors.

Many cultures venerate their family members. Some invoke help from different types of ancestors, such as their kings, chieftains, and persons of great cultural and spiritual achievement. In times both past and present, little altars could be found in some homes, while several countries traditionally have held festive gatherings at the cemeteries of their dead. Many cultures, including Mexicans, South Americans, Estonians, and the Creoles of old New Orleans, create great bowers of flowers and bring enormous feasts of food to the burial places of their loved ones. Some of the most popular ceremonies are reserved for such days as All Hallows' Eve and the Day of the Dead, but there are other days as well, such as the Feast of Lanterns, also known as Bon.

Trick-or-Treat

Perhaps the most well known of these days is Halloween. Indeed, Halloween is one of the most significant of all the festivals that date back to ancient Celtic times. Not only is it the longest continually observed festival, but it's also the only one that remains largely unchanged in date, traditions, and primary purpose in the Western world.

Halloween was called Samhain, the Celtic festival of the new year, which began at dusk. It was the night when the boundaries between the living and the dead were removed. Samhain was the special day when the souls of the dead wandered the world. They were welcomed with the food and drink laid out for them by

2

their loved ones. There were other rituals—such as dressing up as animals, dancing and singing to call up the ghosts and lead them to the edge of town, or carving out turnips or potatoes to hold candles to light the way for the dead. All of these traditions were designed to honor—and sometimes placate—the spirits that were abroad in the world on this special night.

Though these festivities still exist—in some form or another—in the modern world, Halloween has become less about spirit and more about parties and trick-or-treating kids. Yet people's desire to seek the help and presence of their ancestors is even more prevalent and more important than ever before.

Aquarius, the Water Bearer, Leads the Way

The shamans of ancient times filled the role of religious leader, medicine man, and spiritual healer. But one of his most important jobs was to make contact with the dead. In more recent times, this job has been passed to the medium, but even that job has been shifting to the masses. The new Aquarian Age now heralds the time of community. It is the time of coming together. And even the Bible tells us about it.

In Luke 22:7–12, when Peter and John ask where they should go to prepare the Passover, they are told that they should enter the city and find the water bearer, and he will lead them to the place of communion.

Now is the Age of the Water Bearer, the time of reaching out to come together. The energy of global and instantaneous communication, whether through the Internet or even telepathy, is the very essence of the Age of Aquarius.

Countless people from all walks of life want to reach out to their spirit ancestors and loved ones for themselves. And they don't have to go to mediums, much less cemeteries, to do so! In this age of immediate communication, the dynamic energy of Aquarius is here to help everyone open to the ancestral world. And when they do, they'll find many different types of ancestors who wish to give their support and guidance.

Your spirit ancestors connect to all parts of your history, your creative endeavors, your past lives, your spiritual work, and so very much more. This book will help you learn many quick and simple ways to meet all of your different types of ancestors—as well as communicate with them and interpret their messages. You'll discover easy steps—and powerful declarations and command words—that help you link with your ancestral guides instantly. So, as you learn about your different types of ancestors, get ready to stick your toe into the waters of the world beyond!

Those Who Have Gone Before

What exactly is an *ancestor*? That answer might surprise you. Most people define *ancestors* as "those from whom a person is descended." Some believe that they are family members from generations long, long ago. This qualification severely limits the true meaning of the word *ancestor,* which has little to do with any length of time or even biology.

The word *ancestor* originally stems from the Latin words meaning "to go before." The Middle English *ancessour* (like the Old French) simply means "foregoer" or "forerunner." Your biological ancestors would include all of your family members—your recently departed father, your mom's sister, or your great-great-great-grandmother—all of whom could bring assistance to you from the spirit world. But your biological ancestors are just the tip of the iceberg!

There are so many other types of forerunners from different times and places. Beyond the biological link you have with those in your family, consider other strong connections you have felt throughout your life. Take a moment to think about those times when you saw a photograph, read a book, heard a song, or visited a place that moved you in ways past your understanding. You may not have known that person or place, but somehow it seemed to reach into your heart and grab you. This sensation can be a clue to ancestral links that extend far beyond the family—links to the cultures, the organizations, the shared purposes, and even the past lives you have known.

Landcestors

These days many people seem to be intent on discovering their genetic ancestors, as well as the lands and cultures of their origins. They do this by using ancestry registries and even DNA testing that uncover their past lands around the world. I call the ancestors that hail from the cultures and territories of your origin your *landcestors*, and they are much more than just your genetic predecessors. As a matter of fact, they don't even have to be biologically related to you at all. They are those who walk your native lands and carry your cultural heritage.

I have a client, Erin, whose family is from Ireland. She knew a lot about her family history because she had investigated her ancestry fully. When she bought a book of Irish poetry that was over a century old, one of the poets' names made her catch her breath, even though he wasn't connected to her in any way.

After she read his poetry, she was affected even more deeply. Erin is a songwriter, and many of her lyrics were soon inspired by this poet's life and work. On one of her trips to Ireland, she was drawn to an area that was new to her, and she felt compelled to go to a pub in the heart of a small village. She made her way to a booth in the back. And there, in a frame upon the wall, was an old, yellowed picture of this poet who apparently had frequented that pub long, long ago. Over time, this Irish poet came to mean a great deal to Erin. Though he certainly wasn't a part of her biological ancestry, that poet was calling to her. He was a cultural and geographic ancestor—a *landcestor*!

. . . .

Going Home

Take a moment to close your eyes, and just think about the land of your forefathers. See it or sense it in your imagination. Put yourself there completely. Do you know where you are and when it is? Don't think about it, just feel everything. Also notice if there are any people around you. Let yourself really feel your connection to your landcestors.

. . . .

Forerunners from Brotherhoods, Organizations, and Groups

Beyond the foregoers who connect with you through the land, there are also those who were members of the same social, religious, and professional groups to which you belong—the clubs and societies that have been beacons of different philosophies, faiths, beliefs, and activities over the centuries. Armies, navies, law enforcement groups, rabbis, priests, scouts, fraternities, research societies, actors guilds, social clubs, and tribal communities are just a few examples. Your ancestors would include even the most ancient members from the brotherhoods and groups to which you have a connection—or even an interest. These ancestors notice the light of fellowship that goes forth from your aura—just as easily as you would recognize the ring on a Freemason's hand.

. . . .

Joining the Club

Think of a formal or informal group to which you belong or have belonged. Close your eyes, and imagine yourself at one of these group meetings. Notice the people who gather there. What do you feel?

Now think about the many people who have belonged to that group over the ages. You don't have to know their names or who they are. But you soon notice that some of them have come to the meeting, too. Let yourself sense them. If you'd like to ask a question, do so. Sense any image, symbol, or idea you get. And trust every subtle nuance you feel.

Even though you notice that they come from different times and places, there is still a similarity in energy and feeling. It is the fellowship you all share. Take a few moments just to be with them. Let yourself feel the powerful unity of this collective. If one or two stand out for you, notice that, too.

. . . .

Ancestors of Purpose and Action

There are also foregoers who reach out because they share the same passions and endeavors—those activities that have interested you in the past, or that you're now pursuing. This can sometimes overlap with forerunners from clubs and groups because of the purposes they hold.

Yet membership is not required for you to share the same purpose with these ancestors. If you're a painter, spirit painters who have gone before are your ancestors of purpose. So it is with artists, healers, architects, and so on. Remember Erin and her Irish poet? Well, after Erin learned some simple intuitive processes, she forged an active connection with him. She would invoke this poet's help in many ways—especially in creating her lyrics. Erin and he were both writers, which also made him her *ancestor of purpose*—besides being her Irish landcestor.

Of course, ancestors of purpose would include those spirit folk whom many people call their *spirit guides*—those who share the purpose of spiritual awakening and psychic unfoldment. They are the foregoers who have taught you in previous lifetimes and who work with you still. But they are not your only "guides." Everyone in spirit who gives you guidance is a guide to you. So seek to know all your guides, and embrace your ancestors of spiritual purpose. They help you give your spirit a voice.

Actually, all your ancestors of purpose help you express yourself in the world. If you are a sculptor, there will be sculptor forerunners who will help you. If you are a designer, designers who have gone before will be attracted to you and will bring you guidance about your design work. And, of course, there are writing guides—thank God!

There are many stories of ancestral writers helping writers— Harriet Beecher Stowe and William Butler Yeats, to name a few. I have a friend, Julie, who was stuck in a receptionist job that she found dreadful. She had lived in Los Angeles, where she had been a television writer, but she had moved back to her hometown, where writing jobs were few and far between.

One day, after several years in that dead-end job, she found herself going through some of her old boxes that had long been in storage. She unwrapped a very old fountain pen that had the initials M. E. on it. It had belonged to her granduncle M. E. (everyone called him by his initials). He had been a writer, too. Since connecting with spirit was a part of her regular meditations, she decided to reconnect with him and ask for his assistance in getting some writing jobs. He told her he'd help, but she would have to do her part, too—the writing!

She started writing some short articles, many of which were getting picked up by local magazines. Soon she was offered an editorial job at one of those magazines. She quit her old job, and ultimately she became the head editor of a magazine group. Uncle M. E. is still a great presence in her life. He is not only a biological ancestor and an ancestor purpose; he is also a profoundly dear spirit friend.

Your ancestors of purpose don't have to be connected to your family or culture. They are drawn to you by the light of purpose expressed in your aura, and they can help you w ith any endeavor. There are ancestors of purpose for every activity, field, and focus— including bankers, horseback riders, opera singers, pilots, engineers, ship captains, ballet dancers, plumbers, and countless others. Even if you haven't met them yet, your foregoers of purpose are countless, too.

. . . .

A Connection of Purpose

Close your eyes, and think of an interest or activity that you have pursued or want to pursue in the future. Take a deep breath, and call some foregoers who have also shared that purpose at some time. Feel these ancestors approach you now.

This forerunner may be known to you or unknown. Don't think about that; just notice what you sense. Now they give you an image, an idea, a symbol, or a word that indicates your next step in pursuing this purpose. Notice the first thing that you get—no matter how subtle. And trust it completely, even if you don't quite understand it. If something else comes, let that happen, too. When you're finished, say thank you to this guide. Then jot down your impressions and what they might mean to you. Know that you'll be meeting with this ancestor again.

. . . .

Forerunners from Past Lives and Your Ancestral Homes

Another important group of foregoers includes those from your past lives. Maybe you knew a composer in a past life who may be helping you still, or you knew your great-grandmother in a past life, or you sailed on a tall ship with a naval forerunner. There are so very many possible past-life ancestors whom you've known before.

Perhaps the most important person who has gone before in your past lives may actually be you! You have gone before from one lifetime to the next lifetime, to the next—bringing your karma forward each time. Your past experiences planted the seeds for the present. And when you meet your past-life selves, you'll discover some of the actions and karmic lessons that impact you today. You'll also discover more about your relationships—ancient and new.

Of course, there are places that strongly connect with you, too. You have past-life homes. But you also have homes—and even towns and cities—that carry the imprints and energy of the different ancestors who guide you.

. . . .

A Little Visit

Take a moment to recall the travels in your life. There are some places that have compelled you or captivated you in some way—even though you had never been there before. Think of one of those places.

Close your eyes, and take a deep breath. Imagine yourself there now. You may have an ancestor connected to this place. Or perhaps you knew this place in one of your past lives. Feel yourself there completely. Breathe the air. Look around you. Do you see any people there? Notice everything that you sense about this place. How does it make you feel?

Be sure to take some notes when you're done, and revisit this place again to find out more.

. . . .

Your forerunners are with you in so many ways. They can be from your extended family, your adoptive family, your friends, your lands, your groups, your pursuits. Wow, what a treasure trove of helpers!

Now let's look at the simple steps that will help you meet your spirit ancestors in moments!

CHAPTER 2

THE
FIRST DOOR

A mind that is stretched
By a new experience
Can never go back
To its old dimensions.

— OLIVER WENDELL HOLMES

Getting to know your spirit guides and ancestors may be a new experience for you, but it's so much easier (and far less mystical) than you might think. It's not only for people with special talents. It's for everybody, because spirit is there for everybody. And they are there for you.

Only three simple steps are required to turn on your inner—or psychic—senses so you can connect with the ancestral world. Then after you learn these little steps, you'll also discover some other tips and techniques, words and images that can open you to spirit immediately. So let's start taking the steps toward spirit.

Steps in Connecting with Your Spirit Ancestors

1. Create the intention and invitation.
2. Activate your right brain (and let go of the analytical left).
3. Trust *everything* you perceive.

These are the steps that take you to the ancestral world. Of course, there are also easy techniques to get assistance from your ancestors, identify who's who, receive answers to your questions, and interpret spirit's messages. But these three steps will give you the foundation for all your work with the ancestral realms. So let's take a closer look at each one.

Step 1: Create the Intention and Invitation

Creating the intention to know your spirit guides and ancestors allows you to focus on them exclusively—so you can set aside any distractions. You'll know that *everything* you get is from them. You can let go of doubt and embrace your spirit forerunners in every way.

Your intention also sends a call to them, inviting them forward. Actually, you'll find that intention and invitation are inexorably linked. *Just inviting your ancestors declares your intention. And setting your intention will invite your ancestors.* Your call to spirit will fly on the wings of the wind into the ancestral realms.

. . . .

Sending the Invitation

Close your eyes, and take a deep breath. Fill your whole being with the intention to be with spirit. As you hold this as your truth, you continue to relax. With every breath, this intention fills you. It stirs within you and moves into your aura. It shines forth like a beacon, calling to all of your ancestors.

Your intention is an invitation. Say to yourself, I invite my ancestors here. *Soon, you start to feel them gather. The invitation goes farther and farther abroad, and more of your loving ancestors approach. With another deep breath, take a moment to feel their presence completely.*

Simply open your heart to their gentle support. And notice everything that happens for you—everything you sense. After a few moments, say thank you to the ancestors who are here for you. Now bring yourself back, feeling love and gratitude filling your heart.

. . . .

As you do these little exercises, don't let yourself fall into expectations or analysis. Allow yourself to be spontaneous and receptive. And when you're done, always take some notes about your experience.

Step 2: Activate Your Right Brain (and Let Go of the Analytical Left)

Your physical senses (hearing, sight, touch, smell, taste) allow you to experience the physical world. But experiencing the unseen world requires you to use your inner senses (or what parapsychologists call your *extra senses*). For this reason, psychic (or extrasensory) perceptions are subtle, internal experiences. It's important to note that, although words such as *visual*, *seeing*, and *images* are used to refer to the imaging experience of the right brain, your perceptions can be of any inner sense, which we'll discuss in the next chapter. And even *seeing* usually occurs in your mind's eye—somewhat like picturing a memory. For now, just know these perceptions are brought through the right brain, the imaging part of your brain. It's where your imagination lies and where your own spirit and your ancestors reach out to you.

The left parietal lobe (left brain) is the analytical, measuring, judging part of your brain. It is the ego's domain, where your doubts, judgments, and criticisms (of the self and others) take place. If you start to doubt or criticize your perceptions while connecting with your ancestors, it's your left brain that's talking. When that happens, all you have to do is go back to your right brain by *activating* it through right brain imaging (or using your imagination). Creating an image—visually or conceptually—turns on the right brain. It's like priming a pump, and once you activate the right brain, all of spirit's images can flow through.

Because your spirit guides reach out to you through your imaging side of the brain, the perceptions you get will feel like your imagination. This experience can trip people up at first because they say to themselves, *I'm only imagining this; I must be making it up.*

Many people think that their experiences can't be from spirit because they are subtle, internal perceptions. But it's important to understand that, as soon as you ask anything of your spirit forerunners, they will immediately drop an image, word, or idea into your right brain—even before you finish the question (and often before you *know* the question). All you have to do is look to your imaging to see what they put there. *You're not making up the answer; you're just making yourself get the answer that's already there.* And it all happens through your right brain—the home of your imagination.

Therefore, if your perception of spirit feels like your imagination, congratulate yourself. That's how it should feel because that's where it happens. So give your imagination (your imaging) the job, and let it work for you (and for your ancestors) completely. Let's discover the right-brain door now.

. . . .

Open the Door to Spirit

Take a deep breath, and close your eyes. Set your intention to be with your ancestors, and feel how it sends an invitation forth. Now activate your imaging, and see or sense a door—any kind of door—in your mind's eye, or imagine it before you. No matter how you perceive it, make yourself get a door completely.

First, notice everything about the door—its color, its size, everything. After a moment, let it open up before you. When it does, an ancestor steps through and approaches you. Then, perhaps, another steps through, and then another. They are here for you. Whether you know who they are or not, they have come to you.

Don't think; just notice everything you perceive about them. You have opened the door to spirit, and they are with you. What do you see and sense? What do you feel? Who are these people? Don't think—just notice it all, and trust every little nuance.

Take a few moments to do this, and when you've finished, start to bring yourself back. Say thank you to these wonderful spirit ancestors who love and attend you.

. . . .

Be sure to take a few notes when you finish this (and any other) exercise. You can meet your forerunners with this little process often. If you ever start doubting, remember that the easiest way to get back to your right brain isn't by thinking about it; it's by *doing* it! Whenever you use your imagination to activate your right brain, you'll go into the receptive state immediately. Simply create a door in your imagination, and your spirit ancestors will step right through it, sharing their messages. Then the only thing left for you to do is to trust *everything* you experience.

Step 3: Trust *Everything* You Perceive

You can open up to your spirit forerunners and to their symbols and images, but if you don't trust them, you'll invalidate every experience and reject every communication.

> **In spirit communication—**
> **as in any psychic endeavor—**
> ***trust is the coin of the realm.***
> **It is the very currency that gets you**
> **everything you value from the higher world.**

When you validate your perceptions with trust, more perceptions will follow. But when you don't trust what you're experiencing, it drives you into your left brain—asking questions, making you doubt, and pulling you away from spirit even more.

Getting mentally stuck in doubting and judging keeps you out of your imaging right brain, where your spirit ancestors speak to you. So not only do your doubts undermine the perceptions you've had *already*, they also prevent you from having more. It's almost as if your ancestors have told you to meet them in the room on the right at the end of the hall. But you go to the room on the left. You can't meet spirit if you don't go to the right room. And in order to go to the right room, you have to get out of the left!

Doubting is the antithesis to trusting. When you're doubting, measuring, or questioning, you'll find yourself saying minimizing statements. *I don't know what to expect. This can't be real; it's all in my head. I'm not getting anything. I'll never get this right.*

All of these remarks—and so many like them—erode trust through left-brain judging. They interrupt and impede your right-brain imaging, and they stop your ancestors' approach in their tracks. Unfortunately, when you catch yourself judging, you may judge yourself about that, too! Don't do that. Don't even think about it!

You can't *think* your way out of left-brain thinking.
Trying to think yourself out of the left brain
is like trying to kick your way out of quicksand.
You'll only get pulled deeper and deeper into it.

Sometimes, when mediums start to overthink or judge, they say that they're *caught in the weeds.* And the only way to get out of weeds of judgment is to activate the right brain. You saw that opening the door to the right brain allowed spirit to come through. But it is only *trust* that keeps that door open. If you're ever making a connection with spirit, and you find yourself getting pulled into the weeds of doubt and thought, just use any image to activate the right brain again. Now let's take a moment to build some trust with a new imaging activator. (And don't forget—imaginings can be conceptual, feeling, or any other types of sensing, as well as visual.)

. . . .

Snapshot

Close your eyes, and take a deep, relaxing breath. As you set your intention to be with your ancestors, bring to mind a photo of a family member or friend who has passed to spirit. It's a photo that you have seen frequently and know well. Take a few moments to recall that photograph fully. Whether you see it, feel it, sense it, or just recall it, let yourself get it completely.

As you look at this picture in your sensing, you notice

that this person is looking at you and starts smiling at you. That smile gets broader and broader, and soon he or she steps out of the photo and right up to you. With a warm embrace, you can feel the love that flows from this spirit to you. Let yourself just be in this grace-filled moment.

Now, this ancestor wants to send a message to you by giving you a symbol, a word, an image, a feeling, or an idea. Let yourself notice the first thing that you perceive—no matter how subtle it is. And if it changes to another image or idea, let that happen, too. Take another deep breath. And notice what you get, even if it seems small and irrelevant. Trust *everything that happens for you.*

When you're done, say thank you to this spirit. Make a commitment to this person and to your other ancestors to connect with them often.

. . . .

You can use any photograph you have to meet your ancestors—even if you did not know those people when they were living. When you take notes after these little processes, it's a good idea to write about how you *sensed* your perceptions. It will help you get to know which senses are most active for you. (You'll find other processes like this in my audio program *Ancestor Spirit Communication*.)

For a lot of people it's hard to believe that connecting with your spirit ancestors really is that simple. But it is. These visualizations will activate your right brain, turning on your spirit receptors and allowing you to receive even more from spirit. All you have to remember is that left-brain doubts will immediately hang up the phone. But trusting every intuitive perception will open up the whole switchboard. So turn on your right brain with an image, and *trust* every spontaneous perception.

Now it's time to discover some power words that can help you invite spirit and open your senses to them.

Using Power Words to Meet Those Who Have Gone Before

It is quite common knowledge these days that every word and thought has the power to shape a person's life—whether for good or for bad.

**Moment by moment, your mind
creates your reality.**

The right words have the power to soften hard feelings, stimulate change, and galvanize action of mind and body. There are power words that lift your energy, and there are power words that trigger immediate responses. Some of them work gently, some work more spontaneously. And, as in all things, some work for some people, and others work for other people. (You can learn more about word energy and the enormous impact it can have on your life in my book *Power Words*.)

Even simple words that you use every day have extraordinary power. They can help you pursue any goal, achieve specific outcomes, and realize any intention. And that includes your intention to meet your spirit ancestors and receive their messages.

Here are a few spirit power words that you can use to open to spirit in just seconds. You'll also find several others throughout this book. Give them a try to discover the ones that you like best.

Power words for spirit communication are used in the same way you would use power words to impact the rest of your life. The technique is always the same—and always very, very simple.

All you have to do is close your eyes and say the word to yourself. Then take a deep breath, bringing the word into you. Feel the energy and meaning of the word stir within you, bringing an immediate response.

Here's a little process that gently lifts your awareness to your spirit ancestors. It's a simple word process, so keep it simple, and let it flow.

. . . .

Oneness with Your Ancestors in Spirit

Take a deep breath, and close your eyes while you say to yourself the word Oneness. *Fill yourself with the word* Oneness. *And with each breath, you feel* Oneness *gently stir within you.*

You can feel your Oneness *with all that is—and with spirit, too. You are one with every ancestor and guide.* Oneness *means you are connected, and you feel it. There is no doubting, no missing, no waiting. Whenever you use the word* Oneness, *you feel spirit's presence absolutely.*

As you say Oneness *again, you are aware of all the spirit ancestors who drew near. Notice everything. What do you sense, see, or feel? Don't start thinking. Just notice every perception. See who is with you, and sense the images and ideas they send you.*

You can also feel the profound support and love that these wonderful ancestors share. Say thank you to them. Know—with absolute certainty—that every time you say Oneness, *you will sense your ancestors there. They are available to you always.*

. . . .

Take a few notes after you're finished—*not* so you can start to measure and analyze your performance, but so you can get more familiar with your own sensing experience. And if this process didn't work for you right away, keep practicing it. Be spontaneous in your experience and in your trust. Stay out of your left brain completely, and submerge yourself in every sense and perception.

I have found *Oneness* to be a word that lifts my energy and gently opens my awareness to the spirit ancestors around me. But I also love the command words and phrases that trigger a more active response. The following is a single command word that is very easy and very powerful. *Open!* is a call to action that ignites your openness to spirit immediately and absolutely. Give it a try. And remember, keep it simple and spontaneous. Surrender to your imaging and absolute trust.

. . . .

Open!

Take a deep breath, and close your eyes. Now, strongly, firmly, and with the force of pure intention, say the word Open! *This word declares your full intention and opens your awareness to spirit spontaneously.*

With a deep breath, say, Open! *again. In that very moment, a spirit steps before you. Who is it? If you don't know, that's fine. Just open your heart to this person. Notice what you sense and feel for a few moments.*

Now say the word Open! *again. With that, you sense another ancestor—or perhaps two—come immediately forward. They are there completely. Sense any image, word, or idea that pops into your mind. Notice—and trust—what you are getting now.*

Every time you say Open! *you will notice a spirit there.* Open! *turns your focus to spirit completely. Say* Open! *again, and sense who is with you right now. Say thank you to them all. And remember to do this throughout your day whenever you want a few minutes with your ancestors.*

. . . .

As you write about your experience in your journal, make a note, too, about which one of the previous two exercises seemed to work best for you. Which one helped you to feel your ancestors most easily?

I like to use both processes (as well as many others that you'll learn in this book) to link with my spirit ancestors. I use *Oneness* when I want to spend some time with a whole group of my forerunners. I practice the *Open!* command throughout my active, waking day—sitting at my desk, folding laundry, or just walking through the house. When I say *Open!* to myself, I suddenly sense one of my loving ancestors—usually in front of me or beside me. Sometimes I'll ask them a question. Sometimes I just say hi and give them my love, and go on with my work, though I always say thank you whenever spirit shows up.

Of course, if you're more visual, you might like the images (like the door, the photograph, and others in this book). But it's good to practice with the words, too. If you'd like, you can put the two together. Try a little exercise where you say the command *Open!* while you visualize a door opening at the same time. It would be a combination of your senses. Give it a try, and see what happens.

I'm sharing a lot of the techniques that I have used in my many years as a medium. But you can play with them to see how you might want to make them your own. Use them as they are, change them up a bit, or make some new ones for yourself. It's up to you to discover what lifts you to spirit most. But in order to do that, you do need to practice with them. So keep working with all these little techniques. The more you anchor them in your experience, the stronger they will be for you. Then you can start to *Open* to spirit throughout your day. Pretty soon you'll be able to meet up with your ancestors anytime and anywhere—even shopping (yeah!).

CHAPTER 3

SENSING AND SENDING

How Spirit Communicates with You

The world is full of magic things,
Patiently waiting for our senses
To grow sharper.

— WILLIAM BUTLER YEATS

The more you use your inner senses, the more they will grow sharper. They are the intuitive senses that let you *receive* what spirit sends.

Many people think the intuitive senses are felt in the same way as the physical senses. But it's not the same at all. For instance, close your eyes, and take a moment to "see" an image of an apple in your mind. There it is. The apple is there for you because your imaging is there for you. Now, with your eyes closed again, listen in your mind to the song "Happy Birthday to You." Really take a minute to "hear" it all the way through.

In just these few little moments you've experienced two inner senses—seeing and hearing. How did they feel to you? Which one was easiest? Seeing and hearing are the two most common of the intuitive senses. But many people feel they're not real because they're not physical. Well, your spirit ancestors aren't physical, but they certainly are real. And they can give you real guidance through your intuitive senses.

Your Inner Senses

Even though the experience of inner sensing is different than physical sensing, they do coincide in some ways. Visual people tend to be seeing (clairvoyant), audial people tend to be hearing (clairaudient). And feeling (physically and emotionally sensitive) people tend to be sensing (clairsentient). There are also inner tasting (clairgustation) and inner smelling (clairolfaction).

Another way to perceive your spirit ancestors is inner knowing (claircognizance). It doesn't relate to any physical senses, but everyone has experienced it at some time or other. It's much like the gut feelings you've had throughout your life—an immediate awareness or a sudden knowing that seems to come from nowhere. But it does come from somewhere—spirit! It's either your spirit ancestors or your own Higher Self. And they can send you lots of things.

What Spirit Sends

1. Images, symbols, pictures, and visuals
2. Words (including names and ideas)
3. Body language (sensations and references)
4. Music and sounds
5. Aromas and flavors

Your ancestors really do have a lot they'd like to share. First, they want to identify themselves so you know who they are. Second, they want to identify living people so they can get a message to them. And third, they want to share their insights and guidance to help you in life's decisions. I often refer to this third part as the message—though, when your grandma shows up and just says, *I'm here, and I love you*, that's still a pretty important message.

Hearing without Sound

Oddly enough, a very common experience for people just starting out is that they see their ancestors, but their ancestors don't say anything. Many people describe their experience as "He's just standing there, looking at me." "She's just staring; why doesn't she say something?"

This might seem very strange, but it happens all the time. After a while, you'll learn that spirit talks to you telepathically. They talk with their thoughts—not with their mouths. You've probably seen examples of this in old ghost movies, where you can hear what the spirits are saying, but their lips don't move. (In sci-fi movies, it happens with the aliens.) Happily, you're not experiencing ventriloquism—it's spirit telepathy!

A Trip to Highclere

Of course, many, many people who aren't even trying to reach out to spirit have seen their ancestors looking back at them without saying a thing. This kind of speaking without talking is so common that such stories and descriptions can be found across the world—and through the centuries.

One particularly interesting event took place in 1894 at Highclere Castle, a home that most of the world knows as the fictional *Downton Abbey*. Lord Carnarvon (the real-life version of Lord Grantham) had a visitor at Highclere—his good friend Victor Duleep Singh, who was the son of Maharajah Duleep Singh.

That Saturday night Prince Victor had gone to bed in his comfy room, but he was wide-awake. He started looking around him at the paintings there. Then, when he looked at a picture directly opposite his bed, he suddenly saw his father's face looking back at him. It wasn't two-dimensional like a picture, but it had depth, as if he were seeing his father's head. Victor continued looking, and still he saw his father staring serenely back at him, saying nothing. Without alarm or concern, he got out of bed for a closer look.

And there was the picture with his father's face before it. Instead of being alarmed, Victor was relieved and assured his father was happy. It was a peaceful and warm experience for him. He went to bed with a calm sense of his father's presence.

The next morning Victor related the story to Lord Carnarvon and told him that his father had been in ill-health for a long time. Also, his father had often told Victor that if they were not together when he died, he would try to come to Victor. Not surprisingly the night after Victor had his vision, a telegram came to Highclere telling him that his father had died the day before.

Even though the Maharajah hadn't said anything when he appeared to his son at Highclere, his message spoke volumes in the love and the peace that Victor felt. It may be, perhaps, the most important message any spirit can bring, *I am here with you, and I love you*. Of course, spirit ancestors want to bring you all sorts of insights and messages that can help you—from the mundane to the life-changing. But the most important thing they want to tell you is that they are with you and *for* you!

Now let's see—and practice—sensing what spirit sends. There are so many wonderful ways for your ancestors to share their guidance with you!

1. Images, Symbols, Pictures, and Visuals

Most magazines around the world are filled with pictures. That's because most people think visually rather than in words and data streams. There is an old saying, "One picture is worth a thousand words." This is even truer with spirit's messages. One image, scene, or piece of art, with its many components, can capture an entire situation, place, mood, or action. Images can also identify a person or a whole group of people.

For instance, you could get an image of your grandfather's pocket watch, or get an emblem from the club or society he joined. Sometimes you might see the land of your ancient ancestors, or recall a painting on your aunt's kitchen wall.

Again, images can be visual or conceptual—as ideas or memories. And in terms of guidance from your ancestors, visual symbols can be very helpful and informative.

A traffic light is a great example. If you have a yes/no question about something in your life, state it simply with no either/or choices. Then your ancestors could send you an image of a traffic light. If you get green, the answer would be yes. And red would be no. If you get yellow or if it changes color, your ancestors could be telling you that there is more information to come and you might want to decide later. In the next chapter and throughout this book, you'll learn about many such symbols and how to interpret them— as well as other yes/no symbols, too. So let's take a look at pictures and images and what spirit can show you.

. . . .

I See Spirit!

Close your eyes, and take a deep, relaxing breath. Send forth an invitation to your ancestors and say, I see spirit! *Immediately, you do!*

You see a face, or you get an image or memory. Or you may see a piece of their jewelry or recall a photo. You could see just colors or a shape. Let yourself experience whatever you perceive completely. Trust every subtle nuance.

After a few minutes, think of a simple yes/no question so spirit can show you a traffic light. Think of that question, and say to yourself, Spirit shows me! *Immediately, you see or sense a traffic light before you. What color is it? If you get more than one color, notice that, too. If the colors change, that's all right. And if the question changes, that's all right, too. Just experience what spirit shows you for a few moments. When you're done, say thank you to these loving ancestors, and bring yourself completely back.*

. . . .

Write about your experience in your journal. Note the images and symbols that you got. How did you sense those symbols? How did they feel to you?

2. Words (including Names and Ideas)

Spirit's telepathic ideas often come suddenly as a simple knowing experience. When that happens during your active, waking day, they will feel like they are your own ideas! That's how inner knowing works—as an immediate, interior word or thought that suddenly just pops into your mind.

Of course, that's also how you could get names, because names are words, too. Your ancestors can also show you words and names by spelling them out or showing you the first initial or some of the letters. They can also send you images that can *visually* represent words or names. For instance, you can get the color red for the nickname Red.

You can get all kinds of words through spirit's images—even names of streets, towns, companies, and universities. Once, when a client asked where she and her family were going to move to, I received a beautiful image of a cottage on the shore of a lake with pine trees running all down the shore. As I described what I was seeing to my client, I remember saying that I wouldn't mind living there myself! Well, a few months later, she called. They had moved into a happy new home. And the name of their new street was Pine Shore Drive. As you can see, when spirit uses images for words, they can be quite literal.

There are so many wonderful ways that spirit can send you words and names—even through pictures! So let's take a few minutes to get some words from your ancestors now.

. . . .

And Now a Word from Your Ancestors

Close your eyes, and take a deep, relaxing breath.
Say softly to yourself the words, Spirit's with me. *It's*
a tender, inner whisper that is absolute in its truth. And

you instantly sense your ancestors around you and even above you.

Soon, some of those ancestors above you start to trickle down a gentle sprinkling of words. You can read some of them as they float by you like feathers falling softly from the sky. Notice what you see and sense now.

Take a look down, and read some of the words that have fallen around your feet—or even in your lap. If you sense them in a different way, let that happen. Notice that there are some names among them, too. What are they?

After a few moments, you say to yourself, I hear spirit! *Then you hear some words or names, softly being whispered into your inner ear. Get one or two of the whispered words now. And trust everything you perceive.*

Finally, your ancestors want to give you a telepathic message. Say to yourself, Spirit tells me. *Immediately, a few words drop into your mind. Know them completely. Did you get anything else? Trust everything absolutely.*

When you're done, take another deep breath, and start to bring yourself back. Thank these ancestors who love you so. When you take some notes in your journal, write about the different ways you perceived these words. And note which ones you liked the best.

Whenever you practice sensing words from your ancestors, remember to ask for a few names, too. Even if they're people who are unknown to you, it's easier to get closer to them over time if you're on a first-name basis!

3. Body Language (Sensations and References)

To identify themselves, your ancestors will share various physical conditions using subtle sensations—or by calling your attention to parts of *your own* body.

They share these sensations and body thoughts to point out their own distinguishing characteristics or the maladies that they may have had (false teeth, stiff fingers, a limp, and so forth). Of course, you can also get body sensings when your ancestors send you messages, too. We'll take a look at that in the next chapter.

Body Language Can Get You Moving

Gestures and movements are also very helpful when sensing your spirit ancestors and getting their messages. In the physical world, you read people's body language by watching the way they gesture or stand. When sensing spirit, noticing the way *you* want to gesture, walk, lean, move, and stand will help you know who's there and get the guidance they bring.

This is called *kinesthesia*, from the Greek meaning "the sense of position or movement." These movements—like other body sensations—help to identify them. You could feel like you're painting a wall, dealing cards, crocheting a scarf, tap-dancing, marching, saluting, or any other movement.

Of course these gestures and movements can be very subtle at first. Perhaps you might feel a little like swaying, as if there were distant music in the air. Or you might want to slightly move your fingers without knowing why. Again, you could be feeling these through your body or through ideas that spring to mind.

When your ancestors send you gestures and movements, really start to do them and see what happens. You may feel silly at first. (And maybe, if you're in an elevator, you should do them in your mind.) But it's important to respond when you experience kinesthesia. Do whatever movement you feel. And as you do, let yourself start to *exaggerate* that movement. Put yourself fully into the activity. And give it much more energy, more sweep. I call this *kinesthetic exaggeration*. And through it, your body can speak volumes!

· ·

Let the Body Talk

Take a deep breath, and close your eyes. Say to yourself, I sense spirit. *Immediately, you feel them there. With another deep breath, say again,* I sense spirit! *And instantly, your ancestors start to share physical sensations.*

30

Notice your own body, and observe every subtle nuance—a tickle on your hand, a little pressure on your knee, an itch on a foot. Notice everything you feel. Also notice any ideas you get about your own body. Sense everything for a moment. Do these sensations or ideas identify any ancestors you know?

Now spirit wants to give you a message by identifying a part of your body. If you think about your throat, it could be about communication. Or if you notice your feet, it could be about your life's steps. Just notice and trust everything you get. You can work on the meanings later.

After a few moments, your ancestors want to share their movements and gestures. Say to yourself, I sense spirit move! In that moment, you may feel like you want to move. Or you may only get an idea of movement. Even if they're subtle, let yourself sense any gestures, movements, or actions that you'd like to do. Then do them—or imagine yourself doing them—and really exaggerate them, too. Do this for several moments. Be demonstrative. What gestures and actions are you doing? Do they identify spirit, or give you a message, or both? How do these movements make you feel? Sense everything now.

When you're done, start to bring yourself back. Be sure to thank your ancestors. Feel their love and embrace with every part of you. And make a commitment to meet them often. Remember to take some notes when you've finished.

. . . .

These are some of the ways that spirit sends you their body language. (You can find other processes like this in my audio program *Ancestor Spirit Communication*.) Spirit can send physical sensations or gestures and movements or telepathic thoughts about the body. And remember, they walk through your life with you. So stay open for the little, subtle feelings that can come anytime. Your ancestors are a source of love every day.

4. Music and Sounds

Your spirit ancestors can use sounds in literal and metaphorical ways. As with all of these different types of communications, a sound or song can identify spirit, a living person, or act as a message to you. Your inner hearing experience can come through a thought of a sound, or noise in the distance that you can't quite make out. Or it could just be a memory of a sound or song. Everything from a train whistle to a Broadway musical can come to your inner hearing.

Noises can often identify people. A factory whistle, a tea kettle, and a truck horn are all frequent identifiers. Of course, your ancestors send you certain pieces of music, passages of songs, or even song titles. They could be identifying themselves through the songs that you associate with them. Or they could be using lyrics, melodies, or even memories of musicals that can act as messages for you.

I had a client, Sam, who lived in a major U.S. city and had a choice between two good jobs in different parts of the city. Though he meditated on the situation, he was too ambivalent. Throughout the day, though, he found himself whistling and singing the songs from *West Side Story*. After a few days of this, he finally realized that his ancestors were telling him to take the job on the west side. He did. It turned out to be a really great career boost for him. Now he's the one dancing down the streets of the west side! So let's find out what happens when spirit sings to you!

. . . .

Spirit Sings!

Close your eyes, and take a deep breath. With another breath, send forth your invitation to your ancestors. You know they attend you. And look! There they are—already gathering around you!

Now softly say, Spirit sings! *Immediately, you hear a song playing inside you. Or it might be a memory, or a song title that pops into your mind. What song are you getting? Does it identify an ancestor? If so, who is it?*

After a moment, take another deep breath. Spirit wants to give you a message through a song. Say to yourself, Spirit sings! *Immediately, some music stirs within you. Listen with your heart and with your inner hearing for a minute. What song do you hear inside? Notice the lyrics. How does this song make you feel?*

Listen for a few moments, noticing anything else that comes to you. Then start to bring yourself back, saying thank you to your very musical ancestors.

. . . .

I really should remember to ask spirit for a song more often. It's so much fun! My ancestors are musical and funny. Sometimes, when I ask for a song, they put on their tails and top hats. They tuck their canes under their arms and break into a dance from Broadway! I love when they do "Puttin' on the Ritz"!

5. Aromas and Flavors

Aromas and flavors are not a large part of spirit communication, but they do happen. Sometimes you'll get the physical perception, but often it could be more like a thought or recollection—an inner taste or a smell. Sometimes these perceptions act as messages, but usually they identify people.

Being a clairvoyant, I often get an image of people when I perceive tastes and smells—my mother with her perfume, my father with his spearmint candy, my grandmother and her anise cookies. And here's something else you might think a little odd. When I eat their favorite foods, I immediately feel them near—not just because it's a memory, but because their favorite foods, and other things they loved, become invitations to them.

My father was a civil engineer, architect, and contractor. And when I find myself looking at an interesting piece of architecture, I can feel my dad fly in and say, *Let's get a closer look!* Then I find myself inches from the building with my dad. And I'm pretty sure the people walking by are thinking, *Who's that crazy lady touching the stonework on that building and talking to herself?*

I also have a client whose uncle worked as a mechanic in a garage. His uncle would identify himself with the smell of gasoline, as well as an image of cars on a rack, and sometimes a subtle feeling of oil on the skin. But my client always feels that his uncle goes with him when he has to take his car in for repairs. Just thinking about the repairs is an invitation to his uncle!

I share these stories with you so that you can stay open in your own life. You may be doing something your ancestors loved, or eating their favorite cookie, or listening to their favorite song, or smelling their favorite flower. Stay aware. These are all energy invitations to your loved ones, and they are bound to show up. Don't miss the opportunity for a hug!

. . . .

In Your Ancestor's Kitchen

Take a deep breath, and close your eyes. Invite your ancestors to come, so they can bring you some smells and tastes.

Say to yourself, I open my senses to spirit. *And suddenly you get an inner scent. You may think of a scent. Or you may get an image of its source—like seeing a pot of coffee. However you get it, spirit sends you an aroma now. Take a moment to experience it fully. How do you sense it? Does it remind you of someone? Are they there with you now?*

Now ask spirit for a taste that could identify them. You might get a subtle internal taste. Or the thought of a food could pop into your mind. Or you could get a memory of a favorite dessert. Or you may see the person who made it. Take a bite of what you're tasting, and simply notice what you get. Who in spirit brings this taste to you?

After a moment, spirit wants to give you a message. Say to yourself again, I open my senses to spirit. *Immediately, spirit sends you a scent or a taste as a message for you. Get an inner scent or taste. Or just imagine the smell or flavor. Get it any way that it happens for you. What is it? What does it tell you? How does it feel? Notice everything.*

Very well; say thank you to these wonderful ancestors. And start to bring yourself back. Take some notes when you're done, and call these forerunners again soon— especially when you're making dessert!

. . . .

Now you've seen (heard, felt, and smelled) how you sense what spirit sends. In the next chapter, you'll get a chance to work with some of the universal symbols they use in their messages.

CHAPTER 4

THE UNIVERSAL SYMBOLS

Getting Started with Messages

If you wish to learn the highest truth,
begin with the alphabet.

— JAPANESE PROVERB

Spirit can give you literal messages—like the name of a street where you might move or an image of a university to tell you to go to school. But for the most part, your communication with your ancestors will include a preponderance of symbols. There are lots of different types of symbols—including the negative/affirmative, personal, animated, environmental, and more. Indeed, symbols are so prevalent, you could find yourself getting very extensive messages within stories made up of symbols. (You'll learn more about all of these symbols in Chapters 14, 19, and 20.) If there were a single language used by all of your ancestors equally, it would be the language of symbols.

Yet the universals are like the alphabet of symbols—because they are the most basic and broad-reading, having similar meanings for most people. In this chapter, we're going to be looking at the most fundamental universal symbols. They are often symbols on their own, but they can also combine with other symbols to give you more information.

The Basic Universal Symbols

1. Colors
2. Elements
3. Numbers
4. Body and hands
5. Symbols of time

These set the foundation for your work with symbols. So, as you work with them, be sure to use your journal to note how you experienced them and what they meant for you. Also, take some extra time to study these and other symbols on a more in-depth basis. Your symbol perception will expand in ways that you'll find very exciting as you work with your ancestors. So let's get started now with colors.

1. Colors

When lots of people start working with spirit, they often find that colors are the first things they perceive. Besides being the easiest to perceive, colors can also carry the most information.

Colors are not only visual but also carry energy and reflect emotions. After all, you've often heard the phrase "seeing red" to represent anger. But the energy of red certainly isn't limited to anger—or even passion. It can also reflect power, activity, and initiative, where blue can carry the energy of quiescence, reflection, and receptivity. Let's take a look.

Colors from Your Ancestors

Close your eyes, and call to your ancestors to come and show you some colors. Say to yourself, I see spirit. And you do! Only this time they're awash with color. Take a moment to see your colorful ancestors!

Now a few of your forerunners come forward to give you the experience of red. With a gentle touch, you can feel the color red fill your whole body all the way down to your toes and fingers. Just notice what you sense about the color and your own energy with red all through you.

Now take a deep breath, and when you exhale, send out all the red. Empty yourself completely. And soon your ancestors send a wave of beautiful blue energy all around you and through you. Let the blue fill you up completely, and notice how you feel with the color blue within and around you.

After a few moments, take a deep breath, and exhale the color blue. Bring yourself back to your center, and say thank you to these ancestors. When you're done, take notes about everything you felt mentally, physically, and emotionally when you experienced red and blue.

This exercise indicates that even if you don't "see" things clairvoyantly, you can feel colors. When you feel colors, you are able to perceive a wealth of information. You can sense them with spirit guides and even with living people. Colors can tell you about a person's temperament and about people's careers. They can tell you about the purposes that you hold with your ancestors. Colors can also tell you about mental, emotional, and physical energy. So study the following color chart, and practice seeing and sensing colors and their energy. They can reveal so much throughout your life—and through your messages from spirit.

The Qualities of Colors

Color	Chakra	Key Words
Red	Root (first)	Energy; speed; will; high physical activity; heat; power; conflict; excitement; anger; initiative; passion; action
Orange	Sacral (second)	Warmth; vitality; science; logic; detail; regeneration; enthusiasm
Yellow, gold	Solar plexus (third)	Healing; creativity; authority; solar radiance; joy; philosophy; intellect; self-expression
Mild green	Heart (fourth)	Balance; peace; healing; ease; calm
Forest green	Heart (fourth)	Abundance; growth; expansion; prosperity; harvest
Pink, copper, or burgundy	Heart (fourth)	Love; family; devotion; release of conflict; marriage; peace; pursuit of causes
Blue	Throat (fifth)	Communication; calm; spirituality; clairaudience; intuition; psychism
Indigo	Brow (sixth)	Universal consciousness; clairvoyance; unconditional love; vision; meditation
Violet, purple	Crown (seventh)	Spiritual unfoldment; transformation; discipline; mysticism; daily rituals and patterns; initiation; Higher Self
Midnight black		Detachment; meditation; yin; receptivity; rest
Saturnian black		Duty; structure; karma; attachment; limitation; hard work; restriction; obligation; obstacles; effort
Brown		Grounding; stability; inflexibility; follow-through; detail; stubbornness; thoroughness; earthiness
Milky white, silver		Emotions; motherhood; nurturing; reflection; receptivity; psychism; family; changeability; intuition
Brilliant or lighting white	Crown (seventh)	Power of spirit; purity; selflessness; clarity; release of physical; Higher Self; radiant power; higher mind and will

As you become more familiar with these qualities and energies, you'll be able to apply them easily to people's personalities and career activities. For instance, red could show a strong-willed, passionate person or a career that requires high levels of physical activity, particularly one in the military. Yellow could indicate someone who's enthusiastic and expressive or a career that could be very creative. And since blue has a high communication energy, it could indicate therapists, writers, teachers, and other communication endeavors.

Of course, it's possible—and likely—to perceive two or more colors in your messages from spirit. You may be asking a question about a certain business project and perceive both red and blue. They may seem like opposites, but this combination could indicate that your project may require your initiative and action (red) as well as some work in communication (blue).

Color Your Work

Take a deep breath, and close your eyes. Invite your ancestors to come forward and show you some colors. Say to yourself, Spirit colors my world. *Immediately, you notice that waves of color are coming your way. Notice what colors are stirring around you. See and feel everything.*

After a few moments, think of a business or personal project that's been on your mind lately. Ask spirit to give you some colors about it. Take a deep breath, and say, Spirit colors my world. *Immediately, you see and feel the colors spirit sends.*

You may get a word or an idea of a color. Or spirit may give you an image that represents your project. If you get an image, watch as they paint it with colorful energy. See and sense everything that happens.

Now wrap that up, and start to bring yourself back. Say thank you to your colorful forerunners. Take some notes when you're done. And know that you can ask for a color about anything anytime.

Colors When You Meditate

There are just a few, quick things I'd like to share about your meditative colors. If you get violet/purple a lot when you're doing a meditation, that's often indicative that you may be working with one of the Ascended Masters of the Aquarian Age. Purple is the highest color on the visible spectrum, and it reflects a very high vibration. It also has a natural resonance with the Aquarian Age and the teachers who work on that path now. So get to know the higher teachers who work with you and who want to help lift you to your highest truth.

Another thing you'll likely find when meditating is that you will often see or feel black all around you. It is not because there is a "dark" spirit there, but because you are in a deeply restful, receptive yin state. I call this peaceful color midnight black. If, during a meditation, you also sense a radiant, bright white light, it can indicate that you are working with your Higher Self and with one of the higher ancestral teachers—an Ascended Master or an angel. Brilliant white light is the expression of spiritual purity, unconditional embrace, compassion, and the lightning power of Divine mind. When you have such ancestral beings working with you, know that there are contributions you can make together.

2. Elements

Though it's possible to get a sense of an element as a literal message—earth for planting a garden or water for a trip by the sea—the elements can have diverse and profound meanings when you perceive them as symbols in your messages from spirit. People, places, emotions, or activities—any of these can be indicated by a simple image of an element. Let's take a look.

The Qualities of the Elements	
Air	Conceptual thought; intellect; philosophy; writing; mental creativity; Internet; marketing; advertising; flight; teaching; travel; freedom; consciousness expansion; dreaminess; growth; universities; publishing. (Color indications are yellow; turquoise; white; sky blue.)
Earth	Grounding; detail; reliability; science; follow-through; stubbornness; building; planting seeds; farming, mining, and earth-related careers; structure; activities with nature; architecture; engineering. (Color indications are brown; green; light gray; rusty orange.)
Fire	Strength; creativity; power; action; heated situations; military and competitive careers; firefighters and police; anger; conflict; initiation; illumination; energy; burning off the old to create the new. (Color indications are red; orange; yellow; gold.)
Water	Flexibility; intuition; reflection; devotion; nurturing careers such as nursing and counseling; psychism; mediumship; communication; travel on or near water; changeability; emotions. (The type of water you see indicates the type of emotions represented—such as calm and peaceful or rough and turbulent. We'll take a look at extended water stories in Chapters 19 and 20. Color indications are blue; indigo; blue green; silver.)

. . . .

It's Elemental

Close your eyes, and call your ancestors to share an element. Think of a task before you take a deep breath, and say, Spirit shows me. *Instantly, you see, feel, or sense one of the elements. You might even sense a breeze or feel the energy of water flowing around you.*

Consider the possible meanings. If it's earth, do you feel you need to add more structure? If it's air, do you think you might want to travel, or even publish? Take a moment to see and really be in the element you're perceiving. And if you get more than one, sense that, too. Notice everything. How does it feel to you?

. . . .

3. Numbers

Often when your ancestors give you numbers, they can be literal. Your spirit folk could show you an important date, a specific amount of weeks or months required for a project, the number of people involved in a partnership, the amount of money for investments or purchases, and so on.

Your spirit guides could also share information through the symbolic meanings of numbers. The psychological values and characteristics of numbers come to us through numerology.

Numerology, the study of numbers and their meanings, is an interesting and precise area of investigation. But you don't have to study numerology to understand the symbols of numbers when speaking to your ancestors. You just have to learn the basic meanings on the following chart.

You probably already know more about numbers than you think. Consider the number 1. What do you feel? The number 1 stands alone, and being number 1 makes you above all the others. So, naturally, the number 1 reflects leadership, self-reliance, autonomy, and initiative. Thus, if during a meditation you were to perceive a number 1 about a job or a task, you would know that it may require your authority and initiative, and you could realize more autonomy and independence through it.

You can use spirit's insights with numbers in many areas of your life. Imagine that you need to interview people to work for you. If your ancestors give you the number 1 with someone who's applying, you could assume that this person is confident, self-actualized, and energetic. But with every good quality, there is a flip side. Someone who is that independent and goal-oriented may also be dictatorial and uncooperative. These possibilities, too, should be considered. So take a look at our number chart, and you'll see how vast the information from numbers can be.

Numbers as Symbols		
1	**Signifies**	New beginnings; autonomy; leadership; independence; initiative; power; courage; authority; creativity; executive ability
	Challenges	Bossiness; resentment of advice or criticism; "me first" attitude. Needs to learn to cooperate with others and not take things personally.
2	**Signifies**	One-on-one relationships; sharing; cooperation; communication; patience; duality; choosing between two options
	Challenges	Timid; lack of confidence; oversensitive. Needs to learn to keep a clear center of power and sense of self.
3	**Signifies**	Family; leisure; joy; creativity; small groups or partnerships; friendships; generosity; beauty; talent; imagination
	Challenges	Can get scattered in too many directions; needs to learn to keep a focus on work. Don't be impractical or manipulative, and avoid blaming others when things get difficult.
4	**Signifies**	Hard work; foundation building; practicality; discipline; responsibility; dependability; common sense
	Challenges	Stubbornness; intractable when disagreeing with others. Don't take things too seriously, and don't get resentful about cycles that require patience and a willingness to change.
5	**Signifies**	Diversification; flexibility; change; freedom; travel; release of routines; expansion; adventure; versatility; curiosity
	Challenges	Quick to act without forethought; impulsive. Don't be too scattered and restless. Find a way to maintain focus within a sense of freedom.

6	Signifies	Love of friends and family. Global responsibility; fairness; compassion; thoroughness; home; nurture; community service; order
	Challenges	Requires the security of routine; does not like to be alone. Needs to not smother loved ones. Release your need for control and your overprotectiveness of others.
7	Signifies	Intellectual; analytical; studious; intuitive. Faith; philosophy; contemplation; introspection; seeks wisdom and understanding and the inner life through meditation.
	Challenges	Be aware of the polarization between physical and spiritual realities. Learn to integrate new experience of the inner reality into workaday world.
8	Signifies	Success; ambition; achievement; organization; abundance; harvest; hard work
	Challenges	Tendency to sabotage self by questioning deservability. Need to break through restrictions through discipline.
9	Signifies	Selfless love; compassion; idealism; universal self. Completion; end of cycles; letting go; bridge to spirit; higher reality
	Challenges	Tendency to hang on to what's no longer useful
11	Signifies	Inner growth; higher experiences of self-realization; greater mastery of energy; initiation; service; fame; visionary inspiration
	Challenges	Staying out of the ego as greater power and accomplishments are achieved. Difficulty being practical, follow-through with plans, and being prompt for appointments.

Other multiples of 11 indicate higher mastery as well. Read the single digits that make them up, as well as the single digit of their total, and that will show you the areas of mastery that number carries. (For instance, with 33, you would read the qualities of 3 and of 6, their total.)

Now let's get a few, quick insights from numbers.

. . . .

Counting on Numbers

Your spirit ancestors want to share some information through numbers. Take a deep breath, close your eyes, and notice your forerunners there. Now think of an important person in your life. Say to yourself, Spirit gives me numbers. *Instantly, you get a number that tells you about this person. What is it? Trust the first thing you get. Do you get more than one number? Just notice everything now.*

After a few moments, let that all go. Your ancestors are near, and you can feel their loving embrace. No, think of a task or project that lies before you, and say again, Spirit gives me numbers. *Immediately, you see or sense a number before you. Or perhaps you get the idea of it. And if more numbers show up, let that happen, too.*

Don't go into your left-brain thinking about the definitions, just feel them in every way. Now let yourself notice if there are any elements, colors, images, words, or other sensations you feel, too.

After a moment of that, say thank you to these dear ones. Bring yourself back, and take some notes in your journal about everything you experienced.

. . . .

4. Body and Hands

Ancestors use physical nuances to identify themselves and living people—we'll take a look at that in Chapter 6. But your spirit guides may also use them as messages. When your forerunners want to use body sensations and thoughts as metaphorical messages, it is often because they'd like to inform you about the emotional and psychological connections they carry.

Every person will have different related stories and emotions stored within their body, so it's up to you to tap into your own intuition, experiences, and ancestral history for the meanings. However, for further guidance, Louise Hay has given us a treasure trove of insight about how the emotions interface with the body and with physical conditions. A study of her work in *Heal Your Body* and *You Can Heal Your Life* will open a world of understanding for you. So let's move on now to the hands.

What's in Your Hands?

Just as spirit can identify themselves and bring messages by making you notice parts of your body, they can also do the same by pointing out certain parts of the hand or fingers. Of course, if a loved one in spirit had arthritis or was missing a finger, those conditions will often identify those ancestors. But after you know who they are, they can handily continue on with their messages!

I'm very lucky to know ancestors through their body signatures. When my grandmother was little, she had lost the tip of her index finger on her right hand in an accident. After she died, she would let me know she was with me through that signature. I usually don't feel anything physically. Sometimes I would have a sense of my index finger being shorter. And sometimes—whether meditating or just going through my day—I would suddenly notice that I was rubbing (or staring at) the tip of the index finger on my right hand. No matter how I would perceive her, whenever she approached, she would tap me on the shoulder—with a much shorter finger!

I remember on one occasion, I asked for some guidance about whether I should expand my teaching into even more locations. My travel schedule was already overloaded, but I was really pulled to add these interesting new places to my schedule. And there she was, ready to help as always. I immediately noticed my index finger again. But it wasn't just her identifier, because it felt like it was starting to get longer, and my little finger was getting longer, too.

And immediately I knew my message. The index finger, the finger of Jupiter, which rules expansion and travel, was, well, expanding. And so was the finger of Mercury, the ruler of study and teaching. This is a great example of how studying symbols can help your communication with spirit. Of course Jupiter and Mercury have other implications, but my message was clear. It was time to expand my travel and my teaching. I did, and I wasn't disappointed.

As you can see, the astrological connection to each finger and various parts of the hands provides yet another opportunity for spirit to give you a wealth of information through just a momentary tickle, a flash of an image, or even a fleeting thought.

Take a look at the following chart to see what each finger—and some of the other parts of your hand—can mean. There are even further levels of insight when you remember that the right hand, ruled by the left brain, is the expressive, outward-reaching hand. And the left hand, ruled by the right brain, is the yin, receiving hand.

The Qualities of the Fingers and Hand	
Thumb (Venus)	Love; family; relationships; devotion; sensuality; nurture
Index finger (Jupiter)	Goals; expansion; ambitions; hopes; directions; broader horizons; journeys
Middle finger (Saturn)	Duty; discipline; karma; effort; application; industry; commitment; obligation; hard work
Ring finger (the Sun)	Creativity; personal expression; the way you shine; growth
Little finger (Mercury)	Intellect; communication; thought; abstraction; mind and mental action
Palm (Plain of Mars)	Energy; action; healing; movement; heat; power
Mount of the Moon, the fatty mount on inside of hand above the wrist and below the little finger	Intuition; emotions; changes; spirituality; psychism; receptivity
Mount of Neptune, at the base of the palm above the wrist	Dreams; unconscious; mediumship; spiritual awareness; what is below the surface

. . . .

With This Ring

Close your eyes, and take a deep breath. Say softly to yourself, Spirit's here. Instantly, you see and sense the ancestors who are here with you. They want to give you some insight using colors and your hands.

Now say, Spirit shows me. Then one of your ancestors opens his or her hand and shows you a beautiful ring of light and color and energy. See it and sense it completely. Notice everything.

Then suddenly you notice that this ancestor places this glorious, radiant ring on one of your fingers. Which finger is it? How does it feel? Which colors do you see? Do you have an intuition about what it might mean?

Now say thank you to these forerunners, and get ready to take some notes when you're done. As you say good-bye to them, they blow you a gentle kiss of color. What do you get?

. . . .

5. Symbols of Time

It's important to remember, when talking about time, that time is a physical-world thing. For our eternal and spiritual selves, there is no time. But time does matter in our linear, workaday world. And so, knowing how to tell time when spirit is sharing helpful messages is very important, indeed.

Spirit often uses seasonal symbols to show us time as well: pumpkins for fall; Christmas trees for December; the U.S. flag or fireworks for Fourth of July; spring flowers for spring; roses for summer; and so on.

Your spirit ancestors will also use direction to give you a sense of time. In Western society, we read from left to right. Therefore, it's natural for us to feel that what is left has been finished and is in the past. And, of course, what is yet to be read is what's coming—or in the future. So it's through location that spirit shows us past, present, and future people and events.

Some mediums see timelines in front and behind them. So you have to find out how it works for you. For me it's always been left and right. And the distance shown tells me how far past and how far in the future. When you see an ancestor very far to the left, it could indicate a past-life ancestor. And if spirit is pointing for you to go left, they're not sending you backward. You're probably getting guidance to go back and pick up a certain purpose or activity that you wanted to do before but never did. Or there may be something you started but you didn't finish in some way, and you might want to pick it up again.

Of course, these types of things happen for the future, too. I remember a client once asking me when her house was going to sell. Spirit showed me a For Sale sign a few feet to my right. Then they moved it a few feet farther than that. Then they moved the For Sale sign much farther to my right and leaned it against a Christmas tree. I told my client that she would probably meet a buyer in two months and then in four months. But both of those would probably fall through, and she'd sell the house around the holidays. Though she was very disappointed when I told her this, it was all okay a few weeks later, when she found out her job transfer was going to be delayed until the new year.

Besides sensing a direction to signify past and future, you could get some very literal images to show time. Spirit can show you clocks, calendars, and even dates on newspapers. If you have a question about time while connecting with spirit, simply ask to "see" a specific month on a calendar. And if you don't "see" the month, make yourself get the name or number of the month.

Your ancestors use numbers frequently when speaking of time. It's important to consider all possible meanings and note them in your journal. For instance, the number 2 could indicate the second of the month, the month of February, or a period of two days, two weeks, two months, or even two years.

I remember an incident that occurred not long after my goddaughter had gotten married, when she asked me to ask spirit when she was going to have a baby. I broke my own cardinal rule about sharing the exact symbol and *all* of its interpretations. I told her I got the number 4, and it would probably be four years away. It was my logical (read: left-brain) conclusion, since she was so young and newly married. As it turned out, she had her first baby the following year, in the month of April—hence the number 4. As always, the lesson is this: *The symbol is the message.* Always consider all the possible meanings (and share them and the symbol, if the message is for another person).

Time and Its Perception	Can Show
The *past* is indicated when you intuitively perceive an image or spirit guide to the left of you— or behind you.	• Memory • Recall • Past-life ties • Events and relationships that happened in the past • Past lessons and growth
The *present* is indicated when an image is perceived in the center or immediately in front of you.	• Present purpose • Situations and relationships now in play • Present lessons and growth
The *future* is indicated when a symbol is sensed to the right of you—or in front of you.	• Direction • Probabilities and trends • Motivation • Potential and future opportunities • Future lessons and growth

. . . .

What Time Is It?

Close your eyes, and with a deep breath, say to yourself, Spirit's here now. *And in that very moment, you see and sense your ancestors gathering there.*

First, a past-life ancestor wants to help you sense the long past by approaching you from a certain direction. Notice this person approaching. Where does this spirit stand?

Now bring your attention to a situation that has an element of time to it. Consider different options. When are you getting a raise? When should you take a certain trip? When should you take a class? Don't analyze the questions; just hold one in your mind.

As soon as you ask your ancestors, you see one of them showing you a symbol of time—a clock, a calendar, a seasonal image. Notice exactly what you get. And notice if one of your ancestors responds by standing a certain distance to you, too. Let yourself experience everything. And if it changes, notice that, too. Now say thank you to your ancestors, and bring yourself back to today!

. . . .

CHAPTER 5

FAMILY ANCESTORS

Some of Your Busiest Guides

When you are born,
your work is placed in your heart.

— KAHLIL GIBRAN

Your more recent forerunners often come from your biological family. But they can also hail from your adoptive family, your friends, your businesses, and other connections you have made. A lot of people think that family members aren't as powerful (or, sadly, as important) as higher guides. But your family ancestors are much more diverse in their ability to help and guide you than you might think. They certainly help you with the work that they knew well, as well as with spiritual discoveries they've made. They help you with relationships, jobs, creative endeavors, all kinds of projects, and even connecting you with your higher guides. They really are like your personal assistants! Let's take a look at the different kinds of assistance they bring.

Guardians in the Nursery

There are children in the spirit world who are waiting for their opportunity to come to the physical world. And there are ancestors who watch over them. Spirit children can start to draw near long before they get born into the physical world. And, of course, being children, they find each other so they can play!

Some of the children may be from the family, but they likely died young or in a miscarriage. Some spirit children may be from previous reincarnations, and they've come forward because their past-life parents have reconnected in this life. And some children gather around a living family because they know that there are opportunities—or even karmic lessons—for them there. But no matter what their individual reasons might be, the children have seen a light shining into the spirit world that has specifically called to them.

So together they wait in what I call the *nursery*. Now, there is no space or time in the spirit world, so, obviously, there is no actual place such as a nursery. The term *nursery* simply refers to that wonderful gathering of children and the spirit guardians who care for them.

Now it's time to take a peek in the nursery, so you can see who's there.

. . . .

Into the Nursery

Take a deep, relaxing breath, and close your eyes. Start to think now of the children in spirit who are waiting to come. Let joy fill your heart, as you send forth an invitation to those children.

With another deep breath, whisper to yourself, The children are here. *Soon, you seem to hear the gentle sound of children at play. It may seem distant at first, but that's okay. Again say to yourself,* The children are here. *And you immediately see and sense them around you. Some may still be playing, some may be looking at you. Some may even place a gentle, little hand upon you. Notice everything you get.*

After a few moments, turn your attention to the lovely people who care for these children. You may feel as if you want to lift your head up to see the adults. However it happens for you, let yourself see them, sense them, and feel them.

Open your heart to these guardians of the nursery and to the children they love. Do you know any of them? If so, who are they? Don't think or analyze. Just notice everything you sense. Take a few minutes to get it all. And trust what you get.

After a few minutes, say again, The children are here. *Some run to you and give you a hug. Take another look around, and see their joyful, twinkling eyes. And feel the warmth of the smiles from the loving adults with them. Say thank you to all of these gentle spirits, young and old. Make a promise that you'll visit the nursery again.*

Now start to bring yourself back. Remember to take some notes about the nursery and the gentle souls there.

. . . .

You can do this process whenever you're interested in reaching out to the children and grandchildren who are waiting to come from spirit. And if you recognized a little one who had died in recent years, remember that some children who died very young or in a miscarriage can sometimes come back quickly.

Even if children (past or coming) aren't on your mind right now, occasionally connect with the sweet, ancestral caregivers who help in the spirit nursery. These grandparents, aunts, uncles, and other ancestors are busy in many ways. They are your guides as well. And maybe—just maybe—some of them were there when you were in the nursery, too!

The Maintenance Crew

Don't be surprised if your ancestors like to tell you about cars, building projects, repairs, and other things on your to-do lists. In 40 years of clairvoyance, I can't count the number of times that I've seen spirit guys holding their wrenches, toolboxes, or hammers and walking down into basements, up into attics, onto roofs, into garages, and even directly under the ground in order to indicate where and what needed to be fixed. They've rolled in appliances from big-box stores, and they've unrolled architectural drawings for new homes and buildings.

I say "spirit guys," but of course sometimes men take care of the children and women take care of the cars. There is no right or wrong, because your experience of your ancestors is what's important. Whether it's a man or woman ancestor who's meeting you in the nursery or going with you in your garage, how you perceive them is exactly how it's supposed to be.

Some of the guys in spirit who are very active in this "fix it" role are husbands. I know it might seem that husbands wouldn't be ancestors since you were alive at the same time. But they are very much foregoers—just like anyone who has gone into spirit before you. Husbands can help with everything, including helping their wives find new husbands, as well as inspecting the appliances. And when they've done their inspection and find a repair is needed, they can be quite adamant about it!

Gadget Inspector

On one occasion I told a client, a lovely elderly lady named Helen, that I saw her spirit husband put a toolbox on top of the dishwasher, showing that the dishwasher needed to be fixed. Helen immediately started laughing and told me that her husband never fixed a thing in his life. She also said that if the dishwasher ever broke, he would be fine if she washed the dishes the old-fashioned way. I explained to her that, while toolboxes sometimes identify the ancestors who owned them, a toolbox also gives a message that something needs to be repaired (or built).

As I continued with the consultation, her husband kept interrupting other messages by showing me the dishwasher and the toolbox, and I told her about it every time. Finally, he must have decided that he wasn't being demonstrative enough. So besides pointing at the dishwasher, he started stomping his foot. (This behavior is not typical of spirit folk. It only occurs when they think a very important message is being ignored.)

I turned to Helen and told her what her husband was doing. I really wouldn't be able to go on with any new messages from spirit until she took this seriously. So she promised to call a repair man. But she said it with a chuckle, and I wondered if she really would.

Well, her husband's persistence actually worked. Helen couldn't get that image out of her mind, and she called a repair man that very day. After the repairman finished, he showed her a damaged, burned-out heating coil. He told her that if she hadn't called him when she did, the next time she ran it, there would have been a fire. Helen gasped when she heard that. She had the habit of turning on the dishwasher just before going to bed. The fire would have occurred while she was sleeping. It could have been very dangerous—and maybe even fatal.

I actually have gotten similar messages with other clients—especially with dishwashers, hot water tanks, and clothes dryers. (They must not be making appliances the way they used to do!) And many friends have gotten other types of repair and building messages for themselves. Let's take a moment to see who in your ancestral world is on your maintenance crew.

. . . .

Checking the List

Close your eyes, and take a deep breath. Send your invitation to the ancestors who help you with your list of things to do. Take another deep, relaxing breath. Say, Open! *with the strength of full intention to Open to spirit now.*

Immediately, you sense a spirit step up to you. Say the word Open! *again. And you notice other forerunners step forward. What do you see about them? What do you sense? Let yourself get everything exactly as it comes to you.*

Now imagine that one of these spirits hands you a list. See or sense that list completely. From this list a word or image suddenly stands out for you. Let yourself see it or sense it. Trust it completely. What is this one item on your list?

Now spirit is going to send you an image, a symbol, or a sensation that tells you what you can do about this item. Notice every subtle nuance, and trust everything. Is there an action you can take? Does our body feel like moving? Maybe you just feel like picking up a phone to call someone for this job! Just notice what you get.

After a moment, ask any last question about your list—or about anything on your mind. Take a moment to have a little dialogue with this caring spirit.

When you've finished, say thank you to these ancestors. And remember, they can help you in so many ways. So be sure to call your crew anytime!

. . . .

When you're taking notes, consider the plans you might have for this upcoming task and the other things to do. Your ancestors certainly can bring some insight about repairing the porch, getting a new appliance, or just cleaning out the garage. They—and other ancestral guides—can help you with your career, creative endeavors, and relationships. And sometimes they'll even help you find new love.

The Matchmakers

There are a number of spirit ancestors who want to help you find love—from your grandparents to your past-life loves to your spouse from this life. Lots of people doubt that their deceased spouses would do such a thing. They worry that their husbands and wives in spirit may be hurt and jealous even just knowing that they're dating. Of course, spirit people know when their loved ones in the living are dating—they know when keys are lost, when a vacation is coming, and when insurance has lapsed. They know and help you with it all. They love you so much that they want you to be happy. So they would do whatever they can to help you find love and a partner to be there with you.

Even the spirit parents and spouses who weren't very nice or loving in their physical lives will try to help you with practically everything, including finding love. Many people have great difficulty believing this. Remembering how mean some people were in life, it's difficult to imagine that such selfish people could become selfless and loving when they move into spirit.

It's important to remember that the ego is not a part of a spirit's makeup. It is only an aspect of the physical-world self. Indeed, Freud said that it is the ego's responsibility to do commerce with the physical world. In other words, the care and feeding of the personality is up to the ego. It is the ego's job to make sure you are fed and clothed and have a roof over your head. But food, clothes, and a roof over your head are not necessary—or even extant—in the spirit world. The ego is as useless in the spirit world as a fur coat on a hot summer day at the beach.

When people die, they step into their eternal selves, the soul, leaving the ego behind. People—even mean people—discover who they have been forever. It's as if they woke from a bad dream, and they find out that they were the bad guys! Now they see it. They want to do whatever they can to heal things. They want to do things in a new way—the right way. Often, their biggest desire is to make up for the hurtful things they had done and said in life—to turn hate to love and darkness to light.

I recall a client named Elizabeth. When I identified her husband, I told her that he was saying he's sorry. He was sending her his love. She balked and said it must be some other guy because her husband fell *far* short of being loving or apologetic. Nonetheless, I assured her that it was her husband. I had identified him by his career and his heart attack. And when I said his name was either Carl or Charlie, she had to admit it was her husband. She confirmed that his birth certificate name was Carl, but everybody called him Charlie.

Charlie expressed his deep regret and said he was going to do all he could for Elizabeth—from giving her guidance to helping her find a new love. I told Elizabeth that she could help heal her feelings— and her karma—by connecting with Charlie.

She said that it would be too difficult. Just thinking of him was painful because he had been so selfish and belittling in life. Yet she really didn't want this karma showing up again in the future. I told her to try to see him as he was then—a petulant, selfish child, lost in his ego. But now that he's in his radiant self, she could have a new relationship with him. And she could meet his radiant self in her meditations.

Elizabeth called me a little over a year later. She had been meditating and healing her old wounds with Charlie—getting to know him anew. And he was giving other help, too. He helped her find some insurance papers by showing her an image of where they were.

But she didn't get any images when she asked him about her investments. After several days of asking, a certain thought suddenly started popping into her mind. *I should call Jeff.* Jeff was an old banker friend of Charlie's whom she hadn't seen in years. That inner voice telling her to call Jeff persisted. (Instead of an image, this message came as a telepathic idea, which almost always comes in the first person.)

Finally she found Jeff's number and called him. They set up a time for an investment planning meeting, which turned into several meetings. Jeff had lost his wife to cancer three years earlier, and it seems that he and Elizabeth connected on levels much more valuable than finance! Charlie had been her matchmaker, and the match struck fire!

The Welcoming Committee

When it's time for people to pass into spirit, all their many ancestors gather to welcome them home. This includes the ancestors you never met, the loved ones who embraced you always, the father who wants to bring healing, and your old school chums. You might be surprised that the spirits who are often most eager to welcome you are your pets—even going back to your childhood pets. They will climb over your parents to be the first ones at the door to greet you!

There will also be past-life guides, your creative forerunners, your ancestors from different groups and societies, and some of the Ascended Masters who have worked with you for centuries. They *all* come to be there with you, no matter when or how you move into spirit. So, in a way, much of your ancestral world is part of the welcoming committee.

Beyond this welcoming committee, there is another group I call the Early Welcomers. These are the ancestors—often from the family—who have gone to spirit many years, decades, or even generations ago. They come to visit the people who are in various stages of Alzheimer's, dementia, or a coma. These types of conditions provide a way for living people to be able to put one foot into the spirit world while keeping one foot in the physical. This is not a conscious choice, of course; it is simply the road to spirit that is happening for them now.

I remember, for the last several months of her life, my mother, who had dementia, would stare off into the corner of the room. She would tell us that Uncle Al was standing there waving to say hello. Or she would talk with her grandmother, who would share a happy memory. Sometimes she would speak with some of the friends from the company where she worked during World War II, and sometimes she'd tell us about her cousins who had only recently gone to spirit before her. Of course, in between all of these interactions with spirit, there were times when she would speak with us perfectly. She knew we were there, but she also knew her friends from spirit were there, too.

Then, one day, my mom started talking to a new spirit person, Jenny. She told me about Jenny—how young and pretty she was with her blonde hair and sparkling blue eyes. I was a little confused because I couldn't remember any Jenny among her friends or in the family. My mom's health-care worker was there at that time when I asked my mom who Jenny was. The health-care worker said, "That's my daughter. She died in a car accident a few years ago. She often comes with me because she loves talking to my patients. They usually see her and always greet her with open arms." She sighed and said, "It also gives Jenny a chance to say hi to me. I love my job, but when that happens, I'm in heaven." How right she was!

If you have any family members suffering from some sort of dementia, you will, at some point, probably find them talking about (or to) people who aren't physically in the room. They are seeing their loved ones who had lived and died before—sometimes a very long time before. They are the great-grandparents, grandparents, uncles, aunts, cousins, friends, and others who have already gone to spirit.

At various times, the patient will respond to these visitors in different ways; sometimes by staring quietly into what seems to be an empty space; other times the patient may talk to these "invisible people" very demonstrably. If you see these types of conversations with the dead happening, don't assume that the patient is having hallucinations. Feel free to ask questions and let the patient tell you about who's there and about everything that he or she sees and hears.

Most important, be sure to thank these wonderful forerunners who come so frequently and stay so long. They are the great ancestral welcomers. And they are the ones who patiently and lovingly show the way home, even if it may take years.

CHAPTER 6

A FORERUNNERS' WHO'S WHO

Spirit Signatures and IDs

*When people show you who
they are, believe them.*

— MAYA ANGELOU

In building a familiarity with your spirit ancestors, you will find that there are various symbols, images, and energies that will repeat themselves. And if you pay attention, you'll see the patterns emerging.

These are the ways your ancestors tell you who they are. In the world of mediumship, such things are called *evidence*. You can get physical signatures, names, jobs, activities, and so much more. You've already seen some of this, but in this chapter you'll learn more about their identifiers, and you'll get started with a few messages of guidance, too.

As you practice communicating with your ancestors, remember: always be spontaneous. Stay in the flow of an easy dialogue with them. And give yourself permission to ask spirit what you want to know! If you want to know a name, ask for a name. And then trust what you get. If you want to get a symbol, ask for a symbol, and then trust what you get. And if you don't get a name or symbol right away, make yourself get one. You aren't making it up. You're only making yourself see what spirit already put in your mind. So stretch yourself. Trust everything you sense—without measurement or doubt. Your ancestors are there for you, and they know what you're going to ask before you even finish the question.

How Ancestors Tell You Who They Are

There are lots of ways your ancestors identify themselves. And they'll also use the same type of information to identify living people when they have a message for them. Let's take a look.

Evidence and Identifiers

1. Physical signatures
2. Memories
3. Their language and idioms
4. Signs of life
5. Names and initials

As we consider these identifiers and evidence, keep practicing with all of them. Some may seem harder because they are more specific than others. But that doesn't make them more difficult to perceive. It's only your level of trust that determines difficulty. So if you trust *everything*, everything will be there for you!

1. Physical Signatures

As you saw in the section on body language in Chapter 3, physical signs and conditions can manifest in so many ways. You may feel as if you'd like to sit taller, change your posture, or gesture and move in some way. This is kinesthesis. And though it can give you a message, it very often identifies spirit. For instance, I frequently feel like I want to salute when a spirit who was in the military approaches.

You could feel a pressure on your back, or a tickle on your skin, or you could get any number of other physical sensations.

These sensations are often *physical signatures of your ancestors*. For instance, if you feel itchiness or a pressure on your eyes—or even if you just start to think about your eyes, it could indicate an ancestor who was blind or who had vision problems. Or if you feel a pinch or an energy on the bridge of your nose, that could be someone who wore glasses.

Goose bumps are also a significant response to spirit. They often identify Ascended Masters when they're near because your frequency lifts due to their very high vibration. But you can also get goose bumps as confirmation of a correct response. Goose bumps also come when your ancestors are pointing out something that's important. That's something that happens to me very frequently. When I get goose bumps, I know that spirit is very close and that I'm on the right track.

As you've seen before, spirit may only make you *think about a part of your body* to identify themselves. For example, if you find your focus on one of your legs, you could be sensing someone who had one bad leg, an amputation, or maybe just a limp.

You mustn't worry, though, that these symptoms will become yours. When you feel their physical signatures, it's only a temporary, intuitive experience. You are a Divine, eternal being. The sensations you feel are only there to help you identify your ancestral guides—and get the messages they want to share. Also, please don't worry about your ancestors. They don't feel any pain or discomfort.

**The symptoms of your ancestors
are no longer symptoms.
They are now *signatures*.**

Writing in your journal will help you discover the patterns and meanings that spirit's physical cues and movements give you. Now it's time to get some signatures of spirit.

. . . .

Getting Physical

Close your eyes, and take a deep breath. As you invite your ancestors forward, start to see or sense them around you. They want to share their physical signatures with you. Softly say to yourself, I feel spirit. And when you do, you open to spirit's gentle touch. Notice every subtle feeling or sensation. Also notice any thoughts you have about your own body. This is how your ancestors show you who they are. Take a few moments to notice everything you're getting.

After that, they want to give you a kinesthetic sensation that helps you know who they are. Say to yourself, I feel spirit move. And notice what happens. You might feel like marching, or sewing, or sipping a cup of tea. You might get an idea of these movements, or you might want to make those movements with your body. Let yourself sense it—and do it. And then do it with an even broader sweep, and see what happens.

After a few moments, say thank you to your ancestors, and bring yourself back. As you write about your experience in your journal, consider who these ancestors are and what these sensations told you.

. . . .

2. Memories

Memories are some of spirit's favorite ways to identify themselves—and to give you messages. The memories they share can be of dates, places, events, music, and so much more. Your ancestors will remind you of the spaghetti they made every Sunday when you helped with the meatballs. They'll share the memory of their favorite movie that you saw with them, or the trip you took with them skiing in the Rockies.

Memories don't only belong to your biological ancestors, but to all your forerunners—including those who connect with you through groups or purposes. For instance, if you're an artist, they may send you a memory of a painting that you saw in a museum to identify themselves through a style of painting.

I have a client who is an army nurse. She had read a book about the history of nursing in the army. When she was working in the army hospital on base, those early nursing ancestors sent her recollections of that book when they wanted to tell her they're with her. She could feel a whole group of them giving their support and lifting her energy—especially when she was stressed and overtired. Whenever she had a question, somehow an idea would just pop into her mind. This is an example of group ancestors at work.

When it comes to memories, just about anything can be an identifier or a message. (We'll look at memories as messages a little more later.) Your ancestors can send you memories of what your grandmother looked like, or the farm that your great-grandparents owned, or your uncle's pocketknife, or the stories you've heard about those who have gone long before.

Sometimes there can be a challenge when you sense a memory, whether it's for identification or for a message. That challenge—like others—comes when the left brain gets in the way of the right. Because memories come directly out of your own experience, you might find yourself saying, *This can't be real. I'm only remembering this. I'm just getting this because of the book I read or picture I saw.* But the truth is that spirit is telepathically dropping those memories into your mind to reach out to you.

That's also true when people remember their loved ones just going through their day. People don't realize it, but they're actually having a memory of an ancestor because that spirit has just stepped into the room. That happens to everybody because spirit visits everybody. After all, people don't stop loving when they die. Indeed, once they discover the radiant souls that they truly are, they not only *love* even more, they *visit* even more!

So get ready now to invite your ancestors to share their memories. Of course, you may get other perceptions, too. Just let yourself spontaneously notice whatever happens for you. And, as always, trust everything you get.

. . . .

Down Memory Lane

Close your eyes, and send an invitation to your ancestors in spirit. Take a deep breath, and start to notice your ancestors there. Feel their presence and love as you open your heart to them.

Now, with another breath, say the words, I remember spirit! *And immediately, you do! You start to remember their faces, photos, trinkets, jewelry, and any of the other things that you connect to them. Take a few minutes to let these memories flood your mind, your heart, and your experience.*

After a few moments, your forerunners want to remind you of a place. Say to yourself again, I remember spirit! *Right then, your ancestors remind you of some of their favorite places. You may recall a city, a house, or a street. Or perhaps you think of where they were born—or a place where you had visited with them. Take a few moments to see where you are.*

Now they want to remind you of some special events that happened with them—any special day or time. Say again, I remember spirit! *See and sense these events completely. Notice everything. These memories share their love, but they also tell you who's here with you. Experience these memories in every way.*

Finally, your ancestors are going to help you remember something that acts as a message for you. Immediately a memory comes to mind. It can be of anything. See it and sense it fully. Even if you don't know what it means, let it play out.

Now start to wrap that up. Say thank you to these wonderful ancestors who love you so. There will be more memories to come!

. . . .

Don't forget to take some notes when you're done with this process. Over the next few days, take some time to recall these memories again. Put yourself in each one. There could also be a message there. Is there anything else that you can discover when you relive these memories? They may show you some new insights when you do this again.

3. Their Language and Idioms

Ancestral language is a curious thing. Your ancestors will often introduce themselves briefly through the language and idioms of their country—or even their favorite words that you remember them saying. But sometimes, if you tend to be clairvoyant, you may not have as finely tuned *inner hearing* as you do *inner seeing*. Don't be concerned if you can't precisely identify a certain language. Some languages blur a little for me. For instance, sometimes I can only identify languages as being from Central Europe, or I can "hear" an Irish lilt without actually getting the words. So don't make any judgments about how you sense things. Just open yourself to receive.

There is one other very important thing you need to know about your ancestors' language. Though they will often use their own native language or favorite words to identify themselves, it's very likely that you will perceive their messages in *your* language. Your spirit ancestors talk telepathically with their thoughts. This means that those thoughts occur in your own mind—and therefore in your own language.

Some people have a little difficulty understanding this at first because they don't quite realize how telepathy works. I am reminded of the story of Harry Houdini and Sir Arthur Conan Doyle, who took their wives on a vacation to Atlantic City in 1922. Conan Doyle's wife, who was a medium, brought a message to Harry from his deeply beloved mother. She spoke of great love and support to her dear boy, but Houdini rejected the event—because in life his mother could speak very little English, and even that was broken English at best. He didn't understand that messages from spirit are telepathic and are perceived through the mind (and language) of the receiver—in this case, Mrs. Conan Doyle.

Of course, if you already speak the language that your foreign ancestors speak, you could easily get their messages in that language because you think that way, too. So remember, spirit ancestors may identify themselves with a few words or idioms of their native tongue, but you will often perceive their telepathic thoughts in yours.

4. Signs of Life

Spirit's signs of life are exactly that—the signs of who they were, what they did, and how they lived. Although they often start out as identifiers, they can turn into messages, too. Such signs include the scenes, symbols, music, foods, tools, and objects of their lives. They show their careers, the pursuits that mattered to them, the things and activities they loved, the objects they owned, and—of course—the endeavors and purposes they may want to pursue with you! Here are some images and ideas that characterize these signs of life.

Signs of Life	
Scenes	**Objects**
• Trains, stations, tracks, whistles	• Military uniforms and medals
• Horses, saddles, riding gear	• Nurses' caps, stethoscopes
• Bakeries, baked goods, and flour	• Toolboxes and tools
• Football games and fields	• Bookkeeping column pads
• Battle scenes	• Masonic symbols and rings
• Golf courses, golfing, and clubs	• Card tables, cards, and card games
• Gardens, vegetable and flower beds	• Baseball equipment, uniforms
• Baseball games and stadiums	• Musical instruments
• Universities, schools, libraries	• Desks, typewriters, office equipment
• Factories, mines	• Sewing machines, needles, thread

These scenes and symbols are just the tip of the iceberg. There are so many more. Your ancestors will use them, first to identify who they are. For instance, an image or idea of an upright piano could identify an uncle who played the piano and had a piano in his living room. If one of your ancestors had been a cook by trade, you could get a scene of restaurant tables, cooking implements, or even specific kinds of foods. Some of these different types of perceptions could also be symbols for names. For instance, I once got an image of a carpenter's toolbox to indicate the name Carpenter.

Of course, these types of scenes and objects could also relay messages from your ancestors. I remember one of my private students whose great-great-grandfather's pocket watch carried a message all by itself. She had never known him in life, but she felt very connected to him—even as a young girl—when she saw his photographs. The watch had been passed down, and now she had it—saving it for her little boy when he grew up.

In one of our early classes, she told me that she had been sensing the watch frequently that week—and sometimes it's very large in her vision. She assumed that he was visiting a lot, and she was delighted about how present he was for her. But I told her that since he was literally making the watch a *big* deal, he might be trying to get a message delivered. And that message was about time. So I asked her what was happening around her that was of a timely nature. She said that she still had to submit an application for an art class she wanted to take, but the due date was still weeks away. I told her that she better *watch* her time on that. (You know I had to say it!) She sent in the application right away, and she was very glad that she did. She got the last open spot in the class. (Thanks, Grampa!)

This is a good example of an identifier that also acts as a symbolic message. It illustrates something that happens quite frequently in communicating with spirit.

**Once you've identified your ancestors,
if the symbol keeps recurring, they're
trying to give you a message.**

5. Names and Initials

In ancestral communication, names can be perceived with your inner vision in a number of ways. Sometimes you can see letters or initials. Often, when I perceive an initial, spirit will put it in big block letters for a masculine name and in floral script for a feminine name. You can also get visual cues that reflect a name—such as an image of a lily for Lily, a robin for Robin, or a crown for the last name King. I often see a game of jacks when there is more than one Jack in the family. Once, I connected with a client's boss who showed me an image of a man fishing. I thought he was sharing a happy memory, but I discovered that his name was Fisher.

You could get an intuitive peek in other ways. You could see a name on an envelope or a deed. You could get initials on a locket, a signet ring, or embroidered on clothes or hankies. All of these occur for me pretty frequently.

Names can also come through any of the inner senses—even taste and smell. Smell seems to occur when people have the same names as colognes, flowers, plants, or spices (such as Sage). Tastes happen more rarely and are often connected to nicknames. (I have gotten the nicknames Ham, Cookie, and Sugar a lot.)

Some names can indicate an ancestor without necessarily being that person's name. For instance, I once got the names Mary and William, and it identified my client's grandfather who went to William & Mary College. It was still a spirit identifier, but it was through a place name.

Of course, your ancestors also identify living people by name. I remember identifying a number of ancestors for a client, and they were all sharing personal, helpful messages for her. Soon I began to get the name *White* telepathically—through an inner knowing. I continued to perceive *White* many times in many ways, including seeing the name, hearing it, and seeing the color white. But my client assured me that she knew no one living or in spirit by that name.

Still, it didn't concern me that my client couldn't recognize it— after spending a lifetime of trusting spirit. I simply told her that it would be a good idea to write the name down—since spirit often shares names of living people who are coming to be helpful in the future.

Well, some years later, that client gave me a call. She told me that her husband had had a heart transplant, and they had discovered that the donor's name was White!

So, here's a process that'll help you practice getting your ancestors' language, names, initials, and *signs of life* evidence. And you'll also get some messages, too. Open yourself to all of your inner senses. Be spontaneous, be quick. And trust everything.

Collecting the Evidence

Close your eyes, and send forth the invitation to your ancestors. With a relaxing breath, say the words, Spirit's here. *Fill yourself with that truth as you say again,* Spirit's here. *Immediately, you feel your ancestors gathering all around you.*

Now some ancestors want to identify themselves through their language. Let yourself hear—with your inner hearing or knowing—some of their words, whether they're familiar or strange to you. See if you notice an accent, too. Just sense whatever happens. After a moment, ask your ancestors from another land to share a message with you. No matter what their language is, they're thinking this message telepathically at you. What's the first word or idea that pops into your mind?

After you're done with that, quickly let yourself get a name. Perhaps you see a name. Or you see an initial on a piece of jewelry. Or you suddenly just think a name. Whatever happens, trust it.

Now some of your ancestors are even wearing name tags for you! Say to yourself, Picture this! *Immediately, an ancestor steps up wearing a name tag. What do you see and sense? Now notice that a number of your other forerunners are wearing name tags. Take a look around, and see some of those names now. What are they?*

After a moment, your ancestors share a scene or object that indicates one of their signs of life. It could be something they wore or owned. Or they may send you an idea of a career, a favorite activity, a place they loved, or anything at all. Just notice whatever you get. And if something changes, let that happen, too. You certainly have a number of different ancestors with you. So notice all the signs of life you get. Do you know whom these signs identify? It's okay if you don't; just let it all happen.

Now your ancestors use a scene, an idea, or one of their own signs of life for a symbolic message for you. With your complete imaging, see or sense anything that comes to mind. It could be something that belonged to them but also gives you a message—like a watch tells you about time. Notice what you get. If the symbol changes, let that happen, too. Just sense every detail. And trust everything you get.

After a moment, start to wrap that up. Be aware of any last thing that comes to mind from any of your ancestors. Say thank you to all of your forerunners, and tell them you'll reach out to them again soon.

. . . .

Be sure to take some notes after this process. Make some observations about what your ancestors sent and how you sensed it. Make a note about the languages you experienced. What signs of life did you get? How did any of them also turn into messages? And when any memories of your ancestors pop up throughout your day, be sure to say hello. Have a little dialogue with them for a moment or two.

CHAPTER 7

LANDCESTORS

The Cultures and Territories Where You Began

The longer you can look back,
The farther you can look forward.

— WINSTON CHURCHILL

You've already learned about—and met—some of your family ancestors. Now it's time to go farther back to the people and lands of your family's beginnings. I call these people your *landcestors*.

Of course, this group would include your biological ancestors, but there are many more who are related to you through the territories and cultural histories that you share. A lot of people are taking DNA tests that pinpoint their lands of origin—sometimes going back thousands of years. But you don't have to know your lineage to know your landcestors.

Your landcestors know you, even if you don't have a conscious awareness of them. Many of them have been helping you for a long time. With the processes in this book, you can meet— and speak—with your known and unknown ancestors anytime. (You will also find more processes in my audio program *Ancestor Spirit Communication.*)

Changing Fright to Light

There are a great number of ancestors from different times and places who are not yet known to you. But you needn't have any concerns or worries when calling unknown ancestors.

As you expand your reach into the spirit world beyond your family, friends, and biological ancestors, don't fall into the mistake of thinking that your unknown ancestors are something to fear. Your ancestors live in a world of light and love. It is the spiritual world of the soul, not the physical world of ego.

There have been only a few instances when I have experienced "negative" spirits, and in each case they were related to a specific location, not roaming about the ancestral realms. But you don't have to take my word for it. London's Society for Psychical Research investigated a large number of spirit experiences and came to the conclusion that "ghosts of a more persistent type [more physically active] are associated with certain localities and houses" (Sir Ernest Bennett, London's Society for Psychical Research).

Even when I used to "clean houses," most of the spirits we met there were simply members of the families that lived in those houses. Sometimes they would move keys or flash a light here or there, just to say hello. All those families were delighted when they found out that their playful ancestors wanted to speak with them directly.

In the end, there were only a few places—out of dozens—where there was a difficult spirit present, and it was always only connected to the location. In those cases, and in every case, the power to overcome hate and fear was love. You'll get a chance to experience the brilliant perspective of that power shortly.

Another worry that some have is that spirit's messages could be "negative" or something they don't want to hear. There may be some difficult issues in your life. But spirit wants to help you with those issues and give you an opportunity for discovery and growth. Your ancestors also want to help you release past patterns—to clear karma, heal relationships, and lay the ground work for new and happy directions. (We'll discuss more of this in Chapter 9, on ancestral and karmic healing).

The Invulnerable Empath

The final worry that some have with unknown spirits is that the spirit's body signatures could impact them physically. This is especially concerning for people who are very empathic—people who can easily sense others' physical or emotional conditions. It's imperative to remember that—besides being sensitive—you are also divinely powerful. You are invulnerable with eternal strength and light. Hold that truth absolutely and joyfully.

> **As an empath, you can sense the physical perceptions of your spirit ancestors. But you don't have to take them on as your own—because they don't belong to you. Indeed, they don't even belong to spirit anymore.**

Those physical sensations are a part of spirit's past, and you can lay them aside, too. Now they are only signatures. So sense them, let them inform you, and then let them go. You are the invulnerable empath.

Though all of these concerns seem different, they all stem from the personal self and its left-brain, divisive thoughts. Sometimes opening to unknown spirits might make you feel a bit fearful. Or spirits' messages might reveal some buried emotions that must be confronted. Or a heightened, empathetic sensitivity might make you *think* you're more vulnerable.

If any of these concerns come up for you, there is a successful response technique that you can use. You can use this technique anytime you're caught in a moment of fear and worry.

· ·

Your Truths, Your Power

Close your eyes. Take a minute to think about a time when you may have felt fear or hesitancy, or self-judgment. Don't recreate the situation. Just recall it and notice how you feel.

Take a deep breath. Start to think beyond your personal life, and remember who you are—who you have been forever. With your next breath, bring into yourself the word God. Feel that Divine and brilliant energy fill you—moving through all of your body, down to your toes, and out to your fingertips.

Now breathe in the words, God's love. And feel yourself fill with the energy of peace and compassion. Boundless love washes over you and through you— sending away all fear and judgment.

After a few moments, say to yourself, God's light. And instantly, the whole room is alive with light. With the next breath, bring in those words, God's light. See and feel the incandescent and brilliant power fill every cell, every thought, and every part of you. Do you notice any warmth, any colors, and lifting of your energy?

You are a radiant being, and light shines forth from the Divine spark you are. You are flooded with brilliant and limitless love. The boundless energy and compassionate power dispel all fear, worry, judgment, and concern.

Feel the light and love that can never be vanquished or diminished. With a deep breath, bring in the word God again. Feel the Divine source that is your genesis, your energy, your truth. Do this whenever you want to remember the light and love you are forever.

. . . .

Your Cultural Heritage

You don't have to live in the lands of your ancestors to share a legacy with them. They have a connection with you that goes far beyond the miles—or even the centuries. Your landcestors want to help you to become more aware of your cultural heritage— the customs, arts, traditions, skills, and ideas that belong to the civilization you share.

There are countless cultural traditions. Scottish bagpipes, African art and weaving, Swiss watch-making, Russian ballet, Native American natural medicine, and the Argentinian tango are only a few examples of a whole world of customs, music, arts, and pastimes. You may already participate in some of your traditions, or you may have a mild interest in others. It's very likely that there are some you have yet to discover.

My father's father's family hails from Switzerland, where—in days gone by—skiing was a mode of winter transportation. My father took to skiing like a duck to water. When my sister is skiing, she often feels him, and the Swiss skiers who had gone before, on the slopes with her.

I never really cared for skiing—it was too cold! But there are times—especially when a work project loomed before me—that I can feel my dad strapping invisible skis to my feet, making me feel like bending my knees as if I were skiing moguls in the Rockies. If you're not familiar with the term *moguls*, just imagine lots of five-foot-high protrusions sticking out of a very steep mountain face. And your job is to navigate around the moguls while shooting down the steep slope at very high speeds. My mother could beat any man alive at skiing moguls—even at the age of 85!

You need to have knees of rubber to do moguls. And the movement I feel when my dad gives me the intuitive moguls is a message telling me to add speed and flexibility in my approach to a work project before me. I definitely should not pursue the project with a hard, unbendable approach. This has been a very helpful message for me because it has helped me soften my agenda. When I do that, I become open to seeing new options I hadn't known before. Thanks, Dad!

I remember another story about a cultural legacy that involves chocolate. (Yum!) I have a friend from Belgium named Brecht Saelens, who—with his American wife, Sara—used to own a coffee house in New York State. They decided to make and sell their own chocolate bars there, too. Brecht's uncle in spirit had been a chocolate maker in Belgium all his life, and since Brecht is also a medium, he reached out to his uncle. Brecht created a number of recipes for different chocolate bars—award-winning chocolate bars, I might add. Belgian chocolate! Now, that's a cultural legacy everyone can love!

As you can see, your landcestors aren't just your territorial predecessors. They show you the legacies that you can use today, and they help you discover the unknown birthrights that lie deep within you. Let's take a look now.

. . . .

A Look at Legacies

Close your eyes, and take a deep breath. From your heart send a call to your landcestors. Say softly to yourself, My landcestors are here. *With each breath, you sense more and more around you. You may only recognize some, but that's okay. Just be with them, and notice everything you see and feel. They may be wearing clothes from different times and different places. Don't analyze it. Just sense whatever you get.*

Now let yourself think of one of the customs, traditions, arts, talents, or activities belonging to your landcestors that interests you. If there isn't one, just let spirit share something. This is your landcestral legacy— your birthright. It could go back to a civilization that was hundreds of years past, or it could be more current. Say to yourself, I sense my landcestral legacy now.

Instantly, you perceive a sound, a symbol, word, an image, or a thought that gives you a little hint of that legacy. Let your ancestors show you the next step you can take in discovering and pursuing this birth right now. Notice every subtle detail, sensation, and color. And if you get a kinesthetic movement, give it a try!

As you start to bring yourself back, thank these wonderful ancestors who make your history so present for you. Make a promise to connect with them again soon.

. . . .

Of course, take some notes in your journal when you've finished. Even if you don't understand everything you experienced, write it down anyway. Perhaps you got an image that seemed strange. Or there was a word—or part of a word—that was foreign to you. Or maybe there was a symbol that you didn't comprehend. Make a note of it all so that you can have a chance to investigate it more fully in the coming days and weeks.

Lands Beyond

Sometimes landcestral connections can go beyond that culture's native lands. There can even be some cross-connections between places and people, too.

I remember the story of the mother-in-law of Joe Lieberman, the former U.S. senator. His wife's mother had been in a Nazi concentration camp when it was liberated by the U.S. Army. As it turns out, one of those liberating soldiers was the future father of Senator Lieberman's press secretary! It was an ancestral connection that met again across the miles and the generations!

In another incident, one of my clients from Italy met the man of her dreams on a trip to Greece. Her Italian family and his Greek family had both grown olives for generations. It was only after they were married and looking into their ancestry, that they discovered that another such marriage connecting their families had taken place many generations ago. In the 1800s, a man from her family had met a woman from his on a transatlantic crossing to the United States, where they married and—with their children—grew grapes for their winery in New York State.

You'd be surprised how often stories like these occur around the world. Ancestors traveled everywhere—especially coastal and naval ancestors. There are families that stretch from Scotland to Jamaica; from England to South Africa; from Portugal to Brazil.

No matter where your ancestral lands were, there was probably a great deal of movement and travel done by previous ancestral generations before you. You may not be aware of the different places in your landcestral past, but you can find out about them now.

Your Landcestral Map

Close your eyes as you take a deep, relaxing breath. Say to yourself, My landcestors are here. *Immediately, you are filled with a profound sense of their loving presence.*

Now your landcestors want to show you a map of your ancestral territories. You may know some of those territories, but let yourself be flexible with whatever you get. Say to yourself, Spirit shows me. *Instantly, you see a map of the world. If it's only a partial map, or if it's different in some way, let that happen. If you don't see it, let yourself feel it, sense it, or know it.*

However you get it, perceive this map completely. Then say again, Spirit shows me. *And suddenly, certain places on the map start twinkling. Notice the locations that are shining on your map. Take a moment to scan the places you already know. Then bring your attention to one of the locations that is new to you.*

As soon as you do, a few landcestors from that location step up to you. Meet them, and sense them completely. Now they want to share some insights about this location. Say again, Spirit shows me. *As soon as you do, you perceive an image, a word, a thought, an object, a sound, or a symbol that tells you a little bit about this place. What do you get? Notice every detail. Do these perceptions bring up any feelings for you? Sense and trust everything.*

Take a moment to finish that up. Start to bring yourself back. Say thank you to your landcestors. Together you will look into the lands of your history again.

As you take notes about your experience, think back to the travels in your life. Were there any places that seemed to have a compelling energy to you then? Did those places shine on your landcestral map? It's important to take your journal with you whenever you travel. Note what you sense in your intuition, your meditation, your dreams. You'd be surprised at how often your travels take you back to the lands of your ancestors.

Generations of Outlanders

There was a military tradition in the Scottish Highlands that spanned generations of Highland warriors. They would stand together in their family groups, and as they ran into the battle with swords drawn, they would call the names of their ancestors. Some of them were able to recite their genealogy going back 20 generations. Some would invoke their mythological ancestors, too.

They would call their ancestors in such a way that it was almost a blend of recitation and chanting. Their enemies—usually English troops—would often think that the Highlanders were singing as they were going into the fray.

The Highlanders lost the last great Battle of Culloden to the British in only one hour. Now, you may wonder how much help your ancestors can be if many generations couldn't turn the tides for the Highland Jacobites in their battle. But the British had far outnumbered the Jacobites, and that was a physical-world reality that could not be altered.

Yet the Highlanders had the courage and the passion to go into battle and stand for their land. They wanted support in their courage, strength, and purpose to stand up to the danger before them. So the Jacobites summoned the army of their dead.

Spirit is not physical. Spirit is mind, love, energy, and light. Their primary purpose—among all of their other purposes—is to help us know the power and light in our own minds and hearts. What fire could you ignite in your life with a great army of strength and love behind you?

. . . .

Your Ancestral Army

Take a deep breath, and close your eyes. Make a call now to the great army of your ancestors—your family, your landcestors, your purpose, group, and past-life ancestors—all of them. Say to yourself, My Ancestral Army is here. And start to feel them all gather now. Sense how many there are, and feel their love and undying support.

Take another deep, relaxing breath, and say again, My Ancestral Army is here! *Look around yourself at the vast numbers of them. You feel their strength and their gentility. This is your Army of Compassionate Power, ten thousand strong.*

They are your Army of Light, of Mind, of Force. They press around you, and with them you can feel your energy heighten, your love deepen, and your light grow with every breath. They are all with you now. Look around you. Take a deep breath, and breathe in the boundless energy of a thousand generations. What contribution can you make with this Ancestral Army beside you? See it happening now.

CHAPTER 8

SPRINGBOARD TO SPIRIT

Techniques for Psychic Immediacy

If you're gonna go up
to the bell, ring it!

— JOHN CALLEY

John Calley was the head of production at Warner Bros. Studios when actor Mel Brooks asked him how far he could go in his comedy. This was how Calley told him to take it all the way!

I love his quote. It's an amazing call to action, saying, *If you want to do something, do it!* Don't hesitate, don't hold yourself back, and don't tie your hands with worry or rules!

Breaking the Rules

Any intuitive experience needs to be spontaneous and free-flowing, but that doesn't mean that you should have no form or design. Indeed, having just a little structure can help you be free-flowing in your perceptions.

Still, it's imperative that any structure you use in your ancestral communication must not be dogmatic or rigid. Rigidity impedes an easy flow with your ancestors. Many of the processes in this book are focused on letting you meet up with spirit in a moment—just like you would meet living people. The way you approach spirit is your springboard to knowing them.

The Merriam-Webster Dictionary tells us that a springboard is a "flexible, springy board," used as a starting point for taking off—or a jumping-off place. *Flexible* is the key word here. If you want to *take off* with spirit, you need flexibility and spontaneity. Therefore, any design or form you use must be short and simple—so it doesn't get in the way of your experience. After all, if you're focused on satisfying the demands of your structure, you will not be focused on the experience of your ancestors.

Mediumship, by definition, is identifying and communicating with people in the spirit world. There are some mediums who have very rigid structures in their spirit communication. The techniques they use and even the information they get from spirit must meet certain, and often limiting, requirements.

**Whenever you say there's only one way
that something must happen, you prevent it
from happening any other way.**

For instance, some mediums draw a very hard-lined distinction between what's physic and what's mediumship, and this is based solely on the content of the information perceived. They believe that, when you're perceiving your ancestor's evidence and identifiers, you're a medium. But when you're getting information about your life or your friends' lives, it's not spirit who is telling you. You're *only* being psychic. You're just picking up information that seems to be floating in the air.

This view of spirit seems a little myopic to me. If spirit people are capable of telling you who they are, why wouldn't they be capable of talking to you about your life?

Trying to decide what's psychic and what's mediumship is a problem on the face of it. First, since everything anyone perceives is through the psychic sense, everything is psychic—even identifying spirit. Second, since it's the spirit people who are communicating the information—even the information about your life, it's spirit communication, or mediumship.

Now, it's true that there are some psychics who don't know that spirit is working with them or don't know how to identify spirit. In that case, it is not mediumship when evidence of spirit wasn't given. But if a medium identifies your spirit ancestors with strong evidence, you know that spirit is there. Your spirit people will also be there with the information you need. Your ancestors certainly aren't going to leave before they give you some help and guidance about your life. After all, when your grandmother was alive, I'm sure she never called you on the phone to say, "Hi, I'm wearing my rose-print dress and my pearls, but don't ask me about your life, because I'm not going to talk to you about it."

If you start to make rules important, you'll spend your time analyzing if you're meeting those qualifications instead of meeting your ancestors.

Please understand, I'm not trying to convert you to my way of spirit communication. You must create your own way. I'm really just sharing what I've discovered after many years in this work. Too many rules can be the tall weeds that entangle you. So whatever structure you may design, be sure it's simple. Of course, there are *lots* of fast and simple techniques that you can add. You've experienced some already. They're the icing on the cake! But you don't *have* to do them.

Always remember that you are the architect here. You must create your work with spirit in the way that fits you best. If you want rules, see them more as guidelines.

Don't make listening to rules more important than listening to spirit.

That's why I share these fast and immediate exercises—because they break through barriers of thought and help you reach your ancestors. These techniques have worked for me—some more than others, and some at different times than others. But you have to see how they fit you. So please consider them all; try them, and play with them all. Create some of your own, too. Design the approach you want to take for yourself. No one knows better than you what works best for you. But keeping it simple also keeps you open, spontaneous, and free.

Diving into Spirit

The techniques and ideas in this chapter can help you quickly and easily spring into your connection with spirit. Let's take a look.

Your Springboard to Spirit

1. **Absolute trust** gives you the freedom and spontaneity that make it all happen.

2. **Speed** helps you stay in the receptive state.

3. **Immediacy** gives you instantaneous responses to what you see and hear.

1. Absolute Trust

Even though I use lots of different techniques, I think the only rule really necessary in all spirit communication is: *Trust every perception absolutely.* This is the one truth that never waivers for me. I may not know whom the perception describes or what it means. But whatever I see, sense, or feel, I trust it without question or hesitation.

Healing studies have shown that when doctors have created positive expectations, positive outcomes occurred. You can create extraordinary outcomes in communicating with your ancestors by defining your experience in very positive and powerful absolutes.

Immediate Moments with Your Ancestors

Here are some declarations that you can make frequently. When you do, feel them deep inside you, and hold them as your visceral and unimpeachable truth. With some of them, I have added some mini-moment processes in parentheses. Do them immediately, and see what happens.

- *I never hesitate* when linking with spirit. *(Close your eyes and, without hesitation, notice an ancestor with you now.)*

- *Everything* I perceive when I'm talking to spirit is from spirit. *(Close your eyes, and get a word from your ancestors now.)*

- I know my ancestors *completely. (Close your eyes, and feel a loved one touch your heart.)*

- I react to spirit *immediately. (An ancestor is handing you something now. What is it?)*

- Truth, power, and joy are my *only* experiences when I link with my spirit ancestors.

- I have *total* spontaneity, freedom, and speed in connecting to my forerunners.

- I experience only excitement and bliss when talking with spirit. *(Close your eyes, and let your heart lift with the joy of feeling spirit beside you now.)*

These are meant to be declared with power, not just said. And you can create more of your own. You can also turn some into a mini-moment process, like I did. I love to proclaim, _I never hesitate when linking with spirit!_ and then instantly see who's there. So use these proclamations and speed exercises frequently. They help you know spirit moment by moment.

Don't Give It Another Thought

If you've decided to communicate with spirit and you find yourself hesitating, it's usually because you're in your head. You might be thinking about what steps to take, or you may be thinking about your abilities. But one thing's certain: you're only thinking.

As Mel Brooks discovered, thinking about ringing a bell isn't ringing it. And thinking about communicating with spirit isn't doing it. Indeed, thinking is an *impediment* to doing it. That is why it's good to develop speed in connecting to your ancestors. But remember, being fast is *not* your goal. It is the way to *reach* your goal.

**If you want to communicate with spirit,
you must be out of your mind.**

You can't be in a receptive state while you're in the mental state—thinking or analyzing, judging or measuring (and that's why rules can be so prohibitive).

Spirit communication is not what you think! It's what you feel, what you sense, what you perceive. And feeling, sensing, and perceiving are all spontaneous and immediate. Without them, you will stay on the surface of every ancestral experience.

2. Speed

Let's take a look at what an old-school medium has to say about thinking and the clairvoyant—or intuitive—experience of spirit. Andrew Jackson Davis is considered by many to have been the father of Spiritualism, though he might not be quick to agree since he wasn't a big fan of organized religion. Born in 1826, he started hearing spirit voices as a child. He was a popular medium with many notable friends. He also wrote many best-selling books on spirituality. Though his books were very popular at the time, they were also like some other books of his time—extremely abstruse and verbose. It's a shame, too, because there certainly are many pearls of wisdom in all those tangled weeds of words.

In his five-book series called the Great Harmonia, Davis lays out the philosophy of the seven states of man—or the progression of humankind. The Clairvoyant State and Spiritual State are the two highest states. Here, I'd like to share with you his conclusions about the perception of spirit in these states.

Insights from Andrew Jackson Davis on the State of Sensing Spirit

- *You're more receptive than reflective.*

   In other words, Davis tells us that you feel more than you think. The bottom line is that sensing is far more important than thinking about what you sense.

- *You possess more clear perception than comprehension.*

   In this, Davis tells us that the lack of clarity in comprehending spirit's message does not indicate a lack of clarity in sensing spirit or even sensing their messages. This may be a little confusing at first. Just imagine it this way: Your uncle hand-delivers an envelope with a letter in it to you. But for some reason, once you open the envelope, you find that the letter is in a language you can't read. Not being able to understand the letter didn't keep you from meeting your uncle, receiving the envelope, and seeing the letter. And that is your first aim with spirit—to meet them and *to receive* the messages they have for you. You can take your time to interpret those messages later.

- *You discern more than you have time or ability to understand.*

   This may be the most important. Davis isn't saying you won't understand your perceptions. He's saying that in the clairvoyant state, time is of the essence. Notice what you feel immediately—whether you understand it or not. You can work on understanding it later. If you try to understand it while you're in the experience of perceiving, you'll take yourself right out of the clairvoyant state.

Now you know the real need for speed. It's not just about being fast. It's about staying receptive.

3. Immediacy

To be immediate means to happen at once, instantly, without delay—*not separated in time.*

Immediacy and speed are very similar. Speed in ancestral communication gives you a fast approach to meeting them. But immediacy requires an instantaneous response to whatever is happening. So, as you do these quick, little processes, open yourself to the instantaneous perception that comes in that very moment, with no hesitation—no *separation in time.* When you experience no separation in time, you will experience no separation from spirit.

We've already worked with some of the declarations and mini-moment processes that help to create immediacy in your work with your ancestors.

These mini-moment processes are great to promote quick action, but they also help to train the right brain to be at the ready, especially if you do these little processes intermittently throughout your day.

Longer visualization processes certainly don't prevent you from having immediate responses. I'm not suggesting that longer processes should be replaced by mini-exercises. Indeed, in-depth processes can really help lead you to more in-depth messages, as you'll see in Chapter 20. But when building speed and immediacy, different kinds of little processes, including mini-moment declarations, power words, and trigger symbols, can be very helpful.

Spontaneous Linking to the World Beyond

As you start using new methods, it's important to keep changing things up a bit. Doing the same thing over and over makes it very easy to fall into a rut. Your energy can drop, and you could get bored. This is not what you want to bring to the table when you're meeting your forerunners.

Besides changing techniques, alternating the trigger words and phrases is important, too. Power words are meant to be strong, sharp, and immediate. If you only use one or two over and over for a long time, they'll start to become dull for you—like a knife used too often. This is called *word fatigue*. There may be a few words that stay sharp. For instance, *Open* and *Oneness* have always worked for me. But many words do get dull. Don't worry if it happens for you—even if it's with the power words that you liked the most. All you have to do is choose some new ones. Later, you can come back to the old ones again, and you'll find that they won't be dull anymore! Also, once in a while, you should try some of the words that you didn't like at first. We all grow and change, and the types of things that we find useful will often change, too.

Having many options also gives you many opportunities. That's the reason that I try to teach *a lot* of different sensing, imaging, and word devices. Then you can change them around and give yourself new options. Be sure to create some of your own, too. There's something very exciting when you create your own, especially when it's a collaboration with spirit.

I've been very lucky in that regard. Spirit has been inserting new methods and symbols into my meditations and consultations for many, many years. My forerunners seem to love showing me new and exciting techniques. And I love it, too! After teaching mediumship for decades, if I want my students to feel that fire, I'd better still get excited, too! In later chapters, I'll share with you some of the intriguing and very telling symbols spirit has taught me. But for now, here's a chance to practice with some new methods and power words—and a chance to reshape some old ones as well.

Power words are designed to evoke spontaneous responses. While they're all power words, I sometimes call them trigger words, commands, and declarations, too. I often use those names interchangeably, but there are some minor distinctions. To me, trigger words can get responses off like a shot. Command words and phrases are meant to direct your focus. They're not to command spirit or even to command you. They're directives on where to place your focus. And declarations (or proclamations) are whole statements that declare a truth so absolute that it becomes reality—a reality in experience, not just in mind. So let's get going with a little declaration *Now*. Your ancestors are waiting!

. . . .

The Truth Is in Here

Close your eyes, and take a deep breath. With each easy breath that follows, you find yourself relaxing more and more deeply.

Say to yourself softly, but with absolute conviction, Spirit is Always here for me. *Immediately, you feel your ancestors and your own spirit, your Higher Self. With your Higher Self, you are filled with the light and love of your eternal truth. Take a moment to rest in that beauty now.*

After a moment, declare again, Spirit is Always here for me. *Instantly, you sense more ancestors and your higher guides, the Ascended Masters, with you. Some may be on either side of you, and some are in front of you and behind you. Welcome them. Let yourself sense everything about them now.*

Be with them for a few minutes. Then start to have a dialogue with them. Ask any question you have. Then notice the first, immediate word, image, or idea you get. Take a few minutes to do this now.

Very well; start to wrap that up. Say thank you when you've finished. Know that, whenever you declare, Spirit is Always here for me, *you will feel the great spirit inside you—and those spirits who are all around you.*

. . . .

As usual, take some notes when you're done with this process. And if you'd like to find audios of other processes like these, just check out my audio program *Ancestor Spirit Communication*.

Power Words for Lightning Linking

I like to change up the words and images I use when opening to my ancestors. Images are softer, but to me, power words are like lightning. They always bring energy and immediacy to the action they name.

Command Words feel more like an interaction with spirit. Even though they don't command spirit, they help to direct your focus and spirit's focus, bringing them together.

One of the stronger commands is one simple word: *Now!* I don't think there's another word that triggers lightning immediacy more. You can create new commands that contain that word, or you can simply add *Now!* to any word or phrase you'd like. Let's try it with some phrases you've already used. Let yourself respond to the *Now!* and see what it does for you.

. . . .

What Do You Sense Now?

With a gentle, relaxing breath, close your eyes, and send a happy invitation forth to your ancestors.

Say softly to yourself, I sense spirit Now. *And right Now you see and sense the ancestors who are with you. Open your heart and all your inner senses to feel them, Now.*

After you wrap that up, say to yourself, I sense a message from spirit Now. *Instantly notice what you get. Is it a word, a symbol, a feeling? What is your message? Let yourself sense everything Now.*

Now finish that up. For a few moments, simply be with your ancestors. Softly say to yourself, I feel spirit's love Now. *Feel this soft embrace for a few minutes. Then say thank you to these ancestors and bring yourself back.*

. . . .

Take some notes after this process. Did you notice that your responses came more quickly by using the word *Now*? If not, try it again. Declare the word *Now* more firmly, and give yourself over to the *Now*.

The following is a list of different trigger words, commands, and declarations with this powerful immediacy word added. After each command, you're asked for an instant response. See which ones are strongest for you. Then pick one you'd like to do for a week. Later come back to this list, and choose others. Refer to this list intermittently so you can be sure to try different ones. Also, you can take command by creating your own list of *Now* commands for yourself.

· ·

Commanding Immediacy NOW!

Open Now!

Who is the first person you sense?

I am one with spirit Now.

Instantly feel your connection with
an ancestor who is with you, even if you
don't know who that person is.

I see my ancestors Now.

Look! Whom do you see right Now?

Spirit speaks Now.

What is the first spontaneous word you get?

I remember my ancestors Now.

In this very moment, you remember a loved one,
and that person is with you.

I feel spirit Now.

Spontaneously get an energy perception
or body sensation right Now.

My ancestors give me a message Now!

You sense a symbol, a sign, a color, or a thought
from your ancestors instantaneously.

· ·

As you read this list, please be aware that these statements are not meant to be affirmations. Obviously, it seems like they would make wonderful affirmations, but that is not their job. As a matter of fact, if you treat these like affirmations and read them over and over, it will only dull the command *Now*. That is why it's so important, whenever you read them, *do them*! *Feel* the energy as you say it, and emphasize the word *Now*. Then, with no separation in time, let your spirit ancestors immediately fill in the blank. In that moment, focus on what you sense, see, feel, and know.

Play with the commands on this list. But don't read them all frequently. Just pick one and use it intermittently throughout the week. Then in the coming weeks, choose another, and then another. Make some extra ones of your own. Putting each one on its own index card will keep you from having to reread the list over and over, and that will keep the declarations sharp.

If you write one on an index card and take it with you, it could be close at hand. You could do a mini-moment anytime and anywhere you want to sense spirit and their responses in moments. Such daily momentary practices will make you feel that you're walking through the spirit world every day—which you are!

CHAPTER 9

THE PRINCIPLES FOR ANCESTRAL AND KARMIC HEALING

The same power that holds the planets in space
is feeding us breath by breath, moment by moment. . . .
As we are healed, we heal the world.

— REV. SHIRLEY CALKINS-SMITH

Many cultures all the way back to ancient times would call on ancestors for healing. In many tribes, the medicine man would summon the spirits of the dead to help heal the sick.

In these chapters we're going to take a look at working with your different ancestors and past-life guides to help bring healing to historical trauma, karmic patterns, and psychological issues. But even though you're working with your ancestors, it's important to remember that you are responsible for your own healing. When we heal ourselves, we help others to find healing in their lives—not just by lifting the energy, but also by acting as an example and teaching others to heal, too. When we break negative patterns in our lives, we help to break the chain of those patterns for future generations.

Getting Started with Karmic and Ancestral Healing

Karmic and ancestral healing can be a deeply profound experience—one that releases long-held negative, damaging thoughts and behaviors. This release can give you unimpeded freedom to know a new self and to create a new future of success and happiness. There could be past-life patterns, or there may be issues that come from previous generations. Luckily, you have a new chance to create supportive and loving relationships with the ancestors who may be involved.

Often, some of the first spirit people who want to reach out to my clients during my private consultations are the very people who had been distant, difficult, or hurtful. These ancestors certainly may have sourced some of these negative issues, but fixing those very issues is what they want to do now. They come in the light of their spirits with the desire to heal.

Healing with your ancestors requires your time, your focus, and your commitment. Understanding the groundwork will help you on your way to your success. The two key elements in this groundwork are knowing the ancestors who want to help you heal and understanding the patterns you wish to heal.

The Ancestors Who Want to Help You Heal

You probably know those who played a role in your difficulties in this life, but some ancestors who are connected to these negative patterns may be from generations past.

Most patterns move beyond one person or even one generation. For instance, it may be important to heal with your father, with whom you had a difficult relationship, but the difficulties may actually have started with his parents, grandparents, and even beyond.

During my private consultations, it often happens that parents in spirit want to say, *I'm sorry.* But usually, right after that, more ancestors step up to take responsibility because they had started or perpetuated that pattern even before. Whatever the parents had done—selfishness, anger, alcoholism, anything—it had been done to them from the previous generations. This is not an excuse, but it is a reason. The generations that came before want you to know that they contributed to the problem you're having now, and they want to help, too.

Another important thing to know is that some of the ancestors who participate in your healing work may actually come from your past lives. The steps in healing past-life patterns are just like healing ancestral patterns. Important past-life patterns often manifest themselves in this life because, of course, it is your karma to heal them. And very often, you have chosen your birth family to give you the opportunity to address that karma.

Of course, the most significant ancestor from a past life is actually yourself! Ancestors are those who have gone before. Where past lives are concerned, you have gone before and before, and before, and before. So, when doing your healing imaging, be sure to see your past-life self engaged in that pattern.

Of course, there are other important ancestors from past lives who are a part of healing, too. For instance, your critical boss in this life may have been your critical father in a previous life. Often during your process, you will intuitively sense who these ancestors are. But if that doesn't happen, don't let yourself get caught up in overthinking it. You will get to know them as you work with them. Trust that the right ancestors will be there to heal with you. If there are some particular ancestors you want to call, just call them.

It's also important to remember that you have nothing to fear with any of these people. Even those who were mean and hurtful were only that way in the egos of their personal, physical lives. But now, in spirit, they are in their radiant selves. They realize the negative things that they said and did in life. They not only want to say they're sorry and bring healing, but they also want to create a new and higher relationship with you. In life they faltered in their relationship to you, and they want to make up for it now.

Understanding the Patterns

Ancestral trauma and karmic lessons become apparent in present-day patterns, emotions, thoughts, actions, and relationships. Most patterns in a person's life are usually indicative of previous patterns, though, certainly, these patterns are not always bad. For instance, a pattern of daily meditation will often indicate a past life (or many past lives) of spiritual development, prayer, and meditation.

The patterns that need to be healed usually carry strong emotional content. This emotional content acts divisively in people's realization of their Divine soul.

Indicators of Karmic Lessons and Ancestral Trauma

1. Self-defeating mental, emotional, and behavioral patterns
2. Patterns of difficult relationships that cause pain and anger
3. The tendency to get caught up in the patterns that others repeat
4. Chronic physical challenges and ailments
5. The persistent tendency to judge people—whether the self or others

1. Self-Defeating Mental, Emotional, and Behavioral Patterns

You might be wondering why healing focuses so strongly on patterns. What about painful experiences that occurred in a single event? Usually, when a single event is emotionally wounding, those emotions will return. They will get repeated over and over, turning into a long, protracted pattern. That pattern can be so pervasive that—over time—the pattern itself can cause a great deal more injury than the initial event.

There are so many different types of psychological and emotional patterns that could trouble you. They might have come down from generation to generation. They could also be supported by members of your current family structure. Many of these issues can come from previous generations, past lives, or this life. But regardless of where they're sourced or how they manifest, they will continue until you take action on their healing.

What are some of these possible patterns and challenges? Self-diminishment, codependency, control and power issues, a poverty mentality, lovelessness, addictive behaviors, worthlessness, and rejection are just some of the painful patterns.

Whether in this life or a past life, you could have had difficult relationships that created a litany of negative self-talk that repeats daily. Or you experienced a complete lack of power or money in your work or life. That may have resulted in great financial urgency and a need for control. So you see, learning where the narrative started is helpful. But what matters most is changing the narrative to a new thought and creating a new life.

In the next two chapters, you'll discover some processes and daily exercises that can help you do just that.

2. Patterns of Difficult Relationships that Cause Pain and Anger

Let's take a look at the pattern of pain and anger. This often evolves out of relationships that are fraught with a lack of respect and reciprocity, hurtful and selfish behavior, and even power plays that attempted to put you in your place.

This pattern could start with a parent, or someone in authority, such as a grandparent, big brother, or even a boss, a current husband, or an ex. Though your experiences may be current, this pattern likely started many generations ago or in a past life.

It's time to take a moment to think about this possible pattern occurring in your own life. Think back to an important person who rejected you or dismissed you in some way. That behavior hurt you and made you feel that you were unimportant or valueless in that person's eyes. You may have started doubting (consciously or unconsciously) your own worth—seeing yourself in a very much diminished way. Now you've defined yourself through another's responses to you. You feel lessened. You may hold yourself back because you're lacking confidence. You're in pain, and you're angry. You're angry at the person who hurt you, and you're angry at yourself for buying into it. As you go through your day, these feelings might come out of nowhere. You may often find yourself hurting and feeling angry without knowing why.

Sometimes this pain-anger pattern can give birth to physical patterns. Your self-diminishment (or self-loathing, if it goes that far) could cause you to sabotage things—from overeating to even self-medicating with alcohol or drugs.

This is the pain-anger pattern. Pain and anger are two sides of the same coin. Whenever you feel pain and anger, recognize them, but don't live in them. Indeed, go deeper than that. See what's under the pain. See what's behind the anger. Write about it in your journal. Learn about it all. There is a questionnaire to help you later in this chapter. If other people or ancestors are involved, start to engage with them in some of these processes so you can work on healing together.

3. The Tendency to Get Caught Up in the Patterns that Others Repeat

Finding yourself caught in other people's patterns can be very frustrating—and hurtful, too. There can be many different configurations of family and group dynamics. Your children may be influenced by their in-laws, or your sisters could be dragging you into their battles, or your co-workers don't give you credit for your work.

These people may not be your ancestors. You may even be the oldest! But these types of patterns don't happen by accident. They usually reflect the feelings you have about yourself born in other relationships. When other people are stuck in their own "stuff," they end up disregarding you, and that gets you stuck in your "stuff." Again, you start to feel dismissed and are left questioning your own worth. It's important to be aware of how these feelings connect to other patterns in your life.

Remember, you can't change what other people have done, and you can't change how other people see you. You can change how you see yourself, how you see the situation, and how you respond to it. If you find that a situation can't change, but it's still playing out and is too painful for you, try to find a way to leave it. But remember, your most important relationship is with your own Highest Self. You will never be disregarded there. Finding your own inner light and truth will always heal you!

4. Chronic Physical Challenges and Ailments

Certainly not all physical problems have their roots in past lives or ancestral trauma. But some do. I remember getting a past-life image for a client: It was the 1800s, and she was very poor. She also had her five-year-old daughter with her. In that life the mother died, leaving her little girl to fend for herself—which she barely did.

Then I saw a new image of the two of them making plans to come back in this life. I could almost hear the girl say to her mother, *You're never going to abandon me again.* So I told my client that her daughter, who came again as her daughter in this current life, would probably be excessively dependent.

My client said that she could absolutely apply this to her life now. She told me that at the age of five, her daughter had suddenly become paralyzed from the waist down. Of course, they took her to doctors. Indeed, they took her for tests to every major specialist in cities all over the country. No one could find anything wrong with her—not structurally or neurologically. Yet she had been living her life in a wheelchair, which obviously prevented her mother from leaving.

Now, I must say, this is a rather extreme example of the physical impact of past lives. But difficult past lives can also be emotionally paralyzing, to be sure. If you'd like to learn more about past-life physical implications, check out my sister Sandra Taylor's book *Hidden Powers of Your Past Lives.*

Again, there are lots of physical conditions that don't have emotional traumas as their source. But it can be helpful to find out. Consider working with a therapist, a regressionist, and different healing modalities to compliment your traditional medical treatments.

5. The Persistent Tendency to Judge People— whether the Self or Others

You might think that judging others doesn't qualify as thinking negatively about yourself. But actually judging others is a clear indicator that you're feeling bad about yourself. You want to make up for that by convincing yourself of the lack you see around you. Often what you say about others is what you fear—or feel— about yourself.

One of the ways you judge yourself is by constantly seeing yourself as a victim. Have you been victimized by someone? Probably— at some point in this life or another. But when that happens, does it drive you to weakness, or does it drive you to power? Calling yourself a victim is a judgment that says you're powerless. This may be the most important pattern to break of all because, with your power, you will break all others.

All of these patterns can lead to an awakening for you—an awakening of new strength, freedom, and joy—an awakening to your highest truth, if you stay alert.

You must watch for these patterns as they happen in your life. Look for the deeper meanings, and write about them and about your feelings in your journal. Also note any of the people, in spirit or in the living, who may be connected with any of these patterns, too. The questions at the end of this chapter can help you.

Knowing Yourself

Perhaps the most important person you need to know in your ancestral healing is yourself. A parent may have started some patterns, which you certainly didn't want as a child. But now it's time to take responsibility—for the negative self-talk, the defeating behavior, or even the difficult relationships.

You may have been a child when they started, but you're an adult now. If you let the patterns continue even though you want to change them, you will neglect your self-care. That will perpetuate the patterns into the future. But don't blame yourself if the patterns are continuing. Just realize that owning your responsibility to change them lets you reclaim your power—in all parts of your life. To reclaim your power, all you have to do is remember your power—remember who you already are.

Remember the eternal self you are in the silence. Realize that clinging to past beliefs leaves your power in the past. But now you can take action of mind, heart, and body to change those beliefs and your patterns. So take responsibility *now*, and you'll find your power now!

About Freedom and Responsibility

Though your ancestors do bring you helpful insights, both in your meditations and during your waking life, they do not control you. You have your own power, which stems from your eternal truth. There is no spirit who is stronger than your spirit.

You also have *free will*. Freedom may be one of the most important factors in any ancestral healing endeavor—and indeed, in *any* of life's endeavors. Because you are free, you can grab every opportunity and make every choice that brings joy instead of negative patterns. But with freedom comes responsibility.

> **Freedom and responsibility go hand in hand.**
> **With freedom you make the choices;**
> **with responsibility you take the steps.**

Together freedom and responsibility give you the power for you to take action on your own healing. If ever there is a slip or a falling back into old patterns, these two forces together will give you a second chance, and a third, and a fourth! So whenever you falter, always recognize that it is through your freedom and responsibility that you can save and serve yourself—and your world!

Discovery for Ancestral and Karmic Healing

In most healing situations, patterns are usually present in some way or another. So it's important to understand the specific patterns in your life, their origins, the feelings and beliefs they trigger for you, and the people involved. You may feel that you'd like to work on all of the patterns in your life. (And some patterns certainly may be connected to others.) But it's most helpful for your clarity and success to start with the most significant one.

Here is a questionnaire to help you focus on the different aspects of your patterns. Write your answers and observations in your journal. Be gentle and patient as you do this. If writing about some of your history becomes difficult, put it down for a little bit, and then come back to it later. But don't put it away! Not dealing with a pattern won't help you change it. Your awareness will. So get out your journal, and let's get started.

· ·

The Patterns and People Worksheet

- Identify a pattern in your life that you would most like to heal. What is it?

- Briefly describe it. Don't get into a long narrative. Just use some key words that specify this pattern for you.

- Was this pattern caused by a single event or by consistent exposure to someone or something damaging?

- How does this pattern manifest in your life—physically, in repeated behaviors; emotionally, with persistent difficult feelings; or mentally, in repeated thoughts? Or does it manifest in a combination of these?

- Describe these behaviors, emotions, and thoughts. How frequently does this pattern repeat? And for how long?

- In what ways do you think that you might contribute to the pattern yourself? For instance, do you keep going back to the thoughts even when you're focused on something else? Or, if feelings of victimization are a part of this pattern for you, do you allow feelings of victimization to creep into other, more neutral situations?

- Who are the people (living or in spirit) who are directly connected to the events that fed this pattern?

- What roles did they play? How do you feel about them? Even if anger is present for you, did you ever feel the need for their approval? Do you still feel that need?

- Do you think there are any ancestors from previous generations, or previous lifetimes, who may have planted the seeds of these events and patterns? Don't be concerned if you're not sure. Just notice any intuitive feelings you have about that, and write them down.

- Think back to the originating moment when this pattern was born. Recall it—but don't relive it. And if you're not sure, let your intuition take you back there. If you're taken back in your imagination to a time long, long ago, let that happen, too. Notice the people who are there, and just watch or sense that beginning event, no matter how you get it.

- After you recall the originating event, consider what false beliefs about yourself it created for you. Write them in your journal. Then write some positive beliefs—like the declarations in the next section—to replace the negative ones.

- Consider some new, healthy mental, emotional, and physical patterns that you can use to replace the old negative ones. You can start with the following list of declarations. Be sure to use them whenever an old pattern returns.

Refer to these questions when the pattern comes up for you again. Continue to take notes—and use this worksheet—about all your other patterns when they happen. That will help you realize how often they occur and become more aware of what you want to change.

This is your discovery. And as your discovery evolves, so will your healing. You can use this worksheet to start healing other patterns as they come up for you—although the work you do on one pattern is usually helpful on others.

The next part of this worksheet will help you to release the old and replace it with new thoughts and actions of reclamation.

Well, I Declare!

Here are some declaration examples to *release and reclaim*. Often, deeply rooted habits or patterns seem impossible to stop. But it's easier when you have something—a new pattern—that replaces the old one.

These declarations will usually start with a statement of release, followed by statements of reclaiming your power and understanding. They replace the old false beliefs with new, higher thoughts about your eternal truth.

So when the old and dark thoughts, feelings, or behaviors appear, catch them right away. Write down a statement of release—even a short one, like *I let this past go.* Or *I release these thoughts entirely.*

Then immediately write down a declaration reclaiming your power, love, clarity, and peace. For instance, *I reclaim my life in the eternal, powerful, joyful now.* Besides just writing it down, declare it! Proclaim it with your mind and heart, and let the energy shine forth to the world. Then take a deep breath, and hold the gentle truth of it within you.

So many people have difficulty saying good and positive things about themselves. It's because they've spent so much of their lives—and lifetimes—saying and believing the negative. They have succeeded in hiding their truth, their good, from themselves.

So, be sure you repeat your new declarations several times whenever the old habit rears its head. If you've been repeating the old, dark mental pattern for years or decades, or, perhaps, even lifetimes, think of how often you would have to repeat the new one in order for it to take hold. But whatever happens, don't let it drag you down if you slip once in a while—or if it seems to take a long time. You are on the ascent to grace, but it takes discipline, courage, and strength. It's okay to slip, and it's okay to take a rest when you need. Then, whenever you're ready, simply take the next step!

Some of the following declarations have blank spaces for your options. But you should also create some declarations and proclamations of your own. Be sure to change up the declarations that you use now and again; it keeps the fire lit in the power they carry.

. . . .

Declarations of Release and Reclamation

I release the pain of my _____ (divorce, childhood rejection, mistreatment, etc.), and I reclaim the unconditional love that springs from deep within me.

I release these past memories, and I remember the brilliant light of my truth.

I release the behavioral pattern of _____ (drinking, drugs, gambling, overeating, etc.), and I replace it with new physical activities of _____ (walking, deep breathing, yoga, exercise, etc.).

Those who have hurt me have done so from a place of their pain and fear. I release that history and I see them in their light. I reclaim my truth in eternal joy.

I am willing to let go of others' misdeeds to me. I also let go of my misdeeds to them—and to me. Our spirits shine like the sun—together.

I release the thoughts that made me feel worthless. I recognize and reclaim my value in the Divine light and love that fill me always.

I release the past and put it behind me. I reclaim my power each moment. I find new opportunities for new thoughts and new light every second of every day.

. . . .

These are just a few examples. You can refer to this worksheet as a template to make some declarations of your own. In the next two chapters, we'll take a look at the power of forgiveness and how to see the players in a new light.

CHAPTER 10

PROCESSES FOR HEALING THE PAST

*Even for a moment, do not think that you are
the body. Give yourself no name, no shape.
In the darkness and the silence reality is found.*

— REV. B. ANNE GEHMAN

Let's start with a look at some of the different types of healing you may want to pursue. There may be health concerns that are uniquely your own. But there are some that you may share with your ancestors—such as diabetes, heart problems, arthritis, or other physical problems. There certainly are genetic conditions that are passed down. You can choose to work on any type of physical healing with an ancestor, but such efforts should not replace professional medical treatment.

As you consider this, look deeply into the psychological challenges that may be connected to the types of physical issues that trouble you. There usually is some kind of emotional meaning linked to them. Healing the body is so strongly supported by healing the mind. (You can learn more about this in Louise Hay's books *You Can Heal Your Life* and *Heal Your Body.*)

If you are adopted, and you'd like to call someone from your biological family, you certainly can do that. Perhaps you might want to find out more about your family's physical traits. Or maybe, because you were given up for adoption, you might be feeling abandoned, and you'd like to work that out. But since you know your adoptive family best, you might want to start with them. Your history with that family is significant, and it's not an accident that you found yourself with them.

Starting Small

There are some longer healing processes in this chapter, but I'd like to start you off with a few little ones that you could do in moments when a difficult pattern comes up. Of course, one of these processes might work better with certain patterns, and the other better with others. You can use these anytime you get caught in the traps of old patterns, and you can create your own process, too.

. . . .

Healing with Your Ancestors

Close your eyes. Take a deep breath, and relax. Recall a belief or behavior pattern that you would like to change. Don't get pulled into it. Just think of it. Now call to the ancestors who want to help you heal, and notice them come forward.

Say to yourself, I heal this pattern with spirit. *Immediately, your Higher Self fills you with light and love. And your ancestors embrace you, too. A wave of energy and light flows through you, around you, and within you, lifting your heart, your joy, and your power.*

With another deep breath, say again, I heal this pattern with spirit. *And the brilliant light within you expands, shattering the dark thoughts and behaviors and dispersing them into the stars above you.*

. . . .

The next mini-process is really meant to work within the little moments that make up a pattern. You can use it in the very instant you're engaged in a single negative thought or sabotaging behavior.

· ·

I Am Free!

When you find yourself in a negative thought, or a defeating action, stop! In that moment take a deep breath, and say to yourself, I am free! *Feel the boundless power and love of your Higher Self fill you completely and shine forth all around you.* This is who you are.

Say again, I am free! *Immediately, you see that negative thought and action move away from you and cease to exist. They are gone.*

Say to yourself, I am free! *See yourself being filled with new thoughts of light and joy and taking new actions of compassion and calm. See it completely—you in a still photograph of your great success, a photograph that shines with light. Put that photo in your ethereal pocket over your heart right now. Take it out and see it again, whenever old thoughts or actions return. Declare to yourself,* I am free! *And become the person of power and purpose you are!*

· ·

Describe what happened in these two mini-processes in your journal. Was one stronger for you? Pick one that you can use in just moments in your daily life. If you wish, you can alter them or make some of your own. Just remember—whenever the patterns challenge you, declare, *I am free!*

Who's Coming to the Healing?

These little processes are very helpful with the little moments of patterns. But there are many layers to work through. So it's time to get ready for healing some hurtful histories. And the first thing to do is understand the ancestors who were involved—both primarily and secondarily. For instance, if your mother mistreated you and your father didn't intercede, both of them could be parts of your process. That's up to you. You can call whomever you'd like. But remember, it's not time to play the blame game. Continuing the blame continues the pattern. Your ancestors want to heal with you. So take back your power by taking responsibility. Forgive all who participated in this pattern, including you, because—in the end—forgiveness is what heals.

As I mentioned before, ancestors from previous generations will often come, too. When someone in spirit wants to say sorry, their parents and grandparents also come to take responsibility because they passed down the hurtful behavior. So be sure to accept the apologies from all of them, including the primary person who hurt you. They had been wounded as children, and they never learned how to get freedom from the pain.

There also may be unknown forerunners who show up who may or may not be connected to this history. But they might have had a similar history themselves. Don't worry if you don't know who they are, and don't go into your left brain analyzing it. They all bring their support. Some could be landcestors, forerunners of purpose, or any other kind of ancestor, including those from your past lives.

Another thing you need to know is that you may call some ancestors who might not appear right away. It's not because they don't love you or they don't want to heal things. It's not even because they're not there. Some feel deeply responsible for wrongdoing, and they have remorse. Others may regret not being there for you in some way. Have you ever seen a child when he did something wrong and he knew it? First, he makes himself scarce. And when you do find him, he's not very talkative.

Even as an adult, if you've ever done anything that made you feel shame, seeing the people involved would have been uncomfortable at best. So let yourself make the call a few more times. These ancestors are present and will show themselves to you because they truly do want to heal. They want to have a new relationship with you, too.

A New Relationship

Some of the people who teach about ancestral healing tell you that you should visualize the ancestors who mistreated you and ask them to change. That's one way to help you see them differently.

But actually, if they're in spirit, they already have changed. They have sloughed off their personal, temporal selves and have become their eternal spirits. Their change occurred at the moment they died—their moment of waking up.

You have an opportunity to create a new relationship with them, which is something they dearly want. All they want is to fix things—to be there for you and attend you in ways they weren't able to do before. In their old, physical-life perspective, the only person they could see was the one in the mirror. But now they see it all, and they want you to know that.

Your ability to see them anew, to realize who they are now, is a very crucial component of your ancestral healing. When you can see them in their light, you can meet on common ground—because you can see *you* in your light, too. You don't have to die to see the light of heaven; you just have to open your *larger* eyes!

What a gift it is—this chance to recreate your relationships with your spirit loved ones, your ancestors. You could work with someone to heal a past hurt. Or you could have a second chance with someone who had difficulty communicating. Or you could get closer to someone who was distant to you—geographically or emotionally.

Seeing Them in a New Light—Literally

Here's a little event that happened to my friend Dee Wallace. She's a wonderful teacher of consciousness creation, and an extraordinary actress in film and television. (You may know her as the mom in the movies *E. T.* and *Cujo*.) Here's her story.

Her father had had a long battle with alcohol after he served in World War II. She spent many of her childhood nights making sure he didn't get too close to her mother—protecting her from physical abuse. But the verbal and emotional abuse scarred everyone. Finally, her mother moved them away into another house. A few weeks later, her father shot himself in the head behind a bar.

After that, Dee was staying at her grandma's while her mom was recouping. Dee slept on a sun porch, surrounded by windows on three sides. As she was trying to fall asleep, a light in the mirror woke her up. She went back to bed, but the light woke her up a second time. Then she watched it as it slowly left the mirror and moved to the center of the room. She wasn't frightened. It seemed really . . . loving. And then she "heard" the message.

"It's me, Button Nose." (Her dad's nickname for her.) "I just came to tell you I love you, and to get on with your life. This wasn't your fault. This wasn't your mom's fault. This was just a part of my lesson here. Your job is to be happy. Go be happy." Then, ever so slowly, the light traveled back to the mirror and softly faded away.

"It's funny," Dee told me, "how peaceful and reassuring the whole experience was. I have been forever grateful for his message giving me permission to go on and be happy in my life." Then she looked up and said, "I have, Daddy. Thank you!"

Let Them Say They're Sorry

Dee saw her dad in a new light, and you can see your once-troubled ancestors that way, too. Here's your chance. Think about those ancestors who want to say they're sorry—who want to help heal the emotional wounds from the past. It might be a little difficult at first, but give it a try.

. . . .

Healing the Wounds

Close your eyes, and take a deep breath. There are some people in the spirit world who may have hurt you in the past. They want to reach out and heal with you. Make a gentle call to these specific ancestors now.

See or sense who is with you. If the people you called don't seem to be there, the remorse they feel may have made them reticent or withdrawn. Make another call from your heart, and slowly start to notice their spirits come forward.

You may see or sense your ancestors as they were in life. But start to sense their new realities, too. There is a light there that expands from their very beings. They are in their Divine spirits now.

Take a moment to have a dialogue with these ancestors. Without rancor or blame, tell them about the painful memories of your history with them and about how you felt when they hurt you.

Soon you may notice more ancestors step forward. It could be their parents or grandparents. These new ancestors want to let you know that they, themselves, perpetuated the pattern—a pattern that started even before them. They were broken in their history, too. And they contributed to hurting the person who hurt you.

Now bring your attention back to that person. Imagine him or her as a little child experiencing that painful past. Let compassion move through you and bring forgiveness to your heart. Then this little child before you grows into the radiant being who steps closer now.

Listen with your heart now, and you get a gentle whisper, I'm sorry. *However you get it, notice that it comes again,* I'm sorry. *You can hear the truth of it in your heart.*

Now make your own statement of release of these issues that troubled you in the past. Or simply say, I release this past. I am free of this pain. *Let yourself feel the old harsh words, anger and pain all gently dissipate and fall away from you. Now say,* I reclaim my power and this loving relationship anew. *Immediately, you know your grace and power within.*

Then you hear a whisper from all the ancestors who participated through the generations, I'm sorry. *And these ancestors send you an embrace of their great love. As you feel this, declare to yourself,* Spirit heals. *Feel your ancestors' healing energy wrap around you. All those who are present—including your highest guides and your Higher Self—send you the energy of Divine love. Feel this light and power fill you, as you say again,* Spirit heals. *Take a moment to feel and know this truth.*

Before you finish, take a look around you at all the ancestors who have come. Some may have shared a similar history; some are bringing their loving support. Feel their great presence and say thank you to them.

Also say thank you to all those who have brought their apologies—and to yourself for working with them on your mutual healing.

Feel yourself lift with a new strength, freedom, and wisdom. See these ancestors awash in the radiance of their Divine truth—and yours! Start to bring yourself back as your heart flows over with a new peace.

. . . .

Be aware that because this pattern is so long-lived, you may have to do this process a number of times—and continue to forgive a number of times. (We'll look more at forgiveness in the next chapter.) Whenever old feelings and difficult memories of this history crop up in your daily life, be sure to say your declarations of release and reclamation. Whenever you do this process, take some notes about the ancestors who came and how you feel about them as your forgiveness grows.

Like Heals Like

It's not surprising that a great-grandmother in spirit who had suffered from arthritis would want to bring healing energy to her descendant's stiff knees. But it might be surprising to some that an alcoholic grandfather would come to help his grandson heal his drug addiction.

The grandson may remember his grandfather's drunkenness, depression, and possibly even meanness. Remembering such things, many people might say, *I don't want that spirit person around me!* But don't forget about the duality between spiritual and personal realities. It was not the grandfather's spirit who chose a life of drinking and self-medicated denial. But it *is* grandfather's spirit who comes to help. Of course, when grandpa—and others like him—come back in future incarnations, they will have some serious karmic lessons coming their way.

For long-term alcoholics, chemical dependents, gambling addicts, or others who have lived with choking emotional suppression, passing into spirit can be less like waking up from a dream and more like waking from a nightmare. They're free from their self-made prison and are now aware of who they really are. They have a clearer vision of their mistakes and bad choices. They look "down" upon those choices, and they ask themselves, *What on earth was I thinking?*

As we've just seen, these ancestors reach back from spirit to bring healing to those they have hurt. But they also want to help heal those who struggle with the same problems they had. They want to help their loved ones make better choices than they did, and they want to give their loved ones the time and attention they may not have been capable of giving before.

For those in the physical world who are suffering from addiction, there are many physical-world treatments available, including counseling and rehab. And in treatment centers and groups around the world, it will be the recovered addicts who will help those in need. If that's the case in the physical world, who in the ancestral realm would be better at helping addicts than those who had walked that same path before? They know where they fell, and now they know how to get up.

Of course, chemical dependency is just a tiny part of life where ancestral healing support can help. You can call your healing ancestors to assist you with anything. Again, they certainly aren't meant to replace professional medical care, but they can share their energy in so many beneficial ways.

Let's take a look at healing some behavioral patterns with your ancestors. These could include any of the addictive behaviors—from alcohol and drugs to food, to shoplifting, to smoking, and even obsessive-compulsive disorders. But there could also be negative habits like avoiding exercise, rumor-mongering, phobias, procrastination, and the like. All of these are also connected to emotions. So as you do this process, be sure to notice those, too.

. . . .

Strength from Spirit

Take a deep, cleansing breath, and close your eyes. Think of a behavior that you would like to release and change for good. Simply hold it in your mind. Send out the invitation to the healing ancestors who can help you with this.

Now, fill yourself with the gentle knowing, Spirit draws near. *Soon, you sense some healing ancestors gathering. Do you know who they are? It's okay if you don't. These ancestors are here to help you with this habit or pattern. As they draw closer, feel the great support they bring you.*

And now, create a short declaration indicating your release of this habit and reclaiming your power. For instance, I release procrastination and take action every day. *Keep it simple. Just create a quick and easy declaration now.*

As soon as you say your declaration, your ancestors send you a message to show you a new action that can replace the old one. You could get an image, a word, a symbol, or an idea. See and sense every nuance, thought, physical sensation, and picture entirely. Notice everything.

If you get a sense of a new beneficial activity, see yourself taking that action. Softly say to yourself, Spirit strengthens me. *You then feel that energy of strength and purpose and even discipline fill you. Though changing the old pattern to the new one may be a challenge, you know you can do it. And your ancestors support you in every way. Say again,* Spirit strengthens me. *See yourself absolutely taking the new action.*

You also feel the light and love and force of your own spirit. Now you say, My spirit strengthens me. *In this moment, you see that the great, Divine power within you frees your future of this old habit. And you know the truth of it.*

See the results—the new action you create, the changing of your life, the freedom you feel. With eternal strength, you can do anything.

Now say thank you to these forerunners. Whenever the old pattern challenges you, and you want to take higher action, say, My spirit strengthens me! *Then take a deep breath, and notice that within you stirs the power of the universe.*

. . . .

As always, take some notes whenever you do this process. Write down your declarations and refer to them frequently. Whenever you want to make some new ones, that's great. As a matter of fact, try to change them up regularly so you can keep them sharp. Put some on cards so you can refer to them in your daily life. As you walk through your day, say, *My spirit strengthens me.* Then, with a deep breath, feel that Divine truth within you.

Now there is another important healing process to do. We've already done a number of processes in this chapter, and if you want to do more, you can take any of these processes and reshape them to your own specific needs—or create some of your own. But the next healing is unique unto itself. It is a healing that would help each and every one of us, yet it's been pushed aside for years, and decades, and perhaps even lifetimes. Let's attend to it now.

. . . .

God Bless the Child

Take a deep, relaxing breath, and close your eyes. Notice that your loving ancestors already have arrived. They've come because they want you to know about a special healing—a healing where you are the healer.

Notice that your ancestors are pointing down to something—to someone. You look, and there, sitting on the floor by their feet, is a little child. Suddenly you realize it's you—perhaps at the age of four or five or six. There you are—looking back at you. It's your own gentle, forgotten inner child—hoping for your attention.

You have built a long-term habit of disregarding yourself. You've been a bit too busy to remember this part of you. This child has been waiting—for your care, for your love, for your time.

You bend and pick up this sweet child and hold your little self tight to you. You relax in this embrace. And love wraps the two of you in warmth. It takes so little to give yourself love; yet it does so much.

Take a few moments to hold this child, and take a deep breath. This heart beats within your heart. This life lives within your life. Ask this little child to show you one thing that you can do to bring more joy to this wee one's life—to your life. And notice what you get.

Now this child's cheek presses to yours. Those little arms wrap around your neck, and you hold each other tighter still. Make a promise that this little child will not be forgotten. You will build a life of joy and peace for both of you, and you will hold tight your beautiful little self in love.

. . . .

CHAPTER 11

ANCESTRAL HEALING IN DAILY LIFE

*Success is a collection
of problems solved.*

— I. M. Pei

You've looked at the principles and done some processes for karmic and ancestral healing, but for real success, you have to bring healing actions to the conscious mind throughout your day. If you pursue your healing, moment by conscious moment, you can make it permanent. Your highest well-being will become as real and as natural to you as your own breath.

In this chapter, we'll take a look at the little things that you can do frequently, including mini-exercises, activities, and other helpful declarations. We'll also take a look at the great power of forgiveness.

Who's on First?

I know I've spoken before about the duality in which we live. But I can't emphasize enough how important that understanding is to healing, to spirit communication, and to all growth. This understanding is not a mere mental exercise; it has to be visceral. Every moment of every day you are going to have to decide, *Who's on first?* Will your personal self be the one who first steps forward and takes over in any given situation? Or will your Divine self step up first?

In most of our patterns—and in most of our daily life experiences—it is the personal self who is the first to jump forward. It's just a knee-jerk, habitual reaction. But it doesn't have to be that way. We are not physical beings with a spirit; we are, rather, spiritual beings with a body. Since we already are spiritual and eternal beings, that part of us could be the natural first responder. But it's usually the personality who comes forward first because we have forgotten who we are.

We just have to remember it—and keep remembering it. But that can be hard to do. We live in the personal world, and we tend to respond to it personally. The spirit is waiting for us to look its way, and days can pass before we even take a glance.

If it's so easy for us to forget our souls, imagine how it was for those who never even knew that was an option—until they died. When they passed into spirit, the issues that had troubled them, the difficulties they had created, and the tantrums they had had in their physical lives, all became a part of who they used to be. They used to be selfish children—or at least they used to act like children!

Think back to a moment when you were a little kid and a toy was taken away from you, or you couldn't go out with your friends, or you had some other major upset. Recall the disappointment and anger you felt and the fuss you made. Obviously, if those types of things happened now, they wouldn't trouble you at all. In your older, much wiser perspective, you see those things as silly and unimportant.

Death makes people much older—not decades older, but eternally older— seeing with their wisest, most compassionate perspective. They see that every attack—either by them or on them—was a childish striking-out of the ego. So when you remember the attacks, also remember that it was the personality who showed up first, ready to crush the perceived opposition—whoever that may be.

Difficult Pictures

Getting crushed under the heel of people's hurtful words and actions can make forgiving them extremely difficult. Sometimes you can't even tolerate looking at their pictures. But there are some things that can help. Putting out their pictures where you can see them can be very helpful. It might bring some tension at first, so don't do it before you're ready.

If you want, you can take it slowly. Put out some pictures for a few days, and then put them away for a while. Or you can start with one or two photos in just a few places. Then, when you walk by them, take a moment to stop and do this process.

· ·

A Glimpse at the Photos

Take a deep breath. See yourself looking at the pictures of the people who hurt you. Imagine their childish selves having a temper tantrum of past hurtful actions. Now see their childish personalities start to change and grow into the great light and love of their Higher Selves.

Soon you realize that you're not just looking at a picture. This glorious spirit is standing before you. And then you hear, I'm sorry. *Feel the truth of it. For just a moment, breathe in the word* Forgiveness *and hold it in your heart.*

· ·

Do this little process as often as you can when you see a photo of an ancestor with whom you'd like to heal—or even when that person pops into your mind. Embrace every opportunity to redefine them in their eternal truth—and also to redefine you in yours.

Focusing on Forgiveness

When you're starting to use forgiveness in your ancestral healing, remember also to forgive yourself. Someone may have hurt you, perhaps even significantly. But it's important you understand the full breadth of the situation. Forgiving yourself recognizes that you have power in this situation, too. You have the power to hold on to it, or to let go.

I have heard a number of clients tell me, "I won't ever forgive him," or "I *can't* forgive her." But the truth is, if you don't ever forgive a person, you'll never be free of that person, including in your future lives. Your ability to forgive writes your ticket to put this issue behind you.

Without forgiveness, your well-being—now and in the future— is tied inextricably to those past people and events. In some way or another, you have defined yourself through others' responses to you. You've been carrying that heavy baggage around with you— possibly for many years. Forgiving yourself lets you put that baggage down. You own the power to make choices, and now you're in the driver's seat—to forgive yourself and to forgive others.

As I have said before, creating forgiveness is easier when you can see the people you're forgiving in their immaturity—and in their pain. People who are dismissive, angry, or selfish want things their way. When that doesn't happen, they blame everyone else—just like little children. And when you see them as children, you certainly won't value their opinion as much.

Of course, their anger and immaturity are really signs that they are lost in their own pain and gloom. These lost people can often be very dark, brooding, persistently quiet, or quick to anger. They are so lost in their lack, that they have given joy no quarter in their lives. It is so sad. Forgiveness and compassion are easier responses when you see how vast the emptiness of their lives and hearts can be.

Of course, forgiving people's behavior is not the same as excusing it. It's important not to allow anyone to mistreat you. Let yourself forgive, but if any mistreatment still persists, try to find a way out.

Stopping the War

All of these wounded and hurtful people—the childish, the suffering, the lost, and others—can be helped by therapy and other professional modalities. And, happily, many people do seek that help. But there are others who don't. Some don't because they won't acknowledge needing help, and others don't because they're so deeply entrenched in their darkness, they can't see another way.

I feel that—unless there are chemical imbalances, clinical conditions, or hormonal difficulties present—when people are chronically angry, mean, controlling, or judging, they are defining themselves by their physical-world losses and gains. They have lost touch with their inner truth, and they have built a habit of living in the dark. Even the darkest people have Divine light within them, but they have forgotten it.

Consider this: The level of darkness that people express indicates the distance they have put between themselves and their Divine souls. They have pushed their light away. And, sadly, many don't even know it. So when you seek to forgive them, remember that they are acting out of habit and are lost in the dark. You can help to build a habit of light for yourself by praying for them and sending them light and love, which will also spill over to the rest of the world. Be sure to stay aware of your thoughts through the day, too.

If positive statements are affirmations,
negative statements are *infirm*ations.
They don't inform you, they infirm you, spreading out
to others and making the whole world sick.

We live in a dualistic world, and in order to have the Higher Self show up first, we have to put it first. We have to be ever-conscious moment by moment in order to choose the higher mind and vision. But we don't have to turn every negative thought into a battle with the ego. Those types of thoughts come up so often, we would be doing battle with the ego all day long. So instead, make friends with the ego.

After all, the ego isn't really such a bad dude. It's what helps a baby learn that the little foot he's putting in his mouth is his! It also makes sure that we take care of ourselves. The challenge with the ego is that its focus is on the individual's success only in the temporal world. But your spirit lives in—and is focused on—the eternal world, a world of light and permanence. It sees your personal world losses as opportunities to learn, to serve, and to find your power elsewhere—in your soul, not in your ego.

The ego strives to make you feel important. That's why it always jumps out first! Its natural approach is to make you the center of things. So out comes the measuring sticks, the negative thoughts, and the judgments. Some people might think that, in order to stay in the perspective of your spirit, you have to beat those ego thoughts down. You have to silence the ego. And there you are again, living your life doing battle with a part of yourself that's there all the time. So, what should you do? *Make friends with your ego!*

. . . .

Changing Dark to Light

Take a moment to think of some difficult thoughts that occasionally run through your mind. They may be judgments or criticisms (whether of you or of others) that have come up for you before.

Recall yourself being in that state, hearing those thoughts in your mind. Then in your imagination, you say, Well, hello, ego. You're giving me a clue that I must be needing some love right now. Thanks for letting me know!

In this very moment, take a deep breath. Remind yourself of your eternal truth and your Divine love. Breathe in the word love, *and let the breath of that eternal compassion touch every cell.*

Feel the joy and bright colors you become. Also, notice your ancestors around you, sending their love, too. It's a moment of exquisite peace and grace—initiated by your assistant, the ego. A very surprising source, indeed! Now hold yourself, your ancestors, your spirit, and even your ego in gratitude too—for creating this moment of light.

. . . .

Now it's easy to see that healing really is a team effort. When your ego starts to command your attention, say thank you for reminding you. Then flood yourself with love. It will turn into many glorious moments!

The healing exercises in these chapters are only some templates to help you design your own healing practices with your ancestors. No one knows better than you which things work best for you. It's important to be flexible, too. You may have to try a technique a few times to see how it impacts you. And you might want to change some of these practices occasionally just a little, or redo some entirely.

Daily Healing—Things to Do!

Here are some other things you can do in your waking, daily life to support your healing with your ancestors and putting your spirit self first.

1. Do the Job of Journaling

Journaling is so important in working on healing with your ancestors. It helps you identify and prioritize the issues that you want to heal. It also allows you to look at your family history, consider the other people who struggled with this problem—and those who participated in the patterns in your life.

Using your journal regularly also helps you observe all of those patterns, little and large. If you find that there are any emotional, mental, or behavioral patterns that are very painful and deeply entrenched, you may want to consider getting some therapy to help you with those.

2. Meditate Daily

All negative karmic and ancestral lessons are perpetuated by the unfinished (read: unhealed) emotions and beliefs from the past. Though these psychological constructs may have been born in the past, they are constantly being reconstructed over and over (and bigger and bigger) today. The great Buddhist teacher Chogyam Trungpa tells us: "The birth of karma occurs through the constant reliving of the past."

Trungpa also tells us that meditation is the key to step out of "that karmic situation altogether." Through meditation, you can rise out of the personal perspective (with all of its emotional and mental entanglements) and into the mind and heart of the Higher Self. And that self is as detached from your old personal histories as you are detached from the doll or toy truck you had when you were a kid.

3. Employ Self-Observation

Staying conscious is the first step to having real authority in your life—the authority to change your mind, your actions, and your relationships. But staying conscious can often put you in a constant state of thinking about yourself. One must be self-aware without being self-absorbed.

The best way to become aware of who you are and why you do what you do is through self-observation. Learn to step out of yourself and *witness* your responses to the world. See and understand what motivates you. In your journal note what you witnessed. You may become aware of a response, a feeling, or an action that you would like to change. If so, create—and *use*—the declarations and actions to replace the old reality with the new.

4. Be Aware of Your Patterns, and Respond Immediately

Throughout your day, also be aware of your patterns and your feelings. If you start to feel angry or hurt, go inside yourself for a minute. Notice why it's happening. Take a deep breath, and as you exhale, release those feelings. After you do, say one of your declarations to free yourself from the past and from other's negative responses. Reclaim your power and your grace.

5. Create New Patterns as Sacred Rituals in Your Life

Learn that everything in your life is a ritual. Your success is made from those rituals. Witness yourself in the patterns and rituals in your life. Recognize how they come from your past and how they may impede your future success.

Whenever you see remnants of old patterns come up, recognize them. Immediately replace that pattern with a new pattern—a new sacred ritual—that lifts your energy and light. Do this with your declarations and imaging, and add activities such as exercise, prayer, visiting friends, gardening, yoga, or anything that lifts you. When you combine the new activity with declarations and imaging, the old pattern will change to new.

And you'll see that everything—space, time, your actions, your thoughts, your feelings, your relationships—*everything* becomes a tool for evolution. (What a gift!)

6. Live Consciously and Let Go of Control

As you apply your awareness to each moment of your day, make choices that honor your truth in spirit. Realize that you have absolute power to make changes in your life by changing your own thoughts and actions. You cannot control the thoughts and actions of others, and the more you try, the more you will waste your own energy and the unhappier you will be. So seek to understand it all. And what you cannot understand, seek to trust.

7. Employ Your Healing Declarations Every Day

Frequently use your declarations of release and reclamation to embrace your power and redefine yourself every day. If the declarations get weak for you over time, create new ones. And when you use them, don't just think them. Declare them! Really *feel* the energy they emit. That will let you feel the visceral power of that truth.

Declarations and affirmations are crucial because you can do them frequently throughout the day. The patterns you want to break are long-standing, and repeating your healing efforts—both your visualizations and declarations—will help obliterate the long-standing hold your patterns have over you.

8. Use Imaging and Mini-Visualizations

Do the processes in these chapters when you can. Also create some mini-images where you see yourself in the new pattern and where grace-filled healing is realized.

Another image that can be very helpful is seeing your new relationship with your ancestors. See the healing and happiness you have created together. You have redefined yourself and them, and your new relationship with these ancestors is flooded with light. Take a few moments several times a day to picture this in love.

9. Embrace Self-Compassion

Even when you're not thinking of your patterns or ancestors, know yourself as Divine in the little moments of your life. Knowing yourself as Divine (and loving yourself) is an act of loving God (and an act in teaching other to do so, too). Learn to redefine yourself through the feelings that speak to your Divine power and love. Own the confidence to let go of others' opinions, and honor *your* truth. In short, make every thought and deed in your life an act of love.

10. Hold Forgiveness in Your Heart as a Constant

When something disturbing happens, acknowledge your first emotional response, express those emotions (write a letter, punch a pillow, kickbox—just let those feelings out!), and then forgive.

Seek to understand the people who hurt you. Understand their loss, understand their pain, understand their fear—and forgive. Don't forget to forgive yourself when you forgive others. Treat yourself with compassion always. You deserve it. And when you do, take a deep breath. For a moment, pick up and hold that little child of grace within you, wrapped in compassion and love.

CHAPTER 12

THE STIR AND MURMUR OF GREAT COMPANY

Millions of Spiritual creatures
Walk the earth unseen.

— JOHN MILTON

There is a great company of spirit around you, and you give yourself—and them—a gift when you widen your reach to embrace more of them. You know that intention and invitation combine to open the door to your ancestors. Just shifting your intention can fill the room with more and different forerunners. Let's give it a try.

. . . .

Inviting More Spirits

Close your eyes. Hold the intention to be with your ancestors in your conscious mind. Immediately, you see and sense a number of spirit ancestors with you. Simply take a moment to see and sense who's there. Notice everything you experience and everyone who's there. How do you perceive them? Take a few moments to be with them and get everything now.

After a moment, let that go, and bring your complete consciousness into your heart. Fill your heart with your intention to be with spirit. Immediately more forerunners who connect through the heart are there with you. Notice everything you sense. Let them draw near with their heart energy. Who are these people? How do you feel? Notice everything for a few moments.

Now it's time to bring your complete consciousness— and your intention to be with spirit—into your physical body. Your whole body vibrates with the call to your ancestors. And you see even more of them come to you. They connect to you through body. Feel every sensation, and notice any part of your own body that comes to mind. What do you sense? How do you experience these forerunners?

When you're finished with that, take a look at, now, all the ancestors around you—those who connect through mind, heart, and body. How did you perceive them differently? How do they look and seem as you see them all together?

Thank all your forerunners for coming to your call. Promise to meet them again so you can know them better and work together.

. . . .

When you're writing about your experiences, note the different ancestors who came to you. Was there a significant distinction in your experience of them when you held your intention in mind, heart, and body? Was there one way that you liked better than the others? Try this process occasionally to see what happens and how it may change for you.

The Nostradamus Technique

Michel de Notredame was a French scholar, philosopher, prophet, and astrologer. Known as Nostradamus, he may be the most famous prophet through history. He wrote his prophecies in 10 groups of 100 each, called *Centuries*. They were published in Lyons from 1555 to 1568.

His first quatrains describe his experience. He would receive his visions at night, sitting in a quiet place. As he gazed into a bowl of water placed on a brass tripod, he would begin to see his visions in his mind's eye and then write about what he saw. He said that he could feel "God sitting beside" him.

Along with sitting calmly in a quiet place to increase receptivity, there are two other techniques employed by Nostradamus. The first was transfixing. Functionally, it's like meditating with your eyes open. When you stare at a fixed point (as he did with the bowl of water), it allows your mind to empty so you can start sensing the images you seek—or in our case, spirits in the room.

I teach this process in my classes, but you can try it for yourself. Just pick a point on a blank wall (no busy wallpaper or pictures to distract you), and stare at it. (You can blink whenever you want.) As you stare and stare, you will start to zone out—just like you have done before whenever you stared at the surface of a lake or into a fire in the fireplace. As you zone out more and more, you will start to notice that spirit people are all around you. While you keep your eyes fixed on the wall, you will see and sense them in your intuitive perceptions.

I love this process because it reminds you that so many spirit folk are with you, which is so easy to forget in this busy world. If you didn't feel comfortable with your eyes open, you can also close your eyes to meet the gang!

The other Nostradamus technique that I often use—both with spirit and in my own personal life—is calling my focus to the God beside me. You can use this process to feel God's support in your spirit communications, but that support is also there for you anytime and anywhere. This exercise can help with your healing endeavors, too.

When you do this process, remember it is the God of *your* understanding you are calling—whatever and whoever that is to you.

. . . .

By Your Side

Take a few deep, relaxing breaths, and close your eyes. As you let go of any tensions and concerns, start to go deeply into the very center of your being, your eternal, radiant spirit. With another deep breath, make a call to the God of your understanding.

As you rest in your own beautiful spirit, see and feel that Being of brilliant light come up to you. It is the God of your understanding who touches you now, filling you with radiance, confidence, and sublime peace.

This Divine Being sits beside you, and the air becomes more rarefied. And your vibration lifts. You know that every opportunity can be met and every dream fulfilled.

Now you are guided to notice all the other brilliant, incandescent Higher Guides and Angels who are with you and your ancestor. You may just see glowing lights shining there. And you—in your light—are among them, ready to serve.

. . . .

Like your different ancestors, the World Servers whose light you sensed have worked with you before. Later you will meet some of the Ascended Masters who have gone before and who work with you still.

A Party of Ancestors!

I once learned a great linking device from a very unexpected source. Many years ago I was watching Anne Bancroft, a wonderful actress, in a television interview talking about her husband, Mel Brooks. Mel Brooks is one of America's great humorists who has given the world so many funny plays and movies, including *The Producers, Young Frankenstein,* and my personal favorite, *Dracula: Dead and Loving It.*

During the interview, Bancroft was saying that Mel's humor was an ever-present part of their life, that his funny ideas and hysterical characters seemed to be always with him. Anne said, "I get excited when I hear his key in the door. It's like, 'Ooh! The party's going to start!'"

I immediately thought, *What a wonderful linking mechanism!* I started using it with spirit right away. I would imagine hearing keys at the door, and I would say to myself, "A party's coming." Then so many spirit ancestors would come into the room that it really was a party!

Sometimes I do this process often just to say hi to the gang. It only takes a few moments, but you can spend more time with your ancestors at the party if you want. Let's do this now.

- -

A Party's Coming

Take an easy, relaxing breath, and close your eyes. Center yourself in the peace deep within you. Suddenly, you imagine that you hear keys jiggling in the lock at the door.

Take a deep breath, and say to yourself, A party's coming! *How glad you are as your excitement grows. And you say to yourself again,* A party's coming! My ancestors are here! *Then you hear a key turn in the lock, and they enter and embrace you. The room fills with the great company of your ancestors—from so many places and so many times.*

Take a few minutes now to mingle with your forerunners. Talk to them, and meet some of the ones you didn't know before. What a fun party this is!

- -

I have to tell you that sometimes, when I do this process, my ancestors are all dressed up and come with gifts—just like it's the holidays. Let that happen for you, too. And open some of the presents. Some may be gifts of love. And some may be helpful messages, which surely bring love, too!

The Company You Keep

I have often described meeting spirit as going to a party—a big party. That's what I tell my clients when I'm doing consultations, because I want them to know how many ancestors are there for them. Your ancestors are so excited to get through to you. They still love you and want to help you, so they come to you often—even just to spend time with you. You really have a lot less privacy than you think!

Just imagine how many spirit ancestors are seeking to reach through to their loved ones in the living. For them, talking to the living is like "talking" to fish in an aquarium. No one ever hears or even looks when they "tap on the glass."

It's also very frustrating for spirit ancestors when they want to give their loved ones messages. Just imagine if you called your family and friends over and over, and they never picked up the phone. Luckily, spirit ancestors can get some messages through because they send them telepathically. Then the people who get the messages think those thoughts are their own.

It's so important to remember how often your spirit ancestors are with you. There are all sorts of linking devices, phrases, and words that can trigger your immediate attention. But these are not magic. They're tools. These linking devices and words are just the catalysts that help you focus on your spirit guides, who are often already there.

The Whispers of Spirit

One good example of the constant presence of spirit ancestors occurred many years ago. My husband had died of cancer when our son, Devin, was three. I started to teach Devin about his dad in spirit and his ancestors right away, and he became very used to spirit's presence. He would give me messages from his dad and see people around the house. These things were totally normal for him, and he never had any fear or concern about spirit.

Devin was about five when we moved into a new house, and, of course, everyone in our spirit family came with us. There were a number of times when Devin would call to me from his bedroom in the middle of the night when we were both asleep. "Mommy," he would say, "the people in the living room are being too loud again. I can't sleep." So I would go into the living room and tell the unseen—but not unheard—spirit folk to be more quiet. And they would be!

The murmurs and whispers that kept Devin awake are just a little evidence of the great number of spirit ancestors who are with you. H. G. Wells wrote the beautiful line I used for this chapter title. The narrator in *The Time Machine* was describing the indistinct movements and sounds coming from the dark woods behind them in the night. He wasn't talking about the spirit world. But to me, that line exquisitely puts into words the subtle yet ubiquitous presence of spirit. Spirit is always there—no matter where, no matter when. If you listen with your heart, you will *always* hear the *stir and murmur of great company.*

. . . .

The Stir and Murmur of Great Company

Close your eyes, and take a deep breath. Relax and think about the great company of your ancestors in spirit. You say to yourself, The stir and murmur of great company. *Immediately, you start to hear some gentle whispering and soft murmuring. It seems distant because it's so soft, but you soon realize it's all around you. Take a moment to listen and sense the great company of spirit with you.*

Now you say again, The stir and murmur of great company. *And then you notice a gentle stir of movement, or the soft rustle of skirts. You might feel a mild brush of air passing by you. Let yourself feel the energy and hear the tender sounds of the great bounty of spirits who attend you.*

As you reach out to them more, you notice them around you in a circle of boundless love. Listen as you open to them with these words: The stir and murmur of great company. *Simply hear and feel the bountiful company there.*

After a moment, let yourself receive a few words or images that are messages to you from these guides. Don't worry about who's sending those messages. Just get a word, a symbol, or an idea, and notice what you sense.

Now look around you again. There are so many here for you. Say thank you to these devoted spirits. In the future, wherever you are, you can stop and say, The stir and murmur of great company. *And suddenly you will hear with your heart the bountiful spirits around you.*

. . . .

I love this process, and I do it more often as a mini-moment just walking around my house or office. I'll suddenly stop and say, *The stir and murmur of great company*, and I open my heart and senses, and I see who's there. It's actually like being in a busy office. There are even some spirits hanging around the coffee machine, talking.

So Many Spirits—So Little Time

When you meet spirit, some of them may tell you their names. Some may send you body signatures, like a limp or eye problems. Others may give you visuals about themselves, like wearing a military uniform or carrying a toolbox.

These different identifiers could come to you very fast—or even some at the very same time. That's understandable because they're so excited to let you know they're with you. When they come at the same time, they can start talking—and showing you things—at the same time. For instance, you simultaneously could get the name George, sense a pressure in your hip, and see an image of a toolbox all at the same time. When that happens, it might feel like you're talking to a carpenter named George who had a bad hip. As natural as that might seem, it's actually more likely that you have two or three spirit people sending their IDs to you.

I share this with you because there are some teachers of spirit communication who believe that you must get four or five identifiers for one spirit person before going on to a second spirit.

I can tell you from my experience that the second spirit—and the third, and the fourth—*will not be that patient*! They are tremendously excited to speak with you. They often will approach together, which means you'll get all their identifiers together.

Imagine that you're at a party in a group of four or five people, and you're talking to one of them. If a second person starts talking during a pause, it's very natural to engage with that second person. If someone whom you hadn't seen in a long time ran up to you and broke into your conversation to give you a hug, you certainly would welcome that interruption.

The spirit world comes to you just like a party—in joy and with a lot of people. So enjoy them, and meet them as they come. Whether you're talking with living people or spirit people, let it be free, flowing, and spontaneous. Allow it to happen exactly as it happens.

It's a really good thing to learn different techniques from different teachers. But you must decide what feels right for you. Let yourself be guided by the internal star that is visible within you night and day.

A Gallery of Ancestors

I remember another little story about the great company of spirits. One of my students named Iddy really wanted to get closer to more of his ancestors, including the ones from generations before. He decided to put his family pictures in frames—even the ones from the 1800s. He was lucky because both sides of his family had many photos. He also got some online from ancestry sites.

He hung those pictures all over the walls of his meditation room. And there were certainly a lot of people there! At first he would just sit and look at the pictures, but then he started inviting them forward in his meditations.

They came in droves, and he was so happy to know them. They also brought landcestors and other forerunners from even older generations and different places. He speaks with them often, and he's delighted to meet whoever comes.

You can do something like this, too, only on a smaller scale. You could put some photos on a shelf or table near a chair where you meditate. But you really don't have to have any photos at all—just your imagery. Let's give it a try.

. . . .

A Visit to the Gallery

Close your eyes, and take a deep, relaxing breath. Let your breath come and go slowly, easily. As you relax further and further, imagine yourself now in a comfortable room. Let anything you like come to mind.

Now begin to imagine yourself looking around you, and you notice that there are photographs of your ancestors on the walls. You know many of these ancestors, and may even recall some of the photos. Some of the forerunners you see in the pictures are unknown to you. But they are all pleasant and happy even when they're not smiling in the photo.

Take another deep breath, and say to these ancestors, "I welcome you." And you open your heart to them. Then these ancestors seem to come out of the photos and stride right up to you. They even bring some forerunners whom you didn't know. The room is filled with your loving ancestors. Take a few minutes to simply be in this happy reunion.

. . . .

You can do this meditation to meet your great company of ancestors anytime. But work with your forerunners one-on-one, too. Just like life, it's great to come together with many and with a few. So meet them in the ways you love to do.

CHAPTER 13

MEMBERS
OF THE CLUB

Forerunners from Groups, Societies, and Organizations

With three or more people,
There is something bold in the air.

— ELIZABETH BOWEN

The power of the group can be extraordinary. There are so many different types of clubs and groups, too. Some are formal groups like the Associated Press, the Royal Air Force, Phi Beta Kappa, or the Tolkien Society. But others are far less formal, such as psychology students, violinists, and people who read Tolkien. You don't have to pay dues or sign up for membership in a lot of these groups. Your energy will do that.

The ancestors who belonged to the same groups as you will see that energy in your aura. It will let them know you're in their club. It's a membership card of light and color that you always carry with you.

Invisible Recruits

One of the largest groups around the world is the military, and there are lots of ancestors who were connected to it in some form. My friend Cinnamon Mancini told me about an event that happened when she was in the Marines in Okinawa. She and another enlisted Marine were delivering some tanks and other heavy equipment up a mountain. Each of them were driving an LVSR (Logistic Vehicle System Replacement). When they started their way down, they hit an area of slippery, rain-slicked clay. And the huge vehicles that they drove were articulated in such a way that they seemed to be made for doing donuts! Well, at least it seemed that way to the two 18-year-olds in the driver's seats. So they took the opportunity to have some fun.

As she was doing donuts in the red clay, Cinnamon suddenly got a strong, inner command: *Stop now!* So she immediately did. She and the other driver, who also had stopped, got down to have a cigarette. She walked around her LVSR, and when she got to the other side, she saw that her tires were less than an inch from a cliff that dropped straight down for over a thousand feet.

Needless to say, they never did donuts again. Cinnamon took her long career in the Marines to great heights, later becoming a member of the SRIG, or Surveillance, Reconnaissance, Intelligence Group.

That day, Cinnamon knew that inner voice was from a watchful spirit. Her ancestors had been with her before and all through her career as a Marine. And they are with her still in her work as a medium. Now, that's a different kind of reconnaissance!

Ancestral members of the military have been so helpful in so many ways. There have been hundreds of stories of military ancestors bringing assistance during battles and wars through the centuries. Here's one that goes back to ancient Greece. Plutarch wrote in *Life of Theseus* that the great warrior Theseus had come to the Battle of Marathon. He already had been dead a very long time, yet there he was, seen by everybody. Theseus was in full arms in front of the Athenian soldiers rushing into battle against the Medes—and inspiring the Athenians to follow.

There are military ancestors ready to help you, too—perhaps from your family, your landcestors, or other ancestral groups. They want to help you deal with the little, personal battles in your life—to strategize and overcome those challenges. Let's take a moment with them now.

. . . .

Winning the Battle

Close your eyes, and take a deep breath. Your military ancestors want to help you—not with any campaigns of war, but with a personal battle that may be occurring at work or at home.

With another deep breath, call your ancestral reinforcements. Immediately, you see and sense who's there—men or women, young or old. A few may be in uniforms from different times and different places. Notice everything you get.

After a moment, think about a little battle or challenge where they can bring their assistance. Immediately they give you an idea or a strategy for your approach to this little battle—something you could do, say, or even think that will help you. Open yourself to any word, image, symbol, or sensation you perceive. What is this one step that you can take to bring peace to this battle? Notice everything now.

Take a moment to ask your ancestors any question you may have. Let yourself get whatever happens for you. When you're done, say thank you to these forerunners, and bring yourself back.

. . . .

The Romantic Movement Writers' Club

Some ancestors approach without waiting to be called. They want to reach out to us, too. Sometimes they even come through the floor! Such was the case for Samuel Taylor Coleridge, who was a critic, a poet, and the most significant spokesperson of the

Romantic movement in England. He tells of the time that he met Thomas Gray, who had died a year before Coleridge was born. Gray was the poet and letter writer who was widely considered the forefather of the English Romantic movement, which was a great passion for Coleridge.

In a 1792 letter to Mary Evans, Coleridge told her that on the previous Saturday evening, when he was sitting alone, he had heard a creaking sound. When he turned to look, he saw that a ghost was rising out of the floor! The ghost approached Coleridge with a book in his hand and identified himself as "the Ghost of Gray." He asked Coleridge to present the book to Mary Evans, whose opinion he admired greatly. And Coleridge was eager to oblige.

This was not the only visitation Coleridge had with spirit. Sometimes they came in his dreams, greatly inspiring his poetry. He was very frustrated when he woke too soon while receiving the lines for Kubla Khan. Coleridge never finished this poem, but it continues to be a fragment of beautiful poetry.

If the English Romantic movement were a formal club, Gray and Coleridge would have been on the board. But it's not a club of boardrooms and directors. It is, rather, a club of meetings—meetings of mind, energy, and literary wonder. That's why Gray was drawn to Coleridge. But this is not an isolated case. Energy moves through the world and brings people together in happy union.

Never Alone Onstage

I really can't exaggerate how many times performers have told me about the help they had received from unseen forces during their performances. There are ancestral members of orchestras, acting companies, ballet troupes, and members of the band.

I have one client who had written and performed a one-woman show about a well-known country singer. She could feel that singer on the stage with her while she was performing.

Another client is an actress in London—where, it is said, there are many theaters filled with spectral activity. In one of her performances, she had forgotten her lines for a moment, but someone right next to her whispered them into her ear—even though there was no one standing there.

Once, many years ago, I went to see one of the world's great orchestras with a friend of mine, who was also a medium. We were there not only to hear the orchestra, but also to see the first violinist, who was a dear friend of his. Through much of the concert, my friend and I could sense—and see—a great, tall spirit standing with the conductor and moving about the stage. There were other spirits there, too. Even his friend the violinist said there was often beautiful energy moving through the orchestra—during rehearsals and performances.

Well, these are just a few examples of ancestral groups who come to bring aid in so many ways. When you call a group of ancestors, it's a lot like sending a group text. All you have to do is send your thought forward to the group you want. From nursing to singing, from working in an auto union to an orchestra, from writing literature to acting in a play and anything else you might do—they are there for you. And it's time to meet them.

As you do the next process, think about an endeavor in your life that you would like to share with one of your ancestral groups. It could be something you're doing on your own, but you can contact *all* of the members in that group. So let's send them a message now.

A Group Text

Take a moment to think about an endeavor that has a connection to some group in your life—and in your ancestors' lives.

Take a deep breath, and close your eyes. As you think of this specific endeavor or activity, say to yourself, I call my ancestral group. *Instantly, you see and sense these group ancestors. You may or may not know them, but they have often come to help you before.*

Experience these forerunners as they wrap you in their loving support. Notice everything about them, how they're dressed, and if they're holding anything. What do you sense? Also notice any colors that you get with them.

Now ask any question you have about this endeavor or activity. Immediately, your ancestors send you an image, a word, a feeling, or a symbol. You may also get an idea, a song, or a color with any of these. Notice everything you perceive. What do you get? Sense everything, and trust it all.

Ask any last question, and quickly just perceive one symbol. Then start to wrap that up. Be sure to take some notes when you're done. Say thank you to these ancestors who belong to the most profound union there may be— the union of spirit.

Discovering Your Own Mystical Groups and Societies

Mystical groups and societies seem like they should be part of some old, defunct past. But mystical societies are alive and well right now. Theosophists, Freemasons, and Rosicrucians are a few. Or maybe you belong to a group in less formal ways. Perhaps you're a tarot reader, and there are tarot ancestors from hundreds of years ago who would like to work with you—or astrologers who could go back thousands of years.

Some of your ancient societies may be locational. You may feel connected to the Irish Celts who created ogham, the language of the trees. Or perhaps you feel a bond with one of the Nordic, African, Peruvian, Native American, or Amazonian tribes—or any such group from around the world.

Your link could also be to spiritual or religious groups—going as far back as the Old Testament and the Essenes to the Buddhists and the more modern Spiritualists.

It is likely that you have some kind of connection to a number of mystical and spiritual groups. But in order to keep things simple during the next process, create the intention to discover the one that can inform you the most now.

There may be many people whom you don't recognize. You might get some images, symbols, icons, or words that are unknown to you. Let whatever happens happen for you. Don't get pulled into your analytical mind trying to figure things out. You can look into it all later when you're writing in your journal.

Also, let yourself surrender to the experience completely. If you are taken in a different direction, let that happen. Your discovery will unfold exactly as it should. So get ready now to discover your Sangha—your community of ancestors.

A Trip to the Great Hall

As you close your eyes, affirm the great connections you've had with different spiritual groups and societies over the ages. You have learned and grown and shared your path with many others.

Take a deep, relaxing breath. And say to yourself, My mystical ancestors are here. *Immediately, you notice the Great Hall where these groups and societies gather. As you say again,* My mystical ancestors are here, *you sense a door and step through it into the Great Hall.*

The room is large, but welcoming. You notice small groups of people gathered here and there—some standing, some seated. These little groups are dressed differently, and there are different icons, symbols, and colored lights nearby.

Take a deep breath, and simply be in this place. It may seem a little strange, but somehow, it feels like you've come home. Simply notice everything you see and sense and feel for a few moments.

Now let yourself notice which of these little groups calls to you. You may be interested in a number of them. But for now, simply step up to the group that compels you most. See the people and notice what they are saying and doing. If you're uncertain, that's okay. Just sense the colors, icons, and symbols that seem prominent around this group.

You have past histories, but you have current direc-tives with this group, too. Now say to yourself, Spirit shows me. *Instantly they give you indications of your*

157

work together now. You may get an idea, color, image, or you may sense a movement you'd like to make. What is it? Take a few moments to feel everything now.

When you're done with that, spirit would like to share a symbol that connects to this group. It could be an ancient symbol, or it could be current. Let yourself get the symbol completely and notice everything about it.

Now spirit animates the symbol, and it starts to take action to give you a larger story. Watch it move and change, and sense everything about that movement and those changes. Soon the symbol comes to a rest, and it may be a completely different image. Notice what you sense about this new symbol and about how it makes you feel.

After a few moments, wrap that up. Take another look around the Great Hall, and just catch a glimpse of other groups you'd like to meet in the future. See the color and light around them, and notice any last thing that stands out for you.

As you leave the Great Hall, say thank you to these mystical ancestors. You will meet them again. With a deep breath, bring yourself back. Remember to take some notes about your experience in your journal.

. . . .

World Famous

There are usually two responses people have about communicating with famous spirits. Some people feel like they have no right to call them because they're too important to bother. Others think they're making it up because such great people would never be available to them!

These assumptions are not correct. Fame is a temporal world commodity. But greatness—being Divine—belongs to every soul, every single second of eternity. Just because some people have forgotten their greatness, it doesn't mean that their greatness—their soul—has forgotten them.

So let yourself sense the famous spirits. They want to participate with you—though most people in the physical world ignore them because they just don't know they're there. What a sad, missed opportunity that is! When they were in the world, they may have created breathless beauty, done magnificent things, and made powerful contributions. But don't be surprised that they want to work with you. They can see your greatness, even in those moments when you don't. Let them find you. We can all do so much more when we do it together.

I have a friend who is a musician and a composer. She had been working for quite some time doing research related to a well-known classical composer, with whom she connected during this time. Though the research project is now over, his spirit is with her frequently, continuing to bring help and encouragement to her in her musical endeavors. When she speaks of him to me, it's clear that there is warmth that goes well beyond a mere collaboration. And I know just how she feels.

I had a client who was a health-care worker in New York City. She had devoted spirits who came to her consultations to thank her for the compassionate ministrations she gave them. One of them was Bennett Cerf.

Bennett Cerf was the founder of Random House, as well as a longtime panelist on the TV show *What's My Line?*—my favorite when I used to watch the show as a kid. He was thankful to my client for her care, and he came regularly to her consultations. Now, as a writer, I have often sought the assistance of (and forged relationships with) some of the writers and publishers who reside in the ancestral realms. And I reached out to Bennett, too. Sometimes, after my client's consultations, I would ask Bennett to stick around. We would often talk about writing and so many other things.

One day I told him about my book *Intuition and Beyond*, and I asked him if he could help me find a publisher. He gave me a thumbs-up and smiled. I thanked him with my heart, and then I let it go. (It's very easy to surrender such a task to the founder of Random House— it's a little like asking a weight-lifter to open a jar of pickles!)

I became very busy then. About six weeks later, I was in London teaching some classes on psychic development. A lovely lady came up to me in the lecture hall before my class. She said that she was drawn to my name in the program and asked if I'd be interested in publishing a book with her company.

As you might imagine, I was more than pleased, and I told her so. But when she gave me her business card, I was thunderstruck. She worked for Random House U.K.!

I sent a thank-you up to Bennett immediately—and many times over since then. Not just for that extraordinary help, but for so much more. He has become a spiritual guide as well as a writing guide for me. But most of all, he has become an ancestral friend.

Calling the Legends

Think of all the legends through the ages who have inspired you, the great artists, poets, philosophers, politicians, and leaders. Many people in ancient and recent times have lent their hands to your heart, your mind, and your life. Think of one of those people now, and prepare yourself to call to him or her. Often, when you call one person, a few could come together—like Coleridge and Gray or Mary and Joseph. If more than one comes, you can choose one or talk to both. It's your time with your legendary ancestors, so do it your way.

Don't think, even for a moment, that they are too famous or too important to respond to you. When they were in the physical world, they sought to share their vision. Now they have a chance to do it again—with you!

. . . .

Big Inspiration

Close your eyes, and take a deep breath. Think of the legendary person or people you'd like to call. Say to yourself, I call my legendary ancestors. *Immediately, you sense their energy, colors, and presence. Take a few moments to be with them, and notice everything you get.*

Now think about some important goal in your life where they could give you some assistance. Say to yourself, Spirit shows me. *Immediately, your legendary ancestors share an image, a word, or a symbol about that goal. What do you get? Notice everything. Let them show you an action you could take toward this goal. What is it? Sense it all for a moment.*

After perceiving that, some of these spirits want to share their talents with you. Even though you may not be interested in those precise talents (writing, composing, etc.), there is a creative force in them. Say to yourself, My legendary ancestors fill me. *And they flood you with the talents of their life. Feel those talents fill you and move through you, through your hands, your heart, your voice. Notice the actions you would want to take and the voice you would want to bring to the world as you are flooded with these talents and creative forces.*

After a few minutes, notice any last thing, and finish that up. These great legends of the ages wish to share the ideals, the ethics, and the integrity with which they tried to live. Say again, My legendary ancestors fill me. *And they send that integrity and goodness to you, filling you up and lifting you to a higher plane. Feel that goodness and light fill you now.*

After a moment, say thank you to these great people. Make a commitment to meet them again, as well as other legendary ancestors, great thinkers, leaders, poets, artists, and teachers. And know that you can call them if you ever need a little lift of energy or a moment of inspiration.

Whether throughout your day or in your meditations, you can say, I call my legendary ancestors, *and they will be there with you, helping you discover the greatness in you!*

Legends of Faith

One of the other curiosities when reconnecting with the great ancestral-world servers is that they can appear to so many at the same time.

I have a good friend Simon Caudullo, who used to be a Benedictine monk. When he was in the monastery, he became great friends with Father Matthew, and he was deeply saddened when Father Matthew died.

Later that year, he was at midnight Mass on Christmas. As he was looking at the altar, there, next to the priest who was serving mass, was Father Matthew—and Jesus. It was a powerful experience for Simon, taking him on a course of further discoveries outside the monastery. He is now a medium and a reverend in a Spiritualist church.

This type of experience is quite common. Many people see Mary, Buddha, Jesus, Kuan Yin, and so many others, as well as the Ascended Masters like the Count of St. Germaine. So many from different faiths, beliefs, and philosophies appear to people all over the world.

This really shouldn't be surprising at all. Remember that spirit is not three-dimensional. Those in the ancestral realms are multidimensional. And in the physical world, they have spent lifetimes of study, going through an initiation that took them to a sublime spiritual resonance. They want to bring that upliftment to humankind around the world. So don't be surprised when they come to you. You can step on the path of discovery and service—and walk with them!

CHAPTER 14

COMMUNICATION

The Message of Symbols

A four-year-old child could understand this report.
Run out and find me a four-year-old child.

— GROUCHO MARX

Out of the mouths of old-school comedians! Of course, Groucho's line is funny, but it's also true. It's human nature to make things more complicated than they need to be. We do it in most areas of life. And of course, we also do it in learning to communicate with spirit and working with symbols.

Symbols tell you what they mean—by how they look, what they do, and how they make you feel. A child of four could tell you about all those things. And guess what. You already have a child inside you—and you did promise that child you would come out to play! If you approach symbols with your inner child, simply and immediately, you'll sense what they mean right away. But if you make it complicated and overthink it, you'll block the meaning and even block yourself from getting the next symbol. So whenever you're experiencing symbols, go fetch the four-year-old inside you. And have fun!

A World of Different Symbols

There are many kinds of symbols in spirit communication—and so many ways to perceive them. For instance, you could get a book as a symbol of learning and writing by seeing an image of a book, feeling someone handing you a book, or just thinking the word *book*.

So as you get symbols from your ancestors, perceive them exactly how you get them. You certainly can practice stretching your senses. But don't predetermine how you're going to perceive anything. If your sensing perceptions change, let them change. If you jump from one type of symbol to another, let that happen, too. Just let it all flow, and be in the world of symbols.

The Different Types of Symbols

1. Simple symbols
2. Affirmative and negative symbols
3. Personal symbols and memories
4. Universal symbols
5. Environmental symbols
6. Animated (or action) symbols
7. Extended and story symbols

1. Simple Symbols

The simple symbol is just that. It usually doesn't have many components or layers in terms of your experience of the symbol. But nonetheless, it could have a very profound meaning—or, indeed, a number of different meanings. For instance, you could get a symbol of a single gold coin. A very simple symbol, yet let's see what it might mean. As you saw in Chapter 3, gold is the mineral—and color—of authority. And 1 is the number of initiative, self-realization, and new beginnings. Coins are also indicative of finance, career, investments, and things you value.

So this single gold coin could indicate a new career that supports an experience of higher authority for you. It could also indicate an opportunity for a new investment. Or there could be an important purchase coming your way. There could also be a single project that you do outside of your work that provides some additional income and personal success in your reputation. It seems like there are a number of different meanings for this simple symbol. But as you can see, they all have similar impacts—individuality, authority, financial increase, and initiative.

Simple symbols can be just about anything—a circle, a light bulb, an oak leaf, a triangle, a rose, a book, a clock, or anything you can imagine. (You'll find some symbols and their meanings in the Appendix.) Even a vision or sense of a color by itself could inform you on any question you might have.

. . . .

Say It Simply

Close your eyes, and take a deep breath. Call to your ancestors who wish to show you a symbol.

Say to yourself, Spirit shows me. And suddenly you perceive a simple symbol as a message. It could be an image, a word, a feeling, or just a color. Notice what you sense immediately. If it changes, notice that, too. After a moment, say thank you to these loving ancestral guides.

. . . .

If you don't know what that symbol meant, come back to it later. Be sure to take notes in your journal whenever you perceive symbols, colors, numbers, or any sensations from your ancestors. Write about how you experienced them, what they meant for you at the time, and how they made you feel. Your journal will become your lexicon of symbols, and you can refer to it frequently to see how your experience and interpretation of symbols evolve.

2. Affirmative and Negative Symbols

Just like all symbols, you can get *yes* or *no* through images, words, feelings, or even physical or energetic experiences. In Chapter 3, you learned how the image of a traffic light can show you *yes/no* through the colored lights you perceive.

There are many other images that can give you an affirmative or negative. For instance, you could see a door that's open or closed—or partially open, which could make the *yes* somewhat conditional. Always be sure to see what emotions you feel with any symbol.

There was one instance when my son perceived a very particular image for *no*. It was at a time when I wanted to buy a house on the street where my twin sister lives. She and I would often move to the same street. But I had to wait for a number of years to make this last move because houses rarely became available on her block. Finally, one did! I was so happy because now my son could be close to his cousins. This house was right across the street from my sister's, and I enthusiastically wrote a check for *earnest money* to hold it.

Yet, as happy as I was to finally be able to get a house there, I started to feel a sense of *no* whenever I thought about the house. It was unsettling in its persistence. So I asked spirit a number of times about the house, and I would always get a no.

That was not the answer I wanted! So I decided to take my son, Devin, who was eight at the time, to see the house again. He was very used to talking to spirit because he had been practicing with me since his dad died five years earlier. I told him to ask his dad for a picture about the house as we drove by it. He told me that his dad covered the house with a big black blanket—a blanket so big that he couldn't see any of the house at all.

Well, that was all I needed. As disappointing as it was, I called the next morning and removed my offer. I was able to get my money refunded, and I resolved to wait until the next house came up for sale.

A little over a year later, while visiting my sister, I saw that a house was being built on a small vacant lot at the top of her street. I stopped and asked the foreman about it, but alas he already had a buyer for the house he was building. I gave him my card so he could call me if anything changed. This time, as I drove away, I was getting the exact opposite energy than I had gotten with the other house. This time, I was getting a *yes* on a house that wasn't even available.

I started to go the construction site several times a week, but nothing had changed. Nonetheless I kept getting a *yes*, and I kept going to the site. I watched as the footers and basement floors were finished. Then one time I stopped and the foreman told me that the financing for the other buyer had fallen through. The house was mine! After years of waiting, I not only got a house on my sister's street, but it was just my style in every perfect way.

But the story doesn't end there. About a year after we moved into our new house, I met the lady who had bought the first house that I had rejected. She told me that they had discovered a soot infestation left by the previous owners who had *never* cleaned the fireplaces. Black soot had built up inside all the walls and under the floors. The old owners had redone the finishes so you couldn't tell, but the new owners had to demolish and rebuild the interior. The black soot turned into a visual black blanket—a very helpful symbol of *no.*

3. Personal Symbols and Memories

In Chapter 6, we saw how memories from your personal life can help you identify your ancestors. But they can give you messages, too. Your memories, interests, areas of study, and every part of your life can provide symbols for your ancestors to use—because they all have meaning! Absolutely *everything* that you experience, learn, read or study—from a painting you've seen to cooking classes to astrology—can become a potential personal symbol. So the more you learn, the more your ancestors can use to speak to you. But of course, your personal symbols extend far beyond things you learn in classes. They can come from any part of your life's history and experiences. So let's take a look now to see how your personal symbols can work for you.

A Personal Symbol for You

Take a deep breath, and close your eyes. Say to yourself, My ancestors are here. *Instantly, you start to feel them all around you. Now think of a relationship or situation in your life about which you'd like some insight. These ancestors now send you a personal symbol that gives you a message about this relationship or situation.*

You may hear a song inside you. Or you perceive a word or image—or even a piece of jewelry—like your grandfather's pocket watch or your grandmother's ring. Whatever you get may identify an ancestor, but it also acts as a message for you. Notice every word, image, idea, or sensation you perceive. Also notice every aspect about it—size, textures, colors, and any movement you may sense. How does it all feel? What does it mean to you? Take a minute to experience this personal symbol. And say thank you to your ancestors as you bring yourself back.

Personal symbols can come as a simple image, word, or feeling. Or they can be extended stories and memories. However they come for you, don't analyze. Just perceive it and notice how it feels. If you don't have a sense of what it means right away, jot it down so you can interpret it later.

Remember When

I had a client, Jimmy, whose Uncle Larry in spirit wanted to bring a message of assistance about Jimmy's possible new job choice— either writing at an ad agency or at the local newspaper. Uncle Larry shared an image of the two of them shopping for Jimmy's first car together. But Jimmy told me that hadn't happened because Uncle Larry had already died before then. Nonetheless, Uncle Larry showed me that image again.

It took me a moment until I realized that Larry was saying his spirit went with Jimmy to help him pick out his car. When I told Jimmy, he was delighted! And he did remember thinking about Larry a lot that day.

Yet, even after I shared that with Jimmy, Larry continued to show me the day when Jimmy bought his first car. Always remember, when an image keeps returning over and over—even after you think you've identified who or what it means—it shows that there's something more to be discovered.

So I asked Jimmy if he could remember anything else that was happening that day. He thought for a moment. Then he said, "Yes! That afternoon I had to get back to school to work on the school newspaper. I loved working on the school paper!" I told him that maybe Larry was trying to tell him the newspaper job might be the answer for him now. And it was! Jimmy took the job and loved working at that paper, too!

This little story illustrates a number of things to keep in mind as you work with your ancestors. I first thought Larry was in the living when he was car shopping with Jimmy. Well, Larry was there, but he was in spirit. This shows that an image is still correct even if you misinterpret it. So trust the images you get, and consider the different ways of looking at it. Also, if any image or symbol persists after you think you're done with it, your ancestors are trying to tell you more. Finally, if you're ever doing this for any of your friends, ask what the imagery means to them—the way I did with Jimmy. They'll know—just like Jimmy did!

4. Universal Symbols

In Chapter 4, you learned about some of the basic universal symbols, such as color, numbers, and so on. But there are many other universal symbols, too. There are symbols that can cross cultures and have a similar meaning for people all over the world. Red roses mean love, a suitcase represents travel, white symbolizes purity, a sword means war, a pen stands for writing, and so much more. (Look in the Appendix for some universal symbols.)

There are universal symbols represented by the body, too—including eyes for vision, ears for hearing, mouth for communication, hands for how you handle things, and feet for the steps you take.

Of course, there are times when the symbol you sense isn't a metaphor. Freud said, "Sometimes a cigar is just a cigar." So let yourself sense if the symbol could be a literal message. If you're not sure, write about it in your journal and notice how it makes you feel.

Universal Universities

I have a friend who had been trying to decide whether to take a class in online marketing. It wasn't a big investment, but he wasn't sure he would like it—even though he was in advertising. When he called his ancestors to ask for their insight, his grandfather, who had been a naval officer, came and gave him an image of Annapolis, where his alma mater is.

I told him that images of universities are symbols for greater learning, so he might want to try the class. He did, and he excelled at it—leading him to take more and more classes. He also forged a stronger relationship with his grandfather, who often went to his classes with him!

. . . .

A Universe of Symbols

Take a deep breath, and close your eyes. Call to your ancestors, and begin to notice them there. Now think of a situation or relationship in your life about which you would like some insight.

Hold that in your mind for a moment. Say to yourself, Spirit shows me universal symbols! *Immediately, a universal symbol comes to mind. You could perceive a word, a picture, a feeling, or an idea. No matter how you get it, take a moment to see it, sense it, and experience every detail.*

Also notice how it feels emotionally. Do you know how this symbol applies to the situation? Ask any question, and see what you get. And if things change, let that happen, too.

Now start to bring yourself back—saying thank you to these helpful ancestors. Take notes in your journal when you're done, and consider the different meanings this symbol may have for you.

. . . .

5. Environmental Symbols

This experience happens when your ancestors use things in your surroundings to give you a message. It could be an ad in the paper, or a picture hanging on the wall, a sign at a local business, or the clock on your desk. Now, in and of themselves, these things aren't symbols. After all, a rose can be a symbol, but it's just a rose until spirit—or Shakespeare—uses it as a symbol.

Yet all these things—pictures, clocks, pens, toasters, whatever— are simply things that you see around you in your daily life. They only become symbols when you notice a *compelling force* with them.

You may be going through your day, wondering how to approach a certain person, or what to do about a project that's been on your mind. Then suddenly something grabs you. It's almost as if it pulls you, and your attention gets drawn to a greeting card on the mantel or the clock on the wall. You know right then to greet that person warmly—or to watch your time so you're not late with your project.

Since this can happen anytime, be aware when something in your environment grabs your attention in a powerful way. Then notice what had just been on your mind and how that symbol might apply. If you're not sure, just take some notes in your journal. It will become clear to you in time.

When I teach how to get symbols in the environment, I tell my students to hold a question in their minds while walking around the room looking at their feet. I have them look at the floor because I don't want them going into their left brains searching for the thing that they would *like* to be a symbol.

It's very easy and a lot of fun. After walking for a bit, they stop when they feel compelled to stop. Then they look up, and the first thing in front of them is the symbol! I'll never forget the time in one class that one of my students, a medium from the East Coast, saw a very demonstrative sign—literally. When she stopped and looked up, she found herself looking out the window at a stop sign. The question she had been holding in her mind was, *Should I keep lending my brother money?* Ha ha! Spirit sure does have a sense of humor—and a way of using every sign they can!

6. Animated (or Action) Symbols

You've experienced the animated symbol a little already. A message starts with a simple symbol, but then your ancestors start to animate it. It starts to move, grow, and change. With every little bit of action, it gives you more information and greater insight. It could change color or size or into a whole new symbol altogether.

I have a client who's a nurse. She's also a healer who meditates and connects to spirit often. I recall a time when she learned about animated symbols, too. In her meditation—on a day when she had a double shift—she saw her great-granddad handing her the Purple Heart medal he had won in WWII. She felt good he was there, and he seemed to be honoring her for her hard work. But then in one meditation, she saw the Purple Heart start to change and move. It turned into a beautiful butterfly that flew to a modern building. It was a wonderful image. But she didn't know what it meant—until about a month later when she was offered a head nursing job at one of the brand-new locations of the hospital where she worked!

Now, here's a process that starts with a simple symbol but changes to tell you more. You could ask about your life in general, or if you want some guidance about a specific relationship or situation, hold that in your mind as you start.

. . . .

The Animated Symbol—Spirit Shares with You

Close your eyes, and take a deep breath. When you set your intention to be with spirit, you immediately start to see and feel your ancestors with you. Now say to yourself, Spirit shows me a symbol. *And then you see or sense a symbol completely. However you get it, notice everything about it—the colors, size, textures, and how it makes you feel. Take a few moments to see and sense everything.*

After you're done with that, your ancestors begin to animate that symbol. It starts to move and change and tell a story. This all turns into a little movie of sorts. Sense it, watch it, visually or conceptually, and experience it all.

Notice everything about the movement of the symbol—especially how that movement makes you feel emotionally. That's part of the story, too. Notice if the movement is slow, tedious, fast, hesitant, or exciting.

Finally, the symbol comes to a stop. Notice everything about it after all of the changes. Is it a completely different symbol? This is the outcome symbol. Sense the colors, size, and how you feel. How does it speak to the possible outcome of this situation—or the outcome of this phase? Remember, every outcome is a new beginning for the next phase!

Notice any last thing and start to bring yourself back. Say thank you to all these wonderful ancestors. Take some notes about your experience and consider the meanings that symbol had for you.

7. Extended and Story Symbols

With the animated symbols, you saw how the actions and changes of a symbol can create a little story to give you even more insight. But an extended symbol can give you a lot of layers, too. I remember a student in one of my professional classes who asked spirit for a message about putting her online mediumship practice in an office. She kept getting the image of a bright and airy bakery with loaves of bread in the windows. Of course, any type of actual store would symbolize a brick-and-mortar business location, but she questioned why it was a bakery. I asked her, "What's the first thing you have to do when you make bread? You have to *raise the dough!*" That made sense to her immediately, and she decided that taking some more time to raise more money before getting a place would be a good idea. So you see, this symbol showed her the outcome as well as what action was needed to achieve that outcome.

With extended symbols, there are different techniques that allow you to have a multilayered experience providing much greater detail and depth. We'll take a look at these techniques in Chapters 19 and 20.

Guidelines for Symbol Perception and Interpretation

Here are a few guidelines that have helped me over the years in my work with symbols.

1. The symbol is the message.

Even if the image is symbolic, be sure to consider the literal and the simple meanings first. If you jump into the metaphor first, you could miss the most important part.

I remember identifying a client's father who had recently died. He was holding out four $100 bills in front of me. I leaped into different money metaphors, telling her of coming financial success. It was only after she couldn't understand the metaphors I was describing that I decided to tell her exactly what I was seeing. When I did, she started to cry. He was holding up a memory! His birthday had been a week before he died, and she had given him a card with four $100 bills in it so he could get new golf clubs.

It was then—a very long time ago—that I learned, first and foremost, the symbol is the message. If your friends ever ask you to connect with their ancestors for a message, always share what you're seeing or sensing before you share possible interpretations.

2. When considering the interpretations for symbols, consider all possible interpretations.

Write about them in your journal, and think about their universal meanings as well as their more personal meanings to you. There may be some instances when you won't know how to interpret a symbol. Then, in time, something happens that will make that symbol meaningful to you. And if you're sharing some symbols for your friends, ask them what those symbols might mean to them.

3. Understand the blocks.

If you're ever connecting with your ancestors and are feeling blocked, don't assume it's because you're blocking spirit. You could be getting a symbol or feeling blocked because of some obstacles in your personal life or work. So say thank you, and ask how you can remove any blocks in your world.

4. Everything in the symbol is part of the message. Find the meaning in everything you see.

There can be lots of different elements in a symbol that can be part of the message. I remember a good example of this with one of my students. He gave a message that a woman was sitting in the side car of a motorcycle being driven by her boyfriend. But then the side car broke away from the motorcycle and rode blithely into a field of flowers, while the guy on the motorbike kept driving. My student said that it was an image of a breakup. It was, but I told him there was more to it, too. I asked him to describe how the different components felt. He said the woman had no control because she was in the side car, but she was so happy to be in the flowers—and so happy that she was no longer driven by her controlling ex, who always had to be in the driver's seat. Now she was free.

So this wasn't just a breakup symbol. There were many layers of events and feelings to be discovered in all the different pieces of the symbol.

5. If you're unsure about something, ask questions!

Ask your ancestors to animate the symbol or to give you a color, a number, or more details of any sort. There are lots of different ways they can give you more information—so just ask for it!

Now you've discovered some more about symbols. Keep practicing with them as you grow in your connectivity. In the next chapter, you'll learn to expand your readiness to receive your ancestors and to receive their symbols and support.

CHAPTER 15

CONNECTIVITY

Readiness to Receive

Hold fast to time! Use it!
Be conscious of each day,
each hour. They slip away
unnoticed all too easily and swiftly.

— THOMAS MANN

Connectivity is the state of being open—the state of being ready to receive—without hesitation or doubt. You've already seen many simple techniques that can open you to spirit ancestors and their messages. But you can be even more active with your ancestors if you bring that focus to your daily life.

So, as Mann said, be conscious of each hour and each day. Those hours can help you build a joyful state of connectivity with your ancestors. You'll be ready to receive every gentle whisper from your Higher Self and from all of your ancestors. So let's take a look now at the things you can do to create a state of readiness in your life.

Daily Practices to Build Connectivity

1. Build trust throughout your daily life.
2. Lift your receptivity and focus.
3. Expand your familiarity and knowledge of symbols.

> 4. Meet and know spirit everywhere through your day.
>
> 5. Know yourself as spirit and hold the Divine perspective in all things.

1. Build Trust Throughout Your Daily Life

You already know about the importance of trusting everything you perceive from spirit in your visualizations with them. But building trust must also happen in your daily life. It's so easy to get busy and miss the opportunity to talk to spirit. When you don't talk to them, the only way for them to talk to you is to send a telepathic thought your way.

You can recognize those thoughts because they will be compelling and because they will often repeat over and over again. It's like a phone that keeps ringing and ringing until you answer it. When you react to intuitive thoughts as soon as—or even before—they start repeating, you'll open the lines of communication immediately and build greater trust every time. With this practice, the telepathic messages you get could be extraordinary.

The following story shows just how important it is to trust those inner thoughts and react to them. This happened to my friend, a gifted intuitive student named Karen. A lot of different types of ancestors were involved, too!

Building Trust—Building Saved!

Karen had always been very close to her great-aunt Mary. They had shared their faith and had traveled together to very meaningful destinations, such as Ireland and Lourdes, France. Even after Mary passed, Karen still felt her close by.

Though Karen meditated at home regularly, she would often stop at a church near her home to meditate. In the early evening, it was dimly lit with the soft light of flickering candles. She especially loved to sit under the ceiling paintings of archangels Raphael,

Michael, and Gabriel. Karen said that the time she spent meditating there would bring her so much peace and calm after a draining day at work.

One day on the way home from work, she got a strong inclination to stop at church. But she was tired, and she really wanted to go home. She told herself, *I'll go tomorrow*. But the inclination to go turned into an inner nagging.

Karen later told me that she had heard, over and over, *Just stop for five minutes*. Finally she relented. *Okay, five minutes*, she told that inner voice. But she didn't get to meditate that night.

As soon as she walked into the church, she immediately smelled smoke. She saw swirls of smoke floating under the dim lights, and there was a haze across the quiet, empty church. Even though she couldn't see where the flames were, the smoke was getting thicker. So she ran over to the parish office, where one of the priests called the fire department.

The firetruck came, and the fire was extinguished. Karen was told that someone had set a fire in one of the confessionals intentionally. Karen had arrived at the church at 4 p.m., and the evening service was scheduled for 7. If she hadn't gone when she did, no one would have been there for over two hours. The church could have burned to the ground! Karen felt so happy that she had listened to that driving, compelling inner voice, and she thanked spirit for *driving* her to church (so to speak)!

These events that happened to Karen illustrate how important it is to listen—and to *react*—when you feel a forceful, compelling, intuitive message. It may seem silly and often unimportant. After all, what's a five-minute meditation here or there? But there could be something greater—indeed, much greater than you think—than what the message reflects.

Sometimes you'll discover the reason for the message, as Karen did. And sometimes you won't know at all. But whatever the repetitive thought is, it will always lead to good—as long you trust *and react*!

Another interesting thing would be the spirits involved in this event. There were group ancestors from the Catholic Church, and there were probably some past-life ancestors of Karen's, since her Catholic past lives are clearly evident. These are indicated by her deep connection to the church, as well as the fact that she had found—well—so much sanctuary in the sanctuary! Of course, there were probably more angels present than those just painted on the ceilings, too.

Finally, there were the unsung heroes from the family. Or I should say—families. Not only was Aunt Mary there, but so were the members of another family. It turns out that Mary's best friend—who was also in spirit—was the mother of the pastor of that church! It took a great team of ancestors to drive Karen to the church that day!

Karen has since made a point of listening—and responding— to the intuitive thoughts that come to her. You, too, can make a commitment to build that kind of trust. Respond immediately to any thought that compels or repeats. Stay conscious of even the tiniest messages that come spontaneously through your waking day, a flash of light, a sense of presence, or an insight to a problem. Respond to whatever you see, hear, and feel immediately, and note them in your journal. Writing about them will put you in the habit of seeking out these messages and being more and more sensitive to them every day.

2. Lift Your Receptivity and Focus

You've already seen how important meditation is to healing. But meditation is also absolutely key to keeping yourself open and receptive. It also lifts you to your Higher Self, the source of your light, love, and power, which is why it's so critical to both healing and your heightened psychic awareness.

There are many things in the world that can lift you—great works of art, beauty in nature, breathtaking music, walks in the woods, or inspiring books—and it would be great if you could partake in all of them.

Yet, in order for your spirit and your ancestors to reach you, you need to be still and listen. Of course your ancestors can connect with you telepathically. But when you meditate regularly, it gives them the best and most open path to reach you, because your focus will be lifted to them.

When you don't have time to meditate, you can lift your receptivity by just sitting down, closing your eyes, and taking a few deep, relaxing breaths. Bring your focus within, and hold a simple declaration—or even just a word that lifts you. Create these few minutes of stillness whenever you can, and use declarations to help lift your focus throughout your day. Here are some for you, but you can make up some of your own, too.

. . . .

Declaring Your Readiness to Receive

I am always open to the love and guidance
my ancestors share.

I sense and receive the energy of spirit
in the world around me.

I live in joyful expectation; I am ready
to receive from spirit!

I am always open to my ancestors,
and I know spirit's presence instantly!

I connect with spirit as easily as I reach out
and connect with everyone and everything.

I trust the intuitive messages I receive,
and I respond to them immediately.

Because spirit lives within me,
I know when spirit is around me.

. . . .

3. Expand Your Familiarity and Knowledge of Symbols

It's clear that symbols play a large part in spirit communication. The more you practice with them, the more easily you'll be able to perceive and interpret them. Symbols can identify an ancestor or a living person, and they can give you messages, too. Often, one symbol can do all of those things. Just as telepathic thoughts will keep repeating until you respond, symbols will also keep repeating until you get the message and respond to them, too.

Here's an event that illustrates this quite well. I have a friend, Pam, who suddenly started noticing oranges in a very compelling way as she went through her day. Now, these were the oranges she always saw regularly—in the break room at work, at the market, even on television in orange juice ads. They weren't new to her, but the magnetic pull they had on her was new.

This went on for a few days. Pam seemed to be mesmerized by oranges! Then Pam called to ask me what it could mean. I told her that it might be helpful for her to meditate on the symbol, but for me the most common interpretations of oranges—besides vitamin C—were Florida and California.

"Florida!" Pam gasped. "I forgot that I was supposed to make arrangements for my aunt to visit from Florida!" Pam quickly thanked me and then she was off to call her aunt.

This was a strong experience for Pam, showing how objects in the environment can be symbols when a repetitive, compelling force comes with them. Your ancestors in spirit are just like your family and friends in the living. If they want to tell you something, they won't wait for you to call them. They'll call you! And if it's something important, they'll call you over and over—hence the repetitive symbols and thoughts.

The fact that any—and all—of these different perceptions and symbols can drop into your experience anytime emphasizes the benefits of keeping a journal. It helps you keep a sharp eye on the little things that happen in your day and become more familiar with symbols and their meanings. Here is a list of some things that can help you with that.

Practices for Symbol Expansion

- Try to look at everything as a discovery. Study subjects that pique your interest. Look for the images and symbols in the things you study, read, and see.

- Pay attention as you move through your environment. Watch for any symbols, signs, or objects that repeat or that are compelling to you. Write about them in your journal. Consider how they felt to you emotionally and what possible meanings they have in your life.

- Trust your intuition when it seems to compel you. Your spirit and those of your ancestors talk to you through your intuition, but they can't get through if you don't listen.

- Watch for recurring symbols and themes in your dreams. Notice what your dreams are trying to tell you—about yourself and about your life. Keep a dream journal and take notes about how you feel the first thing in the morning—even if you don't remember having a dream.

- Take the time to study various cultural, mythical, historical, and religious symbols and their meanings. Be open to discovering your ancestors and even your own histories when you study new things.

- Regularly practice the animated-symbol visualization from Chapter 14. Ask a question, see a symbol, and watch it move and change into a new symbol. Trust what you get, and then see how it applies to your life.

- Open yourself to see the hidden meanings in the small and large events in your life. Don't analyze, just consider them. See how those events feel to you.

- Investigate other practices that help open your sensing devices. Try psychometry, perceptive or automatic writing, astrology, runes, tarot, or anything else that might strike your fancy. Besides igniting your psychic receptivity, they are filled with symbols that will expand your symbol lexicon.

So remember to look for your own spirit's perspective in your own life. Talk with your Higher Self and your ancestral guides as you go about your day. Invite their input, and take a moment to listen with your heart. Remember that you live in the world of spirit even more deeply than you live in the physical. Feel your spirit with you in every little thing you do.

4. Meet and Know Spirit Everywhere through Your Day

If you want to be open to receive your ancestors, stay open to all the spirits you know—yourself, your family, everyone on this side and that. Here are some helpful actions you can take to build this openness every day.

- Engage and connect with the important souls in your life every day. Take some time each day to embrace and really listen to your children, spouse, friends, co-workers—everyone. They are as sacred as any—and every—spirit in the universe. When you look into their eyes, *see* the spirit who is there.

- Even when some people may be mean or bitter, recognize that it is their outer shell, the temporal self that insulates and isolates them from their own Divine light. Take a moment to talk to their spirits instead of to their personalities so you can get to know who they *really* are. *Feel* and *know* the presence of God in all.

- Talk to your ancestors in spirit as you would talk to your friends. Make them a normal part of your normal life—because they are.

- Maintain correct thoughts about spirit and yourself. Vulnerability and fear are exclusive to the true nature of divinity—both yours and spirit's.

- Have a brief discussion with one of your ancestral guides every day, and write about it in your journal. Also in your journal, note the spirits you perceived most throughout the day.

- Notice which higher guides and creative teachers work with you during your different activities. Are there any other teachers in spirit with whom you would like to build a stronger relationship? If so, call them and share your purpose with them.

- Always remember your Divine soul. Be sure to lift yourself to that truth whenever you're feeling low. Here's a mini-moment you can do often.

. . . .

Connecting with Your Higher Self

Take a deep breath, and close your eyes. Bring yourself into the serene, eternal soul you are. With another deep breath, feel the grace, love, and gentle power there.

As you rest in this light that you are, bring your focus to the boundless connection you have with all. In your higher perspective, you see everything anew. Just take a moment to be with this grace.

. . . .

These are some of the things you can do to connect with your Higher Self and all the wonderful spirits around you. As you go through your day, remember that your ancestors are right there with you, helping you with all sorts of things—sometimes even doing the most mundane activities.

My business manager, Moe, once told me about the time he was at home trying to unclog a sink drain, which was giving him quite a bit of trouble. He felt his father, who was a plumber, standing right next to him. He heard his dad tell him to walk away and come back to it a little later. Moe listened and did just that. When he came back, it was done in a trice! So don't forget, spirit is there to help you—and they'll even throw in the kitchen sink!

5. Know Yourself as Spirit and Hold the Divine Perspective in All Things

All parts of you combine to create your life. Your physical, mental, emotional, and spiritual makeup—all of these must work in harmony. And harmony comes through the touch, heart, and mind of your Divine reality. All of your connections—to Grandma and to God—come through your eternal spirit. So if things start to upset you, seek to calm your emotions. Don't be *reactionary*—be *actionary*! Emotional, physical, and mental stresses are significant barriers to feeling spirit—and to feeling *your own* spirit. Know that the energy you carry can either take you higher or block your union with spirit everywhere.

In Chapter 8, I mentioned the comedy writer and producer Mel Brooks. He carried his humor—as well as an ongoing party—with him wherever he went. I recall a story about another person who was just the opposite—the doleful and depressed Edgar Allan Poe.

The medium and author Andrew Jackson Davis was a friend of Poe's. Davis once said that Poe would always carry a cloud of darkness with him and around him. So no matter where Poe went, or what room he entered, Poe was constantly stepping into his own darkness. With this Davis gives us a powerful image of how we can bring darkness with us.

Darkness, melancholy, and gloom are a movable feast. But joy, wonder, and bliss are, too. Which movable feast would you like to take with you wherever you go?

So find that bliss and joy by creating a state of Divine communion in all things. You will begin to experience a flow of extraordinary light and power in all parts of your life. You will not only create a state of readiness, you will create a state of Divine readiness. So if you see—and live—every moment as an opportunity to meet God, you will!

CHAPTER 16

PAST-LIFE ANCESTRY

The past is never dead.
It's not even past.

— WILLIAM FAULKNER

Have you ever been interested in a place you've never seen or had a curiosity about people from the past whom you've never met? These types of interests often indicate connections to places and people from your past lives.

Past-life ancestors are unlike other types of ancestors because they've lived with you before. They knew your relationships, your occupations, your talents, and now they can help you with those in this life—and with some of your karmic lessons, too.

But before you meet some of your past-life ancestors, let's take a little look at the nature of karma and reincarnation. Put simply, reincarnation is the birth of a soul into a new body—a new lifetime. Since the soul is eternal, this can happen hundreds of times for each individual. Where and when—and with whom—a person returns depends upon the karma that person wants to address and the talents and interests that individual would most like to pursue.

Karma: Lessons from the Past

There are a lot of misunderstandings about karma. For many people, karma is something burdensome—like debts to be paid or sentences handed down by a judge. But there is no Bureau of Karmic

Statistics and no record-keeping. Karma is not punishment or suffering. Nor is karma a system of paying your dues—or for getting paid back. Your past lives may be the reason why things started the way they did in this life, but they are not an excuse to keep them that way. No matter how strong your past-life histories were, karma never brings a loss of power in this life. There may be a *perceived* loss of power—but never a real one.

You chose your karmic lessons before you were born—lessons about lifting yourself out of negative definitions, emotions, and behaviors created in past lives.

> **Your present was born in the past.**
> **It's where all your definitions began.**
> **But now you can give birth to new definitions**
> **for all of your futures to come.**

Your new definitions take form step-by-step. And the great thing about karmic healing is that whenever you might take a step back or make a slip, it's not immutable. You can create karmic healing in the next moment, and the next, and tomorrow, and next month! This is true even if you've been deeply stuck in a karmic or ancestral pattern for a very long time. It could take quite a while to break, but your free will gives you the chance to make the right choices—choices to find the grace and the power of the eternal self you are. Your free will also lets you choose your karmic approach before each life. Let's take a look at the different approaches to reincarnation now.

Planning a Comeback

While karmic lessons and directives can vary widely from person to person, those directives can usually fit into five basic categories in terms of approach (gleaned from the Edgar Cayce material).

Approach to Reincarnation

1. Desire
2. Compensation
3. Retribution
4. Attachment and repetition of patterns
5. Service

1. Desire

This occurs when a spiritual being simply wishes to experience the physical world and express itself in a certain way. For instance, you may want a lifetime of learning the violin. Or you may want to return with a past-life spouse just to recreate the joyful relationship you had before. Desire is much more a matter of want than of emotional yearning. For instance, if you feel you *must* come back with a past-life lover because of strong emotional urgency, that's an indicator of attachment—not desire. After all, wanting a glass of wine is a great deal different than needing a glass of wine.

2. Compensation

Compensation means returning to alternate aspects of yourself or your activities. For instance, a person who lived in the desert may choose to return to a life by the sea. Or a brother and sister could switch places out of curiosity. Or a man may return as a woman. Again, these are more about discovery rather than urgent emotional needs. But when a skinny, starving person comes back and creates an attachment to food and a life of emotional, fearful overeating, it is not compensation. In this case, the negative emotions from the life of starvation then would combine with an attachment to food, deepening the existing karmic lesson about fear and food, which would need to be healed.

3. Retribution

This often includes some compensatory aspects, but it also usually involves other people. For example, if an individual in one life mistreats his parents or children, he may return with those people (either in the same relationship or others) in a life where he devotes himself to their nurturing. Or someone involved in owning or selling slaves may return divested of his freedoms and be made to live a life of servitude. Or he may return as a person who strives to end oppression and social injustices. Obviously, compensation (in terms of doing something opposite) is a factor, but it becomes retribution because it is driven by strong emotional content.

Unfortunately, many people believe that making retribution will clean the "karmic slate." But actually the release of karma rests not on doing different, but on *being* different. The lower emotional body must give way to a higher reality.

If someone was a slave owner in a previous life, and he believes that retribution will "clear his record," he may reincarnate in the role of a slave. Then he would experience the emotions of victimization, servitude, and the loss of power. These emotions are as strongly out of alignment with his eternal truth as the feelings of hatred that he had as a slave owner. At some time or another, this person will need to detach from all of them.

4. Attachment and Repetition of Patterns

These two approaches are often interrelated. Attachment occurs when a person becomes dependent on something for emotional reasons—such as alcohol, drugs, or food for escape—or certain relationships for satisfying a state of lovelessness. When attachment happens, it's because people are looking for a sense of well-being, but that search is external to themselves. They feel that if someone loves them enough, they'll feel better about themselves. Or they hope that drugs or alcohol will take their fears and pain away—at least for a little while.

Sometimes it is the attachment that stimulates the pattern, and sometimes it's the other way around. With either of these, the karmic lesson is to break the attachment and the pattern—to find one's well-being and love within—not from anything or anyone outside yourself.

One of the challenges with such karma is that you have to be reborn with those people—or with those types of people—in order to confront the karma. So many clients have asked me why they were born to such parents or why they keep falling for selfish partners. Well, the answer is simple. Being exposed to the very difficulty you need to rise above is what gives you the opportunity to rise above it. Unfortunately, once you're exposed, it's very easy to get caught in the pattern—again!

Deep understanding and persistence are required to break the cycle of attachment and repetition of patterns, and you have the great inner strength to do it. (To work on such karma, see Chapters 9 through 11 for help with ancestral and karmic healing of patterns.)

5. Service

This is the condition of reincarnating to assist others along their process of growth without thought of personal gain. The action of service may occur for anyone, no matter where that person is in his or her own growth. And growth and service often overlap—just as someone who is divorced may help others going through a divorce.

There are countless ways to be of service because there are so many people in need around the world. So find a path of service that lights you up. But remember, service is not servitude. Don't create an attachment to service. Don't let it become something to do only so you can feel good about yourself. That's not where your well-being lies.

**Feeling good about yourself
comes from feeling God within yourself.**

I have heard some people say that when they're done with this life, they aren't coming back anymore. While we don't have to come back right away, people will continue to return until they are done with all their karmic lessons. At that time, returning becomes an option.

But the Dalai Lama says that even those who have reached the highest spiritual understanding will continue to return in service as long as there is still a sentient being left on the planet who needs help. These higher beings have arrived at a state of heaven within. The Dalai Lama calls this *non-abiding Nirvana*. It is a sort of *being in heaven without living in heaven*.

You can do this, too. From desire to service, be aware of these different approaches to reincarnation in your life. Work with them all. Live in non-abiding Nirvana, and take it wherever you go—to every person and to every moment. Where better to find heaven than right where you are?

Past-Life Cast of Characters

Trying to talk about the comings and goings of people in past lives is a lot like talking about time travel. You could get caught in an endless loop of who's who and who came when. Then, when you add your other ancestors to the mix, the resulting befuddlement could cause a fog from which there may be no return!

Your past-life ancestors would, of course, include any of those who had lived during your past lives. They could also belong to your biological ancestors and other types of ancestors as well. There are people in your life now—grandparents, siblings, anyone—who were in some of your past lives, too. And here's something else to consider—in a past life you could have been your own great-great-great-grandmother. Are things getting foggy yet?

Beyond all of this, there is another important ancestor—you. As I mentioned before, you are your own ancestor because you have gone before many times over. And you—through your own histories, thoughts, choices, feelings, and deeds—have brought the most influence to bear on who you are now. Of course, you have ancestors who have participated, and that's why they want to bring their help. But the responsibility for your higher awareness and karmic healing rests with you, and you certainly have the wisdom to succeed. After so many past lives, just think of how old you are!

Do I Know You?

In the next process, some of your past-life ancestors will show you some past-life places, people, and events. Let yourself have these experiences in your imaging mind without thinking about who's who. Some may be from your family or from your ancient lands. Some may be from the groups and purposes you hold, and some simply may be from your past lives—without having any other connection at all. Regardless, they are all past-life guides because they bring you guidance from and about those lives.

So when you meet them, dive into your perceptions completely. Your imagination is your tool. You may jump from one life to another. You may get an intuitive sense of who some people were in that life—or if some are people you know now. Let whatever happens happen. Trust everything you sense and feel.

. . . .

Past-Life Guides Show the Way

Close your eyes, and take a deep breath. Softly say to yourself, My past-life guides are here. *And with that you immediately sense some past-life ancestors all around you. See them, and feel them. Notice the clothes they wear. They could be from different times and places. Take a few moments to see and sense everything.*

Now a few guides who were together in a past life with you step forward, and they gently touch your shoulder. You are immediately transported in your imaging to a past life that you had with them. Sense yourself there completely. Look around you and notice the location, the terrain, the climate, the plants, the architecture—everything. What do you sense about this time and place?

After a few moments, you notice that you are different. Look down at yourself. Notice your clothes, your feet, your hands. How old are you? What gender are you? Let yourself sense and know all of this.

Now turn your attention to the ancestors who brought you here. Do you know who they are to you? Also notice any other people in the scene that you're sensing. Do you

*know who they are to you? Can you identify them by
their energy? What do you feel with them all?*

*Take a few moments to finish all of that up. Then
these guides now share an image, idea, word, or symbol
that can indicate some purposes or patterns from that life.
Notice everything. Does anything connect to your life now?*

*After a few minutes, start to bring yourself back. Say
thank you to these past-life ancestors. Remember that
you can visit this incarnation—or any incarnation—
with your ancestors anytime. After you're done, take
some notes about everything you discovered.*

You can do longer or shorter versions of this process, exploring
a number of various incarnations with many different forerunners.
There is so much you can learn when you create active relationships
with your past-life ancestors.

Working with Your Past-Life Ancestors

Besides working on your patterns and karmic healing, you could
also discover your past-life talents, purposes, and passions with your
past-life ancestors.

I have a friend, Dr. Neal Rzepkowski, who is an M.D. as well as
a medium. He also has great spiritual ties and past-life histories as a
Native American medicine man that go back to the early 1500s on the
western shore of Lake Michigan. The medicine man who was with
Neal then is one of his most devoted spirit guides now, helping Neal
with healing, his spiritual development, and alternative medicine
practices as well.

Edgar Cayce is another ancestor of Neal's. Neal has long been
studying and teaching Cayce's healing methods. In his classes, he
shares Cayce's ideas and remedies so naturally—maybe because
Cayce is standing right beside him.

An even more recent ancestor to Neal is Frank Fools Crow, a
very famous medicine man who lived in the Pine Ridge Reservation
in South Dakota and died in 1989. Neal feels Frank Fools Crow's

presence and support—helping Neal in his healing work and Native American studies.

It may seem odd that contemporaries can be spirit ancestors. But ancestors are those who have gone before—gone into spirit, gone into different areas of study, and gone into the embrace of great talent. Neal has a lot of talented ancestors working with hm. Now let's take a look at your talents from past lives.

Karmic Legacies—Karmic Talents

A karmic legacy is something handed down to you from your past lives. It could include your karmic lessons and other responsibilities from the past. But legacies also include your past talents, creative activities, and other pursuits you had cultivated during your past lives. You may have a sense of these karmic talents already.

Because of your histories, these talents lie within you, and you can pursue them again anytime you want. Sometimes past-life talents can become your primary purposes in this life, too. For example, I feel that my mediumship and spiritual work, which have been priorities for me, were extremely important in my previous lives, too.

Something like this may have happened to you. Think back on your life to an activity that compelled you to pursue it. It's likely that you had done this activity in some lifetimes before. You probably built some significant skills, which gives you a leg up on your endeavors now. So whenever you are compelled down a path of such purpose, call your ancestors. Together you can get working on reestablishing a path you probably have known and loved many times over.

Past-Life Echoes

There are other talents and interests that may have interested you before, but only manifested in this life for a short time. This happened to me during college. I passionately loved drawing and took a number of classes. But my academic focus was psychology. Over time, my drawing activity just seemed to drop away.

I call these shorter bits of talent and pursuits from previous reincarnations *past-life echoes*. Like the sound of echoes, after a time, they simply get softer and softer, and then fade away. Past-life echoes fade away usually because they have been replaced by new passions.

A past-life echo often (though not always) occurs early in life, in childhood or young adulthood. Your previous histories are more recent then, and past-life energy seems to run closer to the surface. Though your memories of those lives aren't conscious, the interest and skills are still awake! And, as always happens with free will, past-life echoes can return to higher importance when an opportunity for new growth presents itself.

In both karmic talents and past-life echoes, a high level of proficiency is usually evident. You can tap into those past skills and disciplines today. Let us now do a little process to discover some past talents for you. As always, give your imaging the job and trust everything. Remember, your psychic senses are your talents, too.

. . . .

Talents from the Past

Close your eyes, and take a deep, relaxing breath. As you move into your innermost place of power and trust, say to yourself, My past-life guides are here now! *Immediately, you sense some of those ancestors around you. Take a few moments to notice everything—who they are, how they're dressed, how you feel.*

Now ask them for a memory of a talent from a past life. Soon that memory pops into your mind. What are you doing? Perhaps you can feel something in your hands, or you see yourself with the tools of this creative endeavor. What are you remembering?

After a moment, your guides share an image, a word, a symbol, or a feeling that shows you more about this talent. Notice everything that you get.

As you perceive all of this, consider if you have embraced this talent in your current life, too. If not, are you interested in pursuing it or something like it now?

Now let spirit show you one little step you can take to expand and express your talents and skills today. Notice everything you see, sense, and feel.

After a few moments, start to wrap that up. Say thank you to these wonderful past-life guides. They are here for you anytime. Bring yourself back now, and take some notes about your experience.

. . . .

Getting Clarity on Karmic Conditions

In an interview, the Dalai Lama was once asked, if science could prove absolutely that reincarnation didn't exist, what would he do? The Dalai Lama smiled and answered that if that were so, of course he'd no longer believe in it. Obviously, no one can be sure about past lives until this life is over. But there certainly is a lot of evidence of it that I've seen in people's different experiences over many years of this work. I'd like to share some misconceptions about reincarnation that I've discovered over the years. But remember, as you continue your investigations, it's up to you to draw your own conclusions.

Reincarnation Misconception 1:
Most people come back to a new life soon after they die—especially those who had died suddenly.

This is not typically the case. The spirit world is an extraordinary place with lots of exciting things to do and wonderful people to meet. Even people who died suddenly—such as in accidents or suicides—tend to stay on the spirit side for quite a while.

There are some groups of people who tend to return immediately, such as newborns, babies, toddlers, and miscarriages. They like to try again right away. Other than that, there was one historically significant occurrence of a very fast—and vast—return. A great many of those who died in World War II came back extremely quickly. This extraordinary return was called *the baby boom*.

Reincarnation Misconception 2:
People usually come back to the same family group over and over throughout their incarnations.

Though there are different times and phases when you might come back to the same family and lineage, it certainly doesn't happen all the time—or even most of the time. After all, you wouldn't take only one class over and over in college, or visit only one vacation spot year after year.

Now, in a psychological way, we do "take the same class over and over" when we have to break a karmic pattern. But we don't have to come back to the same family to learn that lesson. And that brings us to our next misconception.

Reincarnation Misconception 3:
If you have a karmic lesson that involves another person, you have to keep coming back with that specific person until the lesson is learned.

Being exposed to the source that triggers the negative thinking lets you confront the issue. But it doesn't have to be the exact same source. For instance, if you have to break a pattern with someone who's selfish, there are lots of people like that. They may be different people, but they make you feel the same way. So you can come back with one of them or with the original person. They all give you the same karmic opportunity to learn.

Reincarnation Misconception 4:
If a person kills another in one life, that person must be killed in a future life to release the karma.

In order to release karma when someone kills another, the killer must heal the faulty beliefs and emotional disturbance that made it okay for him to take another's life in the first place. When tolerance, patience, compassion, and love become natural instincts for this person, the lesson will be learned—without being killed.

Reincarnation Misconception 5:
If someone is born to abusive parents, it's because he or she was an abusive parent in a past life.

Being abused is usually a repetitive pattern—not retribution. An abusive relationship causes the abused to create a paradigm of valuelessness and diminishment. The karmic lesson, then, is to stop the abuse, and to redefine oneself through one's inner higher power and greater compassion—no matter what others say or do. Nothing good could be learned by coming back and mistreating others.

Reincarnation Misconception 6:
There is only one soul mate in the world for each individual.

Many relationships in a person's life stem from past-life histories. In an eternal timeline, everyone makes changes—in families, occupations, purposes, and relationships—several times over. There are countless past-life relationships that can carry strong connections. Tying yourself to just one would prohibit all the other joyful romances and partnerships you could have.

Reincarnation Misconception 7:
If one person has all the power in a relationship, it's meant to make retribution for a previous life when that person was the submissive one. This condition is called *emotional role reversal*.

Though this reversal can happen, it's far less frequent than patterning. Most of the time, submissive and dominant people find themselves in those roles because they've gotten caught in a pattern several times over. In these cases, the submissive person needs to learn self-love and to insist on greater reciprocity in the relationship. The controlling, overpowering person needs to learn to be more sensitive, compassionate, and giving. If this doesn't happen, the submissive person must then take action to create a self-honoring environment, even if it means leaving the controlling person.

Reincarnation Misconception 8:
If there is great intensity in a relationship,
it's an indication of great passion and love.

Of course, intensity is present during the infatuation stage of any romance, but long-term intensity is rarely, if ever, a sign of love. It's usually indicative of karmic lessons, imbalances of power, unfinished business, and wounded feelings. Intensity can also be a sign of your urgency that the other person doesn't value you enough or that he or she might leave.

Reincarnation Misconception 9:
If a person feels compelled to take care of another
individual, it is due to a past karmic debt, and that
debt must be paid. This condition is called *role confusion*.

All parents should take care of their children, and adult children should care for their aging parents, but this misconception is about something entirely different. It occurs when a role you played in a past life now starts to dominate a relationship, even though you are no longer in that role.

There are lots of ways role confusion can happen, but the absolute most common is taking responsibility for another adult. If you ever feel a compelling "duty" to care for another adult (who does not have a special need), it usually indicates that you were very likely a parent, nanny, or older sibling in a past life. This shows a karmic pattern of sacrificing your own directives for another's and also enables the other person to perpetuate patterns of dependence, selfishness, and irresponsibility.

If you ever feel responsible for taking care of another adult, meditate on it deeply. It may have started in a past life, but it could be serving other emotional needs for you now. It could be an attempt to keep the other person from leaving. Or you may be doing it to feel better about yourself. Look into it, and understand all your motives. You can't break the chain if you can't see the links!

Well, this chapter has been about the past lives that could take you back centuries or eons. Now it's time to look at spirit communication that could take you only seconds!

CHAPTER 17

SPIRIT INSTAGRAMS

Insights in Seconds

It is the spirit that quickeneth.

— JOHN 6:63

It's so very sad that most of the people in the world go through their lives without even thinking about spirit. Even those who are curious about connecting to their ancestors often think it can't be done because it's too mysterious, too hard, or only meant for a gifted few. Yet none of this is true.

The truth is that communication with spirit folk is as easy as communicating with physical people. Actually, they're even easier to reach.

In the physical world, you call or text your friends and family—and you put posts on social media. Well, your outreach to spirit can happen in very similar ways. For instance, when you want to speak with one of your ancestors, you simply call that person. When you want to reach out to a certain group of spirit guides all at once, you can send an intuitive *group text*, just like you did in Chapter 13. When you want to reach out to all your ancestors, just send out a mental tweet and watch their comments return.

Legions of Spirit Followers

Just think of all of your ancestors as followers. Can you imagine how many spirit followers you have? Lifetimes and generations of ancestral followers! Your spirit ancestors are more active followers than those on social media because they follow you on so many levels—sometimes even literally! Your posts to spirit come through your energy, your thoughts, your purposes, and your actions. Besides your meditations, it's through your energy posts that you reach out to spirit and sometimes ask for help—often without even knowing it.

In this chapter, you'll find fast linking techniques and new trigger words that can open you to all your ancestors—just like social media. You'll also learn new trigger symbols that will let you get a full meaning in moments. Now let's get started.

Pull Up a Chair!

I love the book *A Christmas Carol* by Charles Dickens. It has some of the most sublime words written in the English language. Near the beginning, Marley's ghost tells Scrooge of his frequent visits, "I have sat invisible beside you many and many a day."

There is more truth in this than, I think, Dickens possibly could have imagined. Oh, if the world only knew in how many rooms and how many chairs the invisible were seated! Do you know who's sitting in the chair right next to you now?

Here's a process that will help you find out. I like to do this process to see who's with me throughout my day. Actually, this is a combination of three little processes, where you meet spirit sitting next to you, around you, and opposite you. Remember, as you meet these ancestors, be spontaneous and quick, noticing your first intuitive responses instantly.

· ·

Spirit Takes a Seat

Close your eyes, and relax. Take a deep breath, and hold the intention to be with spirit in your heart. Imagine that there's an empty chair next to you. Say to yourself, Spirit sits with me. *Immediately, you notice that one of your ancestors sits there.*

Take a few moments to sense everything you get with this forerunner. Do you sense the clothes or jewelry? Let yourself get a scent, a symbol, a song, or a word. If you're not sure who this person is, just notice everything you get.

Finish that up now, and say to yourself, Spirit sits around me. *And you start to notice there are other spirits sitting in other seats around you, even in the other rooms, too. You can sense them and see them with your intuitive eye sitting in the chairs there. Don't start thinking. Just feel and see the spirits all around you. And notice everything you get with them.*

After a few moments, turn your attention to another spirit chair that's right across from you. If there isn't an actual chair there, use your imaging to see this. And say to yourself, Spirit sits there! *Instantly, you see, seated there, a smiling spirit who loves you deeply. Let yourself look with your heart and your inner vision at this dear one.*

Take a few minutes to be with this person. Feel the exquisite peace and love that come from that sweet smile and gentle heart. The years fall away, and there is nothing left but love.

Start to finish that up now. If you'd like, take a moment to ask a question of any of these ancestors. As soon as you do, you see or sense a symbol, a color, a word, or an idea. Just notice what you get.

Now start to bring yourself back, saying thank you to all your ancestors who took some time to sit with you. Open your eyes, and take some notes about your experience.

· ·

Usually, I don't ask any questions at all with this process. Just being with these beautiful souls is so very important, too. I generally do different parts of this process at different times. The ancestor who sits next to me is often there to help with work, and sometimes I'll ask that ancestor a work question.

The second part of the process—just noticing the ancestors who are sitting around and hanging out—is something I do sitting at my desk or walking through the house. Wherever I am, I love to glimpse at who's sitting on the couch, at the kitchen table, or even my spirit cats sleeping on the bed!

The third segment of the process is very different for me. When I see an empty chair opposite me, I just welcome whoever wants to come—even if it's someone I don't think I know. It's all about the feelings. Our eyes simply meet, and our hearts open. And there is a sense of the most profound love.

A Brother's Visit

This last part of the process was inspired by an event that happened to English poet Wilfred Owen—after he died. It was just after the end of World War I, and Harold Owen hadn't seen or heard from his brother Wilfred in months. Harold, who was camped off Victoria, decided to go down to his cabin to write some letters. When he went into his cabin, he saw his brother Wilfred sitting in his chair.

Harold was shocked and started quietly asking Wilfred how he got there. But Wilfred didn't speak or move. He just kept looking at his brother with his sweet and endearing smile. After a few moments, the fact that Wilfred didn't speak seemed totally normal to Harold. Indeed, just beholding Wilfred was an exquisite pleasure for him. For Harold, Wilfred's presence and their meeting were "undeniably right and strangely perfect."

Harold loved having him there. But then something distracted him, and he looked away for a moment. When he looked back, his brother was gone. Harold suddenly felt exhausted and dropped onto his cot, immediately falling asleep.

When he woke up the next morning, Harold knew that Wilfred was dead. And he was right. Wilfred had been killed on the Western Front many weeks earlier, just before the Armistice was signed.

I wanted to share this little process and this story with you because they show, perhaps more than anything else, the best thing about being with your spirit ancestors: love never stops; it only gets bigger. So when you can, take a few minutes to do this one-on-one process with someone you love. It will be a gift to both of you.

Of course, do the other two little processes, too. You don't have to do them all together as you did here. As a matter of fact, they're so quick and easy, you can do any of them whenever the mood strikes. And be flexible, too. Maybe a different ancestor than you expect will appear. Or it could be someone you don't know. Whatever happens, it's all good.

In my audio program *Ancestor Spirit Communication*, you'll find an audio process a little like this, but it uses different command words and imagery to place spirit around you. A lot of my students have found these techniques helpful. One of them, Jodi Weaver, said that when she uses them for herself, she often gets people she doesn't know personally. Instead, she gets very interesting spirits who are linked to the things she's doing. When Jodi uses these types of trigger words in her mediumship practice to meet her clients' ancestors, the same is true for them. Of course their loved ones come. But when other types of ancestral guides show up, they bring very pointed and accurate messages, too. This shows how close the spirits you think you don't know really are. Your spirit knows them, and they know you. And their guidance is very real.

So if you don't know the ancestors who are sitting next to you, bring your focus to the energy and support they want to bring to your life's endeavors. The colors and other symbols you sense can help you with this, too.

Remember, there's a good chance that you could see a lot of ancestors in this process. But you don't have to communicate with every one. Just send a loving hello. Anytime during your day, simply say, *Spirit's sitting beside me!* Then instantly notice who's with you or next to you. Send some love. And if you want, you can ask any simple question and get insight in seconds!

Think Fast!

Over the years, there have been many consultations during which I've had to tell spirit to slow down! They really do think fast.

As I have mentioned, the great Irish poet William Butler Yeats was one of the many notable people who not only took an interest in the ancestral world but also worked with spirit regularly. He often talked to his writing guides. Though he didn't know who they were, he was aware that they constantly changed.

He called them *my teachers*. And they told him—when he was asking them questions—to word those questions accurately and ask them without hesitation or delay. He talked about this in his introduction to *A Vision*: "They [spirit] said their thought was swifter than ours." When you work quickly with spirit, it puts you in their natural rhythm. So always embrace their swift thoughts in the very moments they come to you.

Minute-by-Minute Messages

Working with simple symbols can help you practice quick and easy communication with spirit. Developing such immediacy lets you go through your day and get insights in seconds whenever you ask any question of spirit. Then, later, as you'll find in Chapter 20, you can have more in-depth communications and get greater layers of information.

Yet, even as you practice multilayered messages, be sure to keep your questions quick and simple, so you can maintain your rhythm with spirit. Continue to use simple symbols that can give you meanings in moments—like the rose in the next process. These types of symbols are valuable tools you can use for short-burst questions anytime and anywhere. Now let's get some practice with a very fast, very telling simple symbol—the rose.

. . . .

A Rose Is a Rose Is a Message

Call to your ancestors as you close your eyes, and take a deep breath. Think of a particular relationship in your life about which you'd like some guidance. Say to yourself, Spirit shows me a rose. *Instantly, you see, sense, or feel a rose that represents this relationship. Experience it completely.*

Notice the size, the colors, the texture, how much it has bloomed, and how it makes you feel. Is there more than one rose? Is there anything particular about it that stands out? Notice everything in every way.

When you're done, say thank you to your ancestors. Bring yourself back. And take some notes about the details—especially about how you felt.

. . . .

Meanings and Feelings in Bloom

- **A small rosebud or a single rose:** The beginning of a new relationship or the experience of new energy in an old relationship

- **A single, large garden rose:** Though a single rose can indicate newness, this image also speaks to a potential for growth or someone who wishes to nurture and tend.

- **A large bunch of roses:** A long-established relationship or a strong offering of love in a new one.

- **A wilted or dying rose or group of roses:** The wilting of healthy, loving, and nurturing feelings for one or both of the people in this relationship.

- **A rose with some or all of the petals picked off:** Though some love may still be present in this relationship, there are likely to be external pressures that may be tearing at its well-being.

- **A rosebush:** If in the ground, ongoing growth; if it seems ready to be planted, a relationship with the potential to grow; if it feels as if it has been ripped out of the ground, then one or both of the people may feel that this relationship is no longer a sanctuary or a growing place. (Or a move may be coming.)

- **An imitation rose:** Though there may be some beauty in this relationship, there may be something false about it. On the other hand, fake flowers never lose their bloom, so it could be an image of an enduring (yet, in some ways, superficial) relationship. The feelings you experienced during your perception of the rose will help tell you the tale.

- **A rose or a bunch of roses that turns into other flowers:** Each specific incident of this could have a different meaning based on the specific flowers and colors involved—and what those flowers mean to you. Of course, flowers that are seasonal can also be indicators of time.

Trigger Images: Starting the Conversation

In the beginning of this book, you created the image of a door to help you immediately open up to spirit. Trigger images (or trigger symbols) can easily jump-start your conversations with your ancestors. Like the rose, trigger symbols are very easy to understand. They're also easy for spirit to use to expand and tell a story that gives you even greater insight.

When using trigger symbols, you may be the originator of the image, but you are not the source of the message. Spirit will take each symbol where they want it to go. They can mold it, paint it, stretch it, or move it.

And they can completely change it, too. That rose could become a broken cup, a wedding ring, a stone wall, or so many other images that could represent exactly what you need to see about that relationship.

No matter what trigger symbol you may choose, spirit will always create the imagery that will give you the best message. Spirit taught me many of these symbols. They'll teach you some of your own, too. I share these trigger symbols with you so you can also learn spirit's language of symbols.

Obviously, many of these types of symbols can start out very simply. Then they can be animated to give more information as the image changes and develops. You can also get multilayered symbols to receive a whole story, as you'll see in Chapter 20. But no matter what kind of symbol exercise you do, let everything happen just the way it happens. It will make every symbol experience a success.

Career Day

There are lots of different symbols that can represent progress and success in a career. Some include ladders, stairways, cars, trains, paths, elevators, escalators, and so many others. Anything that can give you a sense of movement forward, backward, up or down, or even sideways. (Sideways? Yes, careers certainly can move laterally!)

Of course, all of these symbols can also represent other things besides jobs and careers, too. But for now let's take a quick look at one of these career symbols. You can think of your own career or someone else's, if you'd like to ask for them. And if you'd rather, you can think about the progress of a certain project or creative endeavor in your life.

. . . .

The Stairway to Success

Take a deep breath, and close your eyes. Say softly to yourself, My ancestors are here. *Immediately, you sense them with you. Take a moment to see and sense who's with you.*

Now, as you think about the progress of your career or a specific project, ask them to give you the symbol of a staircase. See it or sense it completely. However you perceive it, notice everything—the size, the shape, the structure, and the colors. How does it feel to you? Experience everything for a few moments.

Now put yourself on the staircase. See or feel yourself there, and notice where you are. Are you standing still or going up? Are you where you want to be? Are there landings where you'd like to stop and rest? How do you feel about where you are and about the progress you're making?

Take a moment to notice any last thing you see or sense—even some small detail you hadn't noticed before. What is it? What does this image tell you? After a few moments, start to bring yourself back. Say thank you to these helpful ancestors who walk up the stairs with you. Be sure to take some notes in your journal when you're done.

. . . .

Now here's a little fast—and fun—process that is absolutely one of my favorites. Here's a book that can give you some of the answers you seek. But I also recommend you do this without asking any specific question, too. You may get an unexpected surprise.

. . . .

The Book of Answers

Close your eyes, and feel your own spirit and the ancestors who are with you. Suddenly, you notice that someone has placed in your hands The Book of Answers. *There are no questions in it—just answers. Think of a simple question, and open the book to any page. Instantly, you notice the first word, image, or sensation you see or sense. What is it?*

Now close the book and clear your mind. Without thinking about any question, open the book again. Immediately notice what you get. You don't have to know the question to embrace the answer! Just perceive any word, image, or symbol that pops into your awareness immediately. And if a breeze blows the pages and reveals a new answer, notice that, too!

Now say thank you to your spirit ancestors. Bring yourself back and take some notes. Make a commitment as you go through your day to pick up your Book of Answers whenever you need.

. . . .

I love to do this little process even without asking any particular question—just to see what I get. Being a clairvoyant—and because it's a book—I often see words. But, like some dictionaries, there are images on those pages, too.

Sometimes I'll get a great surprise when I open the book and a three-dimensional symbol pops right up—just like a pop-up book. Once I opened the book and a cupcake with pink frosting and one little, lighted candle popped up. I interpreted the symbol: a single candle for a new endeavor; on a cupcake—instead of a cake—making it a small endeavor; and the pink frosting indicating someone or something I love. Though I could interpret the symbol, I couldn't apply the reference to my life. A few weeks later I got a request to write an article about my card deck, *The Akashic Tarot*, from a New Age magazine in London, a place I love!

Looking at the Future: Spirit Sees Around the Bend of Time

There's something important to consider as you ask for spirit's vision about your future. No matter how or when you get a message, there may come a time when something you sense from your ancestors may not be exactly what you'd like it to be. That's okay because your free will lets you make different choices and take different actions, so you can change things.

**When spirit shows you potential outcomes,
it's like having your own personal GPS.
If there's a traffic jam ahead, you can change
directions and go to an entirely different place.**

. . . .

What to Know about Looking into the Future

- Those in spirit are not restricted by the physical world. Because of this, they can see around the bend of time a little better than we can.

- Just because they can see a little more forward, it doesn't mean that what spirit sees is written in stone. Nothing is predetermined. There are always other options and other roads for you to take.

- What spirit sees—and shows you—are simply the strongest likelihoods and trends based upon your decisions, patterns, and actions.

- You always have free will. Even when things may not be trending your way, your new thoughts and new actions can take you down a new path.

- You can ask your Higher Self and your spirit guides to show you the options you have and the changes you can make. They can help you make better decisions and take the best actions possible. Through your free will, you can create the future you want!

. . . .

CHAPTER 18

FORERUNNERS OF PURPOSE AND ACTION

*I long for eternity because there
I shall meet my unwritten poems
and my unpainted pictures.*

— KAHLIL GIBRAN

Would you like to discover any unwritten poems or unpainted pictures of your own? Or perhaps you'd like to design clothes, create buildings, establish a business, or do other things that you haven't yet done. Happily, there are many ancestors in the eternal world who can help you realize those ventures in the here and now. They are the forerunners who pursued similar creative, personal, business, and spiritual endeavors.

You may not be descended from them biologically, but your kinship may be even more abiding because of the profound connection you have in your shared passions, activities, and purposes. These ancestors want to participate with you now—in music, art, sports, motherhood, writing, publishing, spiritual studies, political leadership, invention, and any other passion that strikes a fire within you.

Ballet Buddies

Noted ballet dancer and choreographer Aras Ames danced with a number of different companies in New York and California, including the San Francisco Ballet. He often worked with his good friend, the Russian ballet dancer Alexander Godunov. But they didn't stop working together when Alexander died. Aras often said that he could feel Alexander with him when he was teaching and dancing. It was a great sense of support to Aras to know that Alexander was still keeping him on his toes!

In this chapter, you will meet your ancestors of purpose. They have been attracted to you through your energy and activities. Now you can get to know them better and join with them in manifesting the passions you share!

Ghost Writers

There are many, many writers who have sought the help of spirits, and some spirits who have helped even when they weren't asked! Shirley Jackson, author of "The Lottery," said that she preferred to keep ghosts "wholly imaginary." Though she "never had much traffic with ghosts," Shirley said that they were after her to write her novel *The Haunting of Hill House*. One morning she even found notes on her desk, set apart from all the other papers there. Though they were in her own handwriting, she had no recollection of them. She immediately got to work and finished the book!

My friend in Toronto Ben Gleisser has written a lot of articles and books, including co-authoring one called *Compassionate Messenger*. He's also a great editor and ghostwriter.

Well, as it happens, Ben actually calls for the help of real ghostwriters when he gets stuck in a block himself. He has a number on hand—like Edgar Allan Poe and Rod Serling, but Ben's favorite author was Philip K. Dick, who was the notable science-fiction author of such books as *Do Androids Dream of Electric Sheep?* and *The Man in the High Castle*. His books and short stories became a number of television series and movies, including *Blade Runner*, *Total Recall*, and *Minority Report*.

When Ben gets stuck—or even when he's just getting ready to write—he often does a brief meditation and calls P. K. Dick to simply be there and help if need be. There are no conversations;

they aren't necessary. Ben knows that help will be there, as it always has been.

I understand this very well. During my writing tasks, I've called upon people like Conan Doyle, Dickinson, Browning, and many contemporary writers like Bradbury. After Ben told me about P. K. some time ago, I decided to give P. K. a call when I needed some help, too.

One day, I found myself rewriting a few sentences over and over—totally disenchanted with every option that came to mind. Then I remembered to call P. K. In that very second, an excellent solution popped into my head that I knew wasn't mine! P. K. had dropped me a telepathic thought.

Another writer who has worked with spirit during her projects is my friend Rosamund Burton, who lives in Sydney, Australia. She's just finishing her most recent book, *The Whispering Wire*. It's about the building of the Overland Telegraph Line, 3,200 kilometers through the heart of Australia from Adelaide to Darwin. She traveled the route, reading the legendary accounts, seeing the locales, and interviewing historians along the way. And, of course, spirit had their hand in it, too.

She had never been able to trace her father's ancestry. But she learned that Robert Charles Burton had been the 1870s surveyor for the Overland Telegraph in the Northern Territory. She felt a very deep connection to him that went far beyond having the same initials, R. C. B. (Having the same names, initials, and birth dates often indicate spirit ancestry and past-life ties.) An Aboriginal elder in Darwin confirmed the connection to Ros, too.

As Ros journeyed across Australia, she interviewed many historians and elders. Before she met these people, she would often connect with their ancestors, asking them to help insure their stories were well remembered. And, indeed, they were.

There are so many ancestors who work with us on the purposes we share. Even though I already work with a lot of different spirit writers, it was fun to add P. K. to the team! I'm sure Ben and Ros have many other spirits working with them, too. Indeed, as Ros's story shows, you could get help from your purpose ancestors, family forerunners, even other people's ancestors. It's called collaboration!

Collaborating with Spirit

There have been times in your life where you've experienced a heightened sense of possibility when a project excites you—especially when you're working together with others. It's a collaboration, and when you are working collectively on a single goal together, it seems that success is surely at hand. This can be even more absolute in your work with spirit, for no one is more interested and invested in your success than they.

Take a moment to think of a purpose that's important to you. It could be something that's brand new to you. Or it could be something you've been doing already but would like to take to a higher level. You probably have a number of different creative, personal, business, or spiritual purposes, but in order to stay clear during the upcoming process, just pick one for now. You can come back and do this process anytime you want to connect with different ancestors about other purposes.

As you do the next process, be sure to be spontaneous and stay flexible. Don't force anything; just let it all come. You may meet some spirits you don't know, and the purpose you've chosen may change to a different one. Let whatever happens happen. As you look down the future path of this purpose, don't get caught up in searching for the outcomes you expect. Always be open to the unexpected and the gifts you could find there. Now it's time to meet the ancestors who share this purpose with you.

. . . .

Collaboration—Ancestors in Action!

Take a deep breath. Let go of your worries and even your plans. With another relaxing breath, think about an important purpose you hold in your heart.

As you focus on that purpose or that action, say to yourself, My ancestors of purpose are here. *Immediately, you notice the forerunners who have embraced that purpose, too. Take a moment to see and sense them. Notice their colors, their energy, their clothes, and everything you perceive about them. Do you know who any of them are—either personally or by reputation? If not, that's okay. Simply be with them for a moment.*

Now they give you an image, idea, or word that shows you some of their own histories with this purpose. Take a few moments to sense everything they share.

After you're done with that, your forerunners of purpose want to open you to your own work to come in this endeavor. They indicate your next step by sharing a word, image, symbol, or feeling. See, sense, and experience everything completely.

Take a few moments to finish that up. After you do, these ancestors are now going to show you the symbolic path that you are taking in this endeavor. See and sense the path, and put yourself there completely. Simply stand upon it and look down the path before you.

Is the path narrow or wide, straight or crooked, clear or rocky? Are there any colors, objects, or people upon the path that stand out for you? Take a few minutes to notice everything.

Now take a moment to create a declaration about this endeavor. My purpose of _____ thrives within me! My spirit lifts me to action every day. *Every time you make that declaration, you can feel the excitement and joy you have in this pursuit.*

Take a deep breath, and say thank you to these forerunners of action and purpose. You can call on them whenever you might like a bit of upliftment and inspiration.

. . . .

After you've finished this process, take some very thorough notes in your journal about the forerunners who were with you and what you sensed about them. You can also use this process with any of your other purposes and guides.

Also write your declarations of purpose on index cards so that you can take them with you through your day. Be sure to really declare them. Affirmations are great because they help you form a mental reality. But declarations can add a great sense of energy and power to that reality.

Surprising Servers

As you did this process, were you surprised by any of the ancestors who came to help? Maybe there were some family ancestors who never seemed to be interested in this particular activity or purpose. But you may not have known everything about these family members.

I remember telling a client that her granduncle Owen was there wanting to help her with her thesis in her music studies. She couldn't understand why. She remembered him as a kind and funny guy who worked in a brokerage firm. She loved him and appreciated his help but didn't know why he would feel connected to music.

I told her that there could be lots of reasons. They might have shared a musical past life together. Or maybe he just really loved music and had an interest in her project. Or he could have had a history with music that was unknown to her. Whatever the reason—he was there, he was very interested, and he was delighted to help.

Well, she called me just a few days later. She had found out that Uncle Owen had been a saxophone player in one of the big bands during World War II, and he'd been great at it, too. But when he met the woman he loved, he wanted to have a family and didn't want to be gone all the time traveling with the band. So he got off the bus and into a business suit!

My client felt a more profound knowing of her uncle. She put a picture of Uncle Owen up on the wall and forged a profound connection with him. She had felt his help often in her music work. So when she had to make some decisions about money and investments, Uncle Owen put on his brokerage thinking cap!

Family Pursuits

Just like Uncle Owen, there are so many ancestors from the family who can help us with different purposes. My good friend Ellie Cratsley is a medium, a stained-glass artist, and a gifted gardener—*and* she has plenty of family members to help her. Her uncle Jackie helps with her garden here on Earth, and her earlier forerunners help her, too.

Her long-ago ancestors from the 1800s come to assist her with her stained glass. You can see their stained-glasswork in the windows of City Hall in Belfast, Northern Ireland. Her grandfather also works with her. He was the first family member brought by another medium. He told her he would help her in *all* her work. This was very moving to me when she told me, because my grandfather said the same to me!

Now, my mother's father was one of those old-world men who thought children were a little too loud and should mostly play outside. But he did let me play with his pipe cleaners. My grandpa died when I was in high school, and the only real memories I have of him are of him caring for his tomato garden, playing pinochle with my dad, and smiling at me while I played on the floor, building little cities with his pipe cleaners as he sat smoking his pipe. Yet he was the first spirit who showed up in my earliest readings from other mediums. That was the first time I learned that those in spirit you don't think are close are really very close indeed.

Whenever my grandfather came, he always had a Bible in his hand. This confounded me immensely, until my grandmother told me that when they met he had been studying to be an Episcopalian minister. But when he fell in love with her, he had to let that go because she was only allowed to marry a Catholic. So he converted, left a spiritual life behind, and worked in a factory.

I hadn't known any of this when he first started showing up at my early readings. Knowing what my spiritual life means to me, it felt so sad to think how he had to give up his. But he certainly is living the spiritual life now!

He's always here. In my meditations and helping me in all of my spiritual work—and especially talking to spirit. I have grown very close to him. He's with me everywhere, and it filled my heart when I saw him standing next to me at church during the service when I became a reverend with my Spiritualist church. It felt like we were becoming ministers together.

Getting Help from Your Telepathic Team

There are lots of ways that your ancestors can bring you their assistance. One is through the *direct communications* you have with them in your meditations or throughout your day. You can have a dialogue, ask questions, and then get their answers through images, words, symbols, and all of your inner senses. These discourses are very important to do regularly. You get to know each other better and deepen your connection. You also get to build your perceptive skills and practice with symbols. It's a win-win for you and spirit.

Of course there are lots of other ways to receive your ancestors' help. You can play with different techniques—try perceptive writing, billets, spirit art, or any other thing that strikes your fancy. Any of these are great fun, but your primary methods of receiving spirit's assistance will be through direct communication and telepathic perception.

As you have seen, telepathic perception is very different than your experience of direct communication. In telepathic perception, your ancestors simply drop a telepathic thought into your mind.

All you have to do is ask a specific question and then go on with what you're doing. In the coming minutes—or even that moment—suddenly you'll know the words you want to write, the investment you want to make, the music you want to play, the plan you want to organize, the house you want to buy, or absolutely any other kind of knowing you can imagine.

So always be aware of the ideas that pop into your mind. You're literally getting insider information!

Sister Talk

On one occasion Harriet Beecher Stowe reached out to the spirit of Charlotte Brontë. And though Harriet and Charlotte were both very notable authors, this is not a story about writing at all. Harriet wanted to connect with Charlotte more personally. Charlotte shared a lot about her sister Emily, as they both spoke about their families.

This little event shows when you reach out to ancestors of purpose, you can also connect about other things, too. You can talk about a little challenge in the family. Or you might want to ask for help in something small—like cooking for a special party, or redecorating a room, or choosing a college.

You can call any ancestor you'd like, whether you know them or not. For instance, if you wanted help cooking for that special party, you could call your grandmother who was a great cook. She may be a family ancestor, but now she's also a purpose ancestor, too. You could also call Julia Child, if you'd like.

Here's a little process that you can use for fast connections and all kinds of purposes, large or small. Keeping it short helps you to be able to use this process quickly—at any time of the day. It will start out as a direct communication. Then it will set the scene for telepathic perception.

. . . .

Purpose and Action—Fast

Close your eyes, and think of a purpose you hold or an action you'd like to take. With a deep breath, say to yourself, My ancestors of purpose are here. Immediately, you sense them with you. Take a moment *to welcome them. And notice everything you see, feel, and sense about them.*

Now ask them anything about this purpose that's on your mind. Suddenly, you get an image, a word, a symbol, or any other sensation that informs you in some way. Notice everything you get. Take a few moments to do this now.

After you're done with that, think of another question about this purpose. This time ask your ancestors to send you a telepathic thought. Then notice the very first thing that comes to mind. Whatever you get, and however you get it, trust it completely.

Now let that go, and know that these ancestors are here for you. They can give you guidance in so many ways. And often the answers you seek will be in your own thoughts and heart. Say thank you now, and feel their love embrace you.

. . . .

Well, now you've met just a few of your many ancestors of purpose and action. Whenever you feel a compelling personal or creative purpose, remember the many forerunners in spirit who share that passion with you. They are always ready to walk your path with you.

CHAPTER 19

TAKE A MESSAGE

Extending and Expanding Symbolic Meanings

I saw the angel in the marble
And carved until I set him free.

— MICHELANGELO

What a wonderful image Michelangelo shares. You can almost see the angel—joints stiffened by centuries in stone, slowly shaking off the marble chips and dust from his wings. Then, after a long-awaited stretch, he flies free. Actually, that's a little like your work with extended symbols. You can chip away at the different elements of the symbol, and set the message free.

As you've seen in previous chapters, symbols don't have to be confusing riddles. They can be simple symbols, like colors. I remember one time when spirit helped a friend of mine determine her ski schedule just by using colors alone.

Or they can be extended symbols that add more detail, like the staircase and your sense of movement on it.

Or they can be deeply layered symbols, as when one of my clients in a difficult relationship received a symbolic boatload of insight from his ancestors about it. (We'll take a look at the extended boat symbol in the next chapter.) So get ready to discover expanded symbols that take your messages further.

The Heart of the Matter

In Chapter 17, you saw that a rose, though it is a simple symbol, could tell you a lot of different things about relationships, based on colors, imagery, size, and other elements of the symbol. Now let's take a look at another simple relationship symbol—the heart.

When you do the next few processes, you can think of any person in your life: a friend, co-worker, child, parent, or lover—anyone.

. . . .

Intuitive Signs of Affection

Close your eyes. With a deep breath, say to yourself, My ancestors are here. *Instantly, you start to see and feel them around you.*

Now think of a certain relationship in your life. Your ancestors immediately show you the symbol of a heart, and you sense it completely. Notice everything about it— its texture, colors, size, and anything else you sense. Also be aware of how you feel with every perception you have. Take a few minutes to do this now. And say thank you to these loving ancestors when you're done.

. . . .

Remember to take notes in your journal about your experience. It helps you watch how symbol meanings evolve. It also allows you to follow, over time, the insights you get about the important issues in your life.

Now, here's a way to expand the symbol of a heart that will give you a broader picture. You can think of the same person—or another, if you choose—as you do this next little exercise. This time you will not only get an image of a heart, but you will also get a sense of that person.

. . . .

Have a Heart

Close your eyes, and take a deep breath. Say to yourself, I invite my ancestral guides. *And as soon as you do, you feel and see them around you. Take a moment to welcome them and be with them.*

Now think about the relationship you've chosen to investigate. Using your imaging, picture this person visually or conceptually in your mind.

Imagine that this person is now extending his or her heart to you. This action reflects the caring and regard this person has for you. See it, sense it, and know it completely.

Notice everything you perceive about the heart—its size, colors, textures, shape, and especially how it feels. Also notice everything you sense about the person and the way he or she is giving you that heart.

How does this person look? What feelings do you sense in this person's eyes, face, or in the action of handing you the heart? Notice everything, and feel it all.

After a few minutes, finish that up. Say thank you to your ancestors for these insights. Bring yourself back, and take some notes in your journal when you're done.

. . . .

Interpreting the Heart's Message

In this process (and the one before it), some people get an image of an actual, physical heart. Sometimes it's even beating, which can show an active affection. The way the heart looks can tell you a lot. If it's pink and healthy, this could be a healthy relationship. If it's large, there is a lot of feeling there. If it's bruised, this person is likely to have been hurt in the past. And if there are different colors, refer to the color chart in Chapter 4 to see what meanings they bring to the message.

Of course, you may have perceived the most traditional symbol for affection—a Valentine-shaped heart. There really is not too much difference between getting an image of a physical heart or the traditional symbolic heart. The Valentine heart can tell you everything a physical heart can through its size, color, and imagery. Images of paper hearts can be beating, too!

An image of a broken heart is just that—someone who (because of his or her history) is in a state of emotional disrepair. Sometimes you might get a symbol of an incomplete heart or a very small heart. This is not too hard to interpret either. A tiny heart or a fraction of a heart alludes to a diminished commitment, an inability to trust, or a lack of love that person has for others or for the self.

Action Expansion

There are sooo many ways this heart imagery can happen. Here are some that I've perceived in my consultations. In one instance there was an image of a very big, pink paper heart being torn into little pieces of confetti and thrown back at my client. The largeness of the heart told me that my client gave a large part of herself in this relationship. Tearing it and throwing the confetti showed that he had only wanted her for a good time and then he was done.

Another image had an embroidery ring with a heart and flowers drawn in the cloth and the needle dangling from a thread. It was being put aside before it was done, just as the relationship had been.

I have often seen a paper heart that had been torn into two or three parts and taped back together again—or sewn back together. That showed a clear attempt to mend the relationship.

Clearly, as is the case with all symbols (like the animated-symbol process in Chapter 14), action will extend and expand the message.

I remember one student, Oliver, who actually perceived his new boyfriend shoving his heart into Oliver's face. (That relationship didn't last long!)

Many of these actions are clear in their interpretation. Sometimes the heart is freely given. Sometimes it's withheld, which can indicate withholding love, respect, kindness, or commitment. Throwing the heart (whether in joy or in frustration) can indicate a person who may sabotage his or her relationships through carelessness. Throwing it in anger could definitely show very deep-seated issues. A heart suspended in the air—or a heart that is repeatedly given and taken back—shows someone who is ambivalent about the relationship.

Feeling the Message

When you're interpreting expanded symbols, simply consider the different elements of the image as well as the feelings of each of those elements.

It's possible for similar images to elicit very different feelings. For instance, someone withholding a heart could easily allude to someone who's selfish, clutching, and controlling. On the other hand, if the heart is being held back meekly or with hesitation, that person may be shy or may need to become more assured before taking a leap.

Remember that emotions in symbols are not only shown by people in the image but also by all the different elements of the symbol. So always ask yourself with every little part of a symbol, *How does that feel?* When you do, you'll find a wealth of meaning there.

More Symbols to Extend the Message

Let's take a look at some more expanded symbols now. Spirit often uses these symbols to depict many different areas and activities in your life. But you must look at them through your own perspective, too. Some of these symbols can mean something different for you. These also make great trigger symbols for your ancestors to mold and shape and paint a picture for you.

Just think of a specific situation in your life about which you would like some guidance, and then ask spirit to share the symbol you want to use. Close your eyes, and take a few minutes to really sense everything about that symbol that spirit shares. If it changes, let that happen, too. Since we're working with relationships, let's do a little one now.

What a Soft Blanket—or Is It?

Close your eyes, and think about a relationship you have with someone in your life. Your ancestors are going to put a blanket that represents that relationship around your shoulders.

See and feel everything now. What colors do you see? Is the blanket soft or rough to the touch? Is it in good condition, torn, or in tatters? Is it big enough to cover you? Or does it fall far short and make you feel exposed? What does this blanket tell you?

Take a few moments to sense and feel everything about this blanket, including how it makes you feel emotionally. Then bring yourself back and say thank you to your ancestors for this insight.

I have to tell you that whenever I've led this process in a class, everyone has told me that the symbology was an accurate depiction of their relationships—whether for good or bad. Some people may not have wanted confirmation that their relationship was coming up short. But that's the way of life when you're psychic—there are lots of things you already know!

The following list will give you options of different symbols. Try them for different purposes in your life. After all, a staircase can represent movement in a career, but there are other career symbols as well. So try them in different ways. Practice creating some of your own expanded symbols, too. (You'll find a short list of more symbols and their meanings in the Appendix.)

Expanded Symbols	What They Represent
Stairway	Ascent of career, reputation, or talent
Train and train tracks	On track with a career or single project
Weather systems	Emotions, situations that are cloudy or clear
Stove top with pots cooking	Status of many projects at once
Chessboard in play	Interactions of many people drawn together
Suit of clothes	Position at work; nature of a single project
Blanket	Embrace, comfort, and warmth of relationship
Rose or roses	Love, romance, and reciprocity in relationship
Flowers	Different talents and opportunities blooming (dependent on color and kind)
Tree or trees	Life, growth, project, family

Let's consider how a few of these longer, extended symbols might be experienced. As you read the following descriptions, notice how clearly the elements of the symbol can give you their own meanings.

Getting on Track

Spirit often sends me images of trains and tracks when they want to show me if someone is "on track"—often regarding career or projects, but about other things, too. Take a moment to create your own little exercise now. Think about your work, a certain project or a relationship. Close your eyes, and ask your ancestors to send you a symbol of train tracks and a train. Notice and sense everything you get—even for just a moment. Then come back and write down what happened and what you thought it meant.

When I get this imagery, the first thing I usually see are the train tracks, and I can see them in so many ways. The track could be going straight ahead, in circles, uphill or down, split in half, around a turn, at the end of the line, or more.

Sometimes I only perceive the tracks, and that's all I need for quite a bit of information. But sometimes spirit will also show me a train. It could be old and falling apart; an 1800s steam engine; or a shiny, new bullet train. It could have bright colors, dark colors, or chipped paint; broken windows; no coal cars; and so forth. Also it could be moving; stopped at the station or at the water tower, or anywhere. The train could also be shown going in different directions—backward, forward, right, left, or even around in circles.

Sometimes there could be people in the scene. They could be embarking, waiting impatiently, hesitant to get on the train, running to catch it because they're late, traveling with others, or traveling alone. Often I don't perceive any people at all.

It's amazing just how many different perceptions you can get in an image that takes only a few moments to experience. As you consider all of these symbolic elements, don't get pulled into your left brain. The most important thing for you to do is to stay in your perceptive state; note what happens in your journal; look into the meanings of the universal symbols you see, and *always* ask with each element, *How does this feel?*

The Intuitive Shade

Trees can be symbols of your life, work, home, projects, or family. When your ancestors give you the image of a tree—or group of trees—don't think! Just be with the tree and notice every detail and how you feel about those details.

A Tree Full of Symbols

Close your eyes, and call your ancestors. Feel their embrace, and ask them now for a symbol of a tree. It comes to you immediately. And when it does, you notice the type of tree, the state of its health and growth, its age and height, and anything else you get. Take a few moments to sense how everything feels.

Now look up. Does the tree need pruning? Is it bearing fruit? Notice the season and the leaves. What do these things tell you? How do you feel about them?

As you're looking up, do you see or sense any birds, squirrels, or other animals in the tree? If so, how do they feel to you? As you sense this tree, consider if it needs tending. Is there a step you can take to tend to this tree?

Now take a deep breath, and just listen. There's a whisper of a message as a breeze rustles through the leaves. It may be soft, but you can hear it. Is there a word or an idea there? What is it?

Now take a little step back so you can get a broader image of this tree. Look at everything. What stands out for you? How does it all feel?

After a moment, say thank you to your ancestors, and bring yourself back. Take some notes in your journal when you're done.

Though there are some interpretations in Chapter 4 and the Appendix, it would be good to start practicing with your own interpretive skills. Whenever you do a process—of your own, from this book, or from another source—interpret it yourself before you consult any symbol dictionary.

But never interpret anything during the process! That will take you out of the receptive state. Just write down your meanings in your journal after you're done. Then, if those meanings don't coincide with the dictionary interpretations, don't assume you're wrong. Just note those meanings as additional options. You are in the process of developing your own symbol dictionary. Your meanings are valid, too. So trust yourself. Now let's take a few minutes to get a weather report.

The Highs and Lows on Your Weather Map

Unless you're literally asking spirit if it will be a good day for a picnic, when you tune in to the weather, it is first and foremost an intuitive metaphor for the emotional climate of a particular situation, relationship, project, or time. It can indicate the feelings of people, the level of ease or difficulty of a situation, and the general warmth or storminess of any particular issue. As with all of the intuitive exercises that you might employ, it requires only your spontaneous sensing and imaging and your immediate trust.

As always, you must let yourself perceive your images and intuitive ideas exactly the way you get them without embellishment or contrivance on your part. Don't try to change an image if it's telling you something uncomfortable. Growth may be needed in this situation. Your ancestors are simply reminding you.

. . . .

Tomorrow's Weather

Close your eyes, and invite your ancestors forward. See and sense them as they joyfully greet you.

For a moment think about your day tomorrow. Don't try to remember your agenda; you have a sense of that without going into your left brain. Just hold the idea "my day tomorrow" in your mind. Immediately, your ancestors show you the climate of your day.

Is it sunny, windy, or rainy? Does the weather change often? Be in it, and let yourself sense the weather and the emotions completely. Experience it all, and notice how everything feels.

After a few minutes of this weather experience, say thank you to these ancestral forecasters. And when you're done, use your journal to record the images and feelings you perceived.

. . . .

I know it's hard to take the time to write your symbols and your interpretations of them each time. As you build your *intuitive dictionary*, certain symbols will take on specific meanings that are uniquely your own. And you will want to remember them.

Journaling about your ancestral communications helps you see how new connecting techniques work for you. Last but certainly not least, your journal will allow you to look back and see what you perceived for any certain project, relationship, or event, enabling you to chart your psychic perceptions and your life together.

Now that you've seen the climate of your day tomorrow, let's take a look at your relationship weather. As you do this process, remember that you can ask about any relationship. It could be about you with other people, like your spouse, parent, or co-worker. Or it could be other people's relationship, like your son and his wife, your two sisters with each other; or your father with your mother. Simply hold whatever relationship you choose in your mind.

Relationship Weather

Take a deep breath, and close your eyes. Call your ancestral guides to be with you, and notice that they are there.

Think about the relationship you've chosen. Your ancestors would like to give you some insight about it. Immediately, spirit shows you the weather that reflects that relationship. Really see it visually or conceptually. Notice the whole scope of the weather front before you. Notice any clouds, wind, and all the elements—and how you feel about everything.

Is there any rain or lightning? Or perhaps it's a warm, balmy, sunny day, with just a gentle breeze. Also notice if there are any changes in the weather that occur. If so, sense how those changes feel emotionally. Let yourself get it all now.

When you're done, say thank you to your ancestors for this weather report and bring yourself back.

After you write about these impressions in your journal, make a commitment to check in with the weather about this relationship regularly over the next few weeks to see how it may evolve.

Now, it's likely that you already have a sense of what all these possible symbols might mean. Most of them seem obvious. For instance, there was a long-ago movie when Lena Horne sang "Stormy Weather," mournfully lamenting a lost love. Moviegoers didn't have to think twice about what a storm reflected emotionally. Then and now it's a pretty universal message. But does rain always signify sadness? The answer is *no*! Let's take a look at some of the many meanings the changing weather can predict.

Interpretations of Your Intuitive Barometer

- **Sunshine:** Warmth, growth, happiness, enthusiasm, creativity, joy, and often success.

- **Light clouds:** A very regular emotional experience, when seen with the sun; if the clouds are scattered, they could show intermittent doubts or concerns (yours or someone else's); lots of moderate clouds could indicate dealing with someone who's moody, or someone who's been depressed but may be able to feel lighter.

- **Heavy clouds:** Darker thoughts and emotions belonging to you or others, the portent of a possible emotional conflict coming, a significant shadow cast upon a specific situation.

- **Rain:** Tears and/or sorrow. Except: when seen or felt as a spring rain (nurturing or growth), or a rain that washes and cleanses (releasing and freeing you of negative conditions—sometimes through a somewhat challenging event), or, finally, a rain that comes to a land after a drought (new life or the end of a "dry" period).

- **Lightning:** Great power and intensity. Please note that there is no value judgment attached to this. It could be beneficial or difficult. If the lightning is extreme, the intensity could either damage the landscape or illuminate a dark horizon. This interpretation (as well as others) will depend primarily on *how it feels to you.*

- **Storms:** Very often storms indicate emotional turbulence. Large electrical storms can also indicate power struggles. Hurricanes, tsunamis, and the like can obviously reflect major upheaval—a relationship or situation that could metaphorically drown you.

- **Winds:** Gentle winds indicate energy that refreshes a situation. Winds that clear the air can mean just that—clearing the mind or opening greater channels of communication and understanding. Winds that blow you off your feet reflect a state of imbalance for you (or another) in the situation or relationship (depending upon whom you sense in your image).

As you can tell from this list, tuning in with the weather is just the beginning of the intuitive allegory. The other particulars you see can add many layers to the insight you seek. How does the scene change? Who, if anyone, is in the image? In what kind of place is this weather occurring? Does it fill the whole conceptual space? If not, what's on the right or the left? Dozens of details may spring to mind, and all of them could add a different feeling to the experience. (Always note in your journal that *what you feel* is important.)

So now that we've seen how symbols can extend a message, let's take a look at how broader stories and gestalt symbols can fill in some of the blanks.

CHAPTER 20

WHAT'S THE STORY?

Getting Guidance with Greater Depth and Detail

Listen to the voices.

— WILLIAM FAULKNER

Even though this is a great quote to promote the practice of clairaudience, for me, Faulkner is saying listen to the inner voices. It's the voice of the Higher Self that, all too often, has to repeat itself because we don't listen the first, second, or third time.

As you continue your work with your ancestors, don't forget that your eternal self is an important part of that group. Of course, you're led by your Higher Self in all things—as long as you listen. But your Higher Self can also help you in your symbol work with your ancestors. In this chapter, we're going to be getting more deeply layered stories and gestalt symbols. Don't get into worrying because it might sound complex. Instead, let your Higher Self guide you in total trust. The things you feel compelled to notice are being pointed out to you. These layers of symbology make the meanings easy to sense and know. So just let it all happen.

Starting with Stories

Tom Wilson, the creator of the comic strip *Ziggy*, was a smart, kind, large-hearted man, who was a great friend of my mother's. We were fortunate to be able to visit with him often, including at his L.A. home. He lived in the Hollywood Hills in a home built by silent film star Theda Bara. Wow—talk about interesting spirit stories! If you ever want to meet some of those intriguing spirit film folk, you can call them directly, or get yourself over to an old home from Hollywood's heyday. They love to visit with the people who visit their old haunts!

As we study simple symbolic stories, my mind snaps back to the *Ziggy* comic strip—especially the single panel pieces of only one picture. The one I loved the most—and, perhaps, the most famous one—was the spring flower that had sprung up early, and Ziggy's holding an umbrella over it to protect it from a snowfall. And there it is, the whole story, no words, just one image, one idea. In a single moment of a symbol you get an evocation of sympathy, generosity, gentility, compassion, and love. (You also get a good idea of who Tom Wilson was!)

Physical-world stories can be told by anything as simple as a comic strip and as significant as an 800-page novel. Your ancestors can start to make their messages more comprehensive by expanding a simple symbol. Then later they can give you more layers to bring greater understanding to the story. All you have to do is start with the big picture and then notice what you see (and feel) as other elements are added to the scene.

In all of your work with your ancestors, you can practice by starting with a trigger symbol that gives spirit a blank canvas to draw the picture for you. Let's see what happens with one of the most universal symbols for work and creative projects.

....

The Symbols on Your Work Desk

Close your eyes, and take a deep breath. Say to yourself, My ancestors are here. *Immediately, you feel them with you. Now think about a project or your job or any certain task that's been on your mind. Instantly, your ancestors show you a desk. Take a few minutes to experience everything about it—its size, color, how it's made, and how it makes you feel.*

After a few moments, spirit places an item or items on that desk that represent your project. What are they? Notice everything about them. Is there any movement? Experience everything, including how they feel.

After you're done with that, your ancestors now place on your desk any objects that represent the things that get in the way of your project—whether they be obstacles or distractions. Notice any and all items that come upon your desk. What are they? Where are they placed in relation to any other items? Now watch and see if you notice any movement with them or interaction with other items on the desk. How do you feel about all of these different elements?

Now start to wrap all of that up. Say thank you to these wonderful ancestors. Take some notes in your journal about your experience.

....

This type of symbol interpretation is based upon the principles of gestalt psychology. The relationship that the elements have to each other and to the whole scene provides new layers of understanding this message about your project.

The word *gestalt* has no direct translation in English, but in general, it has been taken to mean "shape, form, figure, or wholeness." The background is called the *field*, and the different elements upon that background are called *forms*. The gestalt model of *field* and *form* is uniquely appropriate in doing this type of message work. Though the form is considered distinct from the field (or background), it is perceived as never actually being so. They are separate but interdependent, a part of the whole.

Considering the Project and Work Symbol

The desk is the field (or background) that acts as the metaphor for work or effort, including working on different tasks. Then spirit places the form that represents a specific project on the desk. (Also notice where anything is placed. As you remember from Chapter 4, left is past, center is present, and right is future.) Then you see if any other objects appear on the desk that might be part of the project. Those objects and any action taken will continue the message for you. Then, of course, the new items that represent the obstacles or distractions to your project will bring even greater understanding.

This seems like a lot to consider, but please do *not* get pulled into your left brain worrying about getting any of this right. Just getting the imagery is doing it right. So let everything go, and give your imagination the job. Then interpret it later when you're done.

The Story Will Tell You the Story

Desk stories often can be very active. When I do this process for myself or for my clients, spirit will put lots of action things and tiny people on the desk. Their activity on the desk will provide a lot of insight—co-workers who don't do the tasks they're given, children who need to be taken in little cars to soccer, and planes taking off from the desk to show travel. Once there was a little, three-inch boss dressed up like a clown. Now, there's a message!

Of course, these are some of the more uncommon (and funny) images I've seen on desks. I often get very traditional work symbols, such as coins, column pads, and calendars. The condition of the items and where they're placed will tell the story. But whether the items that are placed on the desk are checkbooks or tiny people, the insertion of those forms onto the field is always done entirely by spirit. Those images are how spirit paints their messages on the blank canvas—or the field—of the desk.

Even when I ask for a desk, I don't predetermine what it's supposed to look like. That's spirit's job, too. You could get a grand-looking ornate desk, a teacher's desk, a child's desk, a dining-room table, a desk with broken legs, or even a dollhouse desk.

There are so many variations of symbols. So whenever you ask your ancestors for a particular symbol to act as a field, just let it all flow.

Don't start thinking about what kind of symbol it is—simple, extended, form, or field. It's your job to *perceive* them. The reason we categorize different kinds of symbols is simply to help us work with them and understand them more easily. It really won't serve your purpose to block your perceptions with analysis.

All symbols can inform you. There are a lot of symbols that don't necessarily have a field-form component. So whether you have a simple symbol or gestalt, don't worry about what it is; just experience it!

So work with any of the symbols in the following chart. Some may be very simple, and some may be complex. Try them in different ways, and play with them all!

Gestalt Symbols	What They Represent
Garden	Life and growth of the seeds you plant
Car and road Places of business (stores, offices)	Career or life and one's authority within it Work, career, expression
Boat and water	Condition of relationship, career, life
Desk, papers, and other items	Work, work projects, organization
Path	Spiritual evolution, career, or life in general
Ice skaters on rink or pond	Foundation and interaction in relationship
Poker table, chips, cards	Getting in the game; taking a risk or a gamble
Monopoly board and pieces	Real estate; business; wealth

The Little Man with the Monocle

One of the most regular gestalt symbols I get is the Monopoly board. It usually comes with real estate questions from clients, but I also see it regarding investments, business, finance, and moving.

The Monopoly board—the field—is laid out in front of me and spirit inserts different forms into the scene. Sometimes they use the original game pieces, but usually they use images that will further the story of the message.

Often my clients—or little versions of them—become the pieces. But they rarely walk around the board taking the traditional game-directed route.

With one client I immediately saw two very little people on very little motorcycles, crisscrossing the board back and forth going their own way. They never even stopped; they just kept going up and down, left to right, and every which way on the board.

After I described what I was seeing to my client, I asked her who the two people were. (Monopoly can show clients their children, bosses, partners, parents, and even animals!) She told me about the real estate business she owned with her husband. They had income properties in many states and in the Caribbean. I told her that business is booming—and will continue to do so. But it might be a good idea for them to take some time to nurture the relationship, too.

Sometimes people aren't on the board at all. I can't count the number of times I've seen tiny clients standing right next to the "Go" square, hesitating to get into the game and start their own business.

For the animals, I see them frequently in different ways. But one time I saw several little horses walking and grazing on different property squares all over the board. When I told my client, she said that she owned a horse ranch and really wanted to move it to another place, but she couldn't even decide on which state. Her little horses were a wondrous sight for me. I can't tell you how fun some of the images I see are!

Setting Sail on Symbols

There are many symbolic fields that can set the stage for stories to unfold. Water has long been a common universal symbol for emotions, making it a perfect field to start the investigation of relationships.

In this next gestalt process, you'll begin with imaging a body of water, the background or field. Notice how the water feels. Then a form, the boat representing the relationship, will be placed into the scene. See how it responds to the water. Then the people involved will be placed in the scene. The interaction they have with the boat and with each other will reveal more understanding for you.

Then, of course, your ancestors can insert any other forms—objects or people that give you more layers of insight. So give your imagination the job now, and embrace everything you perceive.

Just as in the weather process, you can think of any relationship about which you'd like some guidance. It could be a relationship you're having. Or it could be a relationship between two other people you know. No matter who it is, just determine that relationship now. But if the people change during the process, let that happen, too.

. . . .

The Love Boat

Take a deep breath, and close your eyes. Say to yourself, My ancestors are here. *And sense their loving presence all around you. Hold the relationship you've chosen in your mind.*

Ask your ancestors to give you an image of a body of water. You see it immediately. This water reflects the emotions in this relationship. Notice everything you see and sense. Is it a large lake, an ocean, a fast-moving river, a little creek, or is it something else? Notice all of the elements of this scene in your imaging. And sense how everything feels to you.

After a few moments, spirit wants to give you the image of a boat that represents the relationship. Say to yourself, Spirit shows me. *Instantly, you perceive the image of a boat. What kind of boat is it? Is it large or small—a yacht or a little rowboat? Is it old or new, seaworthy or needing repair? Also notice how—or if— the boat is on the water. What's happening? How does it feel? See and sense everything—if the boat's moving, which direction it's going, and what colors you sense. Notice anything else that grabs your attention. And, of course, sense how you feel with all of it.*

Take a moment to finish that up, and turn your mind to the people in this relationship. Say to yourself, Spirit shows me. Immediately, your ancestral guides insert those people into the scene. Are they both present? Are they on the boat together, on the land, on separate boats, on islands? Precisely where are they, and how are they acting?

Also, how are these people interacting with the boat? Is one at the wheel? Is one above deck or below? Or is one on the land, watching from a distance? Notice how these people relate to each other. How do you feel about them and about everything they're doing in the scene?

Now take a moment to sense if anyone or anything else has entered the scene. Is there any last thing that compels you?

Take a few minutes to wrap this up now. And with great thanks to your ancestors, bring yourself back and take detailed notes about what you sensed and how it all felt.

. . . .

As you can see, you can get a wealth of information from the numerous layers of symbols in this exercise. The water is the field— or the background. It can indicate so many different emotions in this relationship: a stormy sea (angry conflict), a dead calm (a lack of emotional stimulus), a dried-up riverbed (the drying up of love), a rising tide (a burgeoning of feelings), a peaceful lake (an idyllic ease)—and these are just some of the possibilities.

Then spirit inserts the symbol of the boat, the form, which shows the relationship itself and how well it's faring on these emotional seas. After you notice all of that, the boat then becomes the field, and spirit inserts new forms, the people. That gives you another layer. The most important thing to remember is to notice how the individual elements (forms) connect and relate to each other—and to the field. And of course notice how everything feels.

A Kayak Built for One

I remember a student, Ovi, who got an image of a kayak with her husband in it. But he had dropped his oar, and the kayak was being buffeted about by the wake of a speedboat driving in circles around it. When you think about it, this tells a very evident story.

The kayak shows that for her husband, there was room for only one person in that relationship. But he had no propulsion and no way to control where he went—especially with the disruption made by the speedboat.

As Ovi told me about her experience after the class, she said that her husband had been distant for almost a year. She said that she had seen a dark-haired woman driving the speedboat, but she hadn't seen herself anywhere in the scene.

For Ovi, this confirmed what had been happening in the marriage for a while. Her husband had been growing more and more isolated—leaving her out of everything. Later Ovi found out he had been having an affair with a dark haired woman, and he was completely in her sway.

Ovi had already been talking to a divorce attorney before she took the class because her life had gotten too empty and dark. But now she decided to take action on it. She moved out, reset her course in her own boat, and rediscovered an inner joy she hadn't known for a long time.

Keeping Complex Symbols Easy—Feel Them!

Even though this type of imagery can show many symbolic details, those details are usually very obvious in meaning. What you see—and even what you don't see—will tell the tale. Don't overthink anything. Though there may be a lot of details, they are easy to understand because they are easy to feel!

The boat is one of the many images that spirit has created for my symbol lexicon. These types of symbols started coming very early in my work as a medium.

A client asked about his marriage, and spirit immediately showed me a boat. He and his wife were on it, but he wouldn't let her take the helm. When I described the image to him, he became very thoughtful. He said that he did tend to control things—and he was going to have to make an effort to change that.

Ever since then, the boat has been a frequent symbol for me. Usually it comes by itself, but sometimes I ask for that symbol. Either way, it always works because it's spirit who creates the scene and fills it with the story.

I recall spirit giving me a boat image for a client, Felix, who was beset with stress about work. In the image he was a slave on an ancient Roman warship, chained to an oar. But his face was on the other slaves, too. And Felix was also the master who beat the drum for the oarsmen to keep time. Such was his story. He was the head of a department in a finance company, and he didn't have enough staff to do all the work, so he was managing and doing the staff work, too. He was chained because—even though he wanted to quit—he was afraid. I told him I didn't think he'd be getting off that ship until he realized he was his own master and had the keys to release the shackles and chains himself.

When I teach the boat process, I usually use it as a relationship metaphor. Many, many years ago I was teaching a class with my friend Colette Baron Reid and my sister Sandra Taylor. I shared the boat process with Colette, and she loved it. About a year later she told me that she and her husband were doing the process together almost every day—only they had changed it to represent their work and creative projects together as well as their relationship.

This is a great example of reshaping the techniques you find to fit your style and your needs. The boat process lends itself well to envision life's journeys as well as work and specific projects— especially when there are a lot of people involved. It can give you a clue as to those who are going to pull their weight or shirk their duties, and those who are going to be team players.

There are so many different examples of this process. I do it for myself for life's journey, too. But usually I use the extended path process. It's very comprehensive. You can see relationships, work, creative projects, spiritual endeavors—everything you'd like to know. All sorts of people can step on and off the path—co-workers, lovers, friends, family, as well as your ancestral guides and the Ascended Masters. You can literally discover where everybody stands in your life! (You can find an audio process of the Life's Path Process in my audio program *Ancestor Spirit Communication*.)

Again, all of these different little details and symbols can seem a little challenging. But don't let them be so. Whenever you do any extended symbol—or gestalt—process, don't go into your left brain about anything. Don't worry about what's form or field. Those distinctions are there only to help you understand how the different symbols relate to each other. And don't hesitate to ask your ancestral guides to use a certain symbol to get started. It becomes the field for their messages to you.

**Remember, setting the stage for the story
by determining the background
will invite spirit to insert symbols
onto that background.**

Your forerunners are free to change and develop any images, words, or sensations they want to share with you. And they do! So play with them! Notice the feelings and embrace everything—especially your wonderful, joyful ancestors who love you and live with you every day.

And they've lived with you for a long, long time—in many places around the world. Now let's take a look at some of the ancestral homes where they lived—and some where you lived with them.

CHAPTER 21

Discovering Your Ancestral Homes, Towns, and Lands

Ah, maybe you've some vision
Of showings beyond our sphere;
Some sight, sense intuition
Of what once happened here?
The house is old; they've hinted
It once held two love-thralls,
And they may have imprinted
Their dreams on its walls?

— Thomas Hardy

When you want to discover your ancestral homes and locations, your spirit ancestors can take you there in your imaging. But there's a very different kind of energy that you can experience in places around the world, regardless of whether those places connect to your ancestors and past lives—or not. It's called an imprint.

The Power of Imprints

This energy is not about sensing the spirits who were there, but—as Hardy said above—it's about feeling *what once happened there*. In a home where there was a lot of love, love will be *imprinted on the walls*. In a factory, production, activity, and industry will be imprinted there. And at a battlefield of war, the imprints of loss and pain will often be palpable.

An imprint is like a memory, but it's not a person's memory. It's a memory of energy—a memory of place—as well as the feelings, actions, and events that occurred in that place. Of course, sensing the imprint of a location doesn't prevent you from sensing some of the spirits who were—and are—present there. But you will experience the energy of an imprint quite differently.

Often, with an imprint, you may not perceive any people at all— just the energy "captured" from the history of the place. Or you may get images of people—busy in the activities they had done there. But they won't respond to your presence or engage with you. Their spirits aren't there. If you sense people in perceiving an imprint, it's like looking at an energetic photograph or movie of them.

That's how you can tell the difference between a spirit and an imprint of a person. Since you perceive both through the imaging brain, your perceptions will feel the same. But imprints of people will not speak to you, turn to look at you, or even notice you. Please be aware that this is not the same as spirits who look at you but don't speak—like Victor Singh's dad at Highclere on *Downton Abbey*. Those are spirits who meet you with their eyes and talk to you with their hearts. Even without speaking or moving, they are fully engaged with you. So just remember, spirit people will reach out but imprints won't. And there are times you'll only get spirit, and sometimes you'll only get imprints, and sometimes you'll get both!

I remember a paranormal investigation in New Orleans that I did that was very intriguing. It was in a narrow Victorian home that was slated for demolition the next year. We were in two small groups and went to see the various rooms separately. It was completely empty, and the first thing I perceived on the first floor was the imprint of a bar that ran the full length of the room to the back wall. I could feel that the place had been very busy. I saw several people sitting at the bar eating and talking to each other, but I didn't get an impression of anything happening in the center of the room.

We were told later that during the 1940s and '50s, the house had become the neighborhood dime store with a soda fountain and lunch counter, which was very popular and busy. The center of the room held the shelves of products that were sold there.

Then, when we went upstairs, I met a spirit who lived there with his wife after it had been turned back into a house. His wife had died before he did, and he had lived there by himself for quite a long time. He took us to his bedroom, where he had been sick and died.

His wife in spirit stepped forward and showed me that she had been by his side the whole time until he died. Since then, they've been in spirit together, caring for their family. They travel the world but come back to the house to say hello to visitors—especially those who want to talk to spirit!

Travel Plans

That paranormal investigation was only one of many different spirit experiences I've had over the years in New Orleans. I wanted to share it with you because it illustrates how imprints and spirit communication can happen in the same place. Whenever you travel someplace that intrigues you, open all your inner senses to perceiving what is imprinted there. It will make history come alive for you! And so will your ancestors when they travel the world with you.

Think back to a time when you entered a town, a building, or even a new area or landscape, and for some reason you were immediately enthralled. Or maybe you felt a little disenchanted or uneasy. At the time you may have thought there's no reason to feel that way. But such responses indicate that you've just entered a place from your history.

An ancestral home can show up in any number of ways. It may have been a place where your biological ancestors lived, a location that figured significantly in your group or purpose history, or a home from one of your past lives. You can see them in your imaging or you can travel there by train!

A Train Ride in Korea

I have a friend, Lucinda Kim Wilson, who was born in Korea. She was adopted before she was two, and she lived with her adoptive American family—Mom, Dad, and three older brothers—on a farm not far from Gettysburg, Pennsylvania.

She decided, in her forties, to go back to the land where she was born. She hired an interpreter and guide who had given herself the name Grace to use with her American travelers. Grace and Lucinda traveled by train to Gyeongju, the ancient capital and home of the old royal families. Lucinda's adoption papers were written in Chinese, so she didn't know where she had been born. But as the train started moving through the mountains, streams, and valleys of Gyeongju, she began feeling the sense of strength and calm she had always known living in the mountains and hills of Pennsylvania.

Suddenly she felt that her ancestors were welcoming her home. Then, on that train ride, Grace looked at the adoption papers. She told Lucinda she had been born there in Gyeongju. Lucinda's family ancestors were welcoming her! Ever since that trip, Lucinda feels all of her ancestors—American and Korean—around her, sharing their love, guidance, and support.

If you are adopted like Lucinda, you don't have to take a train to make your discoveries. You can give this little processes a try. And if you weren't adopted, you can use this process to take yourself to your ancestral lands.

. . . .

The Lands of Your Ancestors

Take a deep breath, and close your eyes. Say to yourself, I call my ancestors forward. *Immediately, you sense them and see them all around you.*

They want to take you to the place of your beginnings. Now say to yourself, I go to the land where I was born. *Or you can say,* I go to the land where my ancestors were born. *And with a touch of a loving hand, you immediately find yourself there.*

Look around you. Notice the terrain, the climate, the plant life, and the animals—everything. Take a few moments to sense it all.

Now see if there are any homes or buildings nearby. Let yourself go up to one and enter. Where are you? What do you see and feel? Notice everything around you, especially anything that grabs your attention.

After a few minutes, finish that up. Start to bring yourself back. And with a loving thank you to your ancestors, open your eyes, and take some notes about your experience.

You can actually do this as a mini-process in moments anytime and anywhere. Whenever you want to take a little vacation to the lands of your forerunners, just sit back and call your ancestors forward. Then say the focusing command, *I see the land of my ancestors,* and they will take you there in your imaging for a little visit.

Feeling Manly

Sometimes you can meet your ancestors in places they've never even been before. That happened to me in Australia. Over the years, I've been very fortunate to teach in Sydney many times over. During my early years there, I would usually stay in Manly. What a most wonderful place it is! It had great restaurants, fun shopping, and original Victorian architecture—and it also had my grandmother. Or, I should say, my grandmother went with me there.

Now, lots of ancestors travel to distant locations with you. So I wasn't surprised to have my father's mother with me. I was just a little surprised that she was with me every step of the way—from the ferry returning from Circular Quay, to shopping along the Corso, to walking along the beach with its stunning Norfolk pines.

We had great fun that first day. I even found—and of course bought—an antique pin that was very similar to one that she had had. As I was walking back from the beach that evening, I asked her why she seemed to like the place so much. She immediately stopped and pointed up. There, about 50 feet before me, was a sharply angled, triangular-shaped building—rather like a miniature three-story version of the Flatiron in New York City. The sign on the building said *New Brighton Hotel.*

I understood immediately. My grandmother had lived and worked in Brighton, England, before she immigrated to the States. She told me that Manly was very much like Brighton. I later found out that Manly was developed for that very purpose.

Henry Gilbert Smith, an Englishman, wanted to re-create his beloved Brighton over 10,000 miles away. The New Brighton Hotel and the other Victorian buildings—and even many of the Norfolk pines—go back to the 1850s and Henry Smith's early work there. His efforts must have been successful since he was able to capture the heart of an original 1920s beauty from Brighton!

Spiritual Travel Guides

As you investigate ancestral lands, you'll find that some of the locations that you visit may not be homes at all. There are times when you're working with group or purpose ancestors that you'll discover places of specific endeavors, such as schools, monasteries, historical sites, or whole towns.

For instance, if you have a focus on architecture, one of your forerunners could bring you to Christopher Wren's St. Paul's Cathedral. If you're an avid golfer, you may find yourself with a forerunner at St. Andrews. If you have a passion for Native American tradition, your ancestral guide may take you to the lands of the Lakota tribes near the Black Hills of South Dakota. And if you have a growing interest in healing or spirit communication, your purpose ancestors may bring you to Lily Dale, New York.

Now, it's possible—even likely—that you could have had one or more past lives engaged in these endeavors in these places. Maybe you were one of the workers on the great dome of St. Paul's in the 17th century. Or you played on the links at St. Andrews. Or you lived and hunted in the Rockies with your Lakota people. You could have been a healer or medium in Lily Dale—or maybe you just studied there. But even if you didn't have any past-life exposure to these places, your ancestors have seen the light of your interest shining forth from you now, and they want to take you there.

So, since this is a book about spirit communication, let's take a quick look at Lily Dale, a sleepy little town in western New York State. It started out as a summer camp in the 1800s, but Lily Dale is now the largest and oldest Spiritualist community and center in the world.

For over 150 years, there has been a summer program of daily mediumship demonstrations, healing services, and classes in spirit communication, healing, reincarnation, meditation, and so many other areas of spiritual development. There are also a number of registered mediums there, some of whom I've mentioned in this book.

Because you're developing your spirit communication skills, those ancestral teachers who had lived or lectured in Lily Dale over the last century and a half may reach out to you.

Your ancestral connection is all a matter of energy. Whether your interests lie spirit communication, Indigenous cultures, golfing, or architecture, your energy goes forth and acts like a beacon, calling the ancestors of purpose and groups to work with you. So, if you do feel an ancestral touch that brings you to Lily Dale, open yourself to that discovery. And if you ever travel to Lily Dale, open all your senses to experience the imprints you find there. After 150 years, there's a powerful history of spirit that you can feel!

Your Dream Journal—a Ticket to Discovery

It's so important to use your journal to record your dreams. Your ancestors come to you so often when you sleep, and they help you in so many ways. So practice building the habit of writing down your dreams—even when you might think that you didn't dream at all. If you just start writing something, even before you sit up, some little ideas and feelings will pop up for you. Doing this regularly will help you train yourself to recall your dreams.

When you do start remembering your dreams, you don't have to write down every little particular of the narrative. Just take a few notes that will help you recall the story, what you experienced, and how you felt.

If you keep your journal next to your bed, you can jot down the things that come to you in the night. Sometimes they won't be dreams. Sometimes they may only be thoughts, words, or just random feelings.

Dreams can divulge so much for you—your hopes and wishes, your deepest feelings, your fears, things hidden in your unconscious that need to come into your awareness, your past-life histories, and so much more. Yet there are two things that happen at night that can end up feeling like dreams but are very spiritual and metaphysical in nature. One occurs when spirit visits you in your sleep, and the other happens through astral projection, when your spirit travels out of your body during states of deep sleep.

Often these two can be combined when spirit visits and then goes traveling with you. But because you are in a deep-sleep state—both during astral projection and during many spirit visits—you are not usually conscious of what's happening while they occur. Therefore, they are often recalled as a dreamlike experience.

That's why dream journaling can be so helpful. Even little pieces can be telling. For instance, you could wake up and remember only bits of a dream—like your grandmother and Big Ben, and nothing more. This could indicate that your grandmother may have come to you and traveled with you to London.

You can also find out a lot about your past lives in your dreams. Places that recur frequently in your dreams are very likely past-life locations. You may not recognize the city, country, or even people you see. But be sure to take notes about them in your dream journal, because, clearly, they want to be known to you.

Mrs. Butler's Dream Home

There are lots of occasions of people seeing astral travels and past-life homes in their dreams. It brings to mind a delightful—and true—story related by Augustus J. C. Hare in his memoirs. It was the late 1800s, and he tells of the Butlers, a lovely couple who lived in Ireland. One morning at breakfast, Mrs. Butler shared her experiences with her husband and her houseguests (of which she frequently had many).

She told them that she had spent many pleasurable hours during her dreams exploring an enchanting, comfortable house. She described it in detail. Though it wasn't too big, it had a lovely garden, conservatory, and so much more! Each day, when she came to breakfast, she told everyone that she had seen "her house" again in her dreams. She had gone about the bedroom and the terrace, and sat peacefully in the library. She exclaimed to everyone that it was the most perfect house.

Her frequent visits to "her house" continued in her dreams for so long that the family and her guests would ask if she'd been to her house on the previous night. She didn't visit it every night, but when she did, she was always excited to describe it in detail to everybody.

But over time her life got busy, and the dreams no longer happened. Or at least she was no longer remembering them. After some years, Mr. and Mrs. Butler tired of their home in Ireland, which was troubled by the danger of political disturbance. They had always wanted to move to England. Their children were grown, and they had enough money to do it; so they made their plans. They moved to London and hired agents in different towns to find houses in the country about 40 miles away.

They looked at many different houses that were not satisfying. Then, finally, one of their agents took them to Hampshire. As they drove up the drive to the house, Mrs. Butler declared that this was her house! When they went inside, she knew every hall, every room, and every passageway. She knew how to get to the library, the drawing room, the kitchen, the garden, and everywhere! It was—quite literally—her dream house.

She was delighted in the extreme, and they bought the house immediately (though they wondered why the price was so cheap). They labored over all the details of their house purchase. Then, when everything was completed, they decided to go to the seller's agent. They wanted to find out why it could be bought so cheaply—a question no one else would answer.

When they walked into his office, the agent gasped and was quite startled. He told them that the house had been for sale for quite a long time, but no one would buy it because some years ago the house got a widespread reputation for being haunted. And one night he, himself, had seen the ghost. He then told Mrs. Butler that she need not be concerned at all, because *she* was the spirit he had seen!

What had happened all those years ago was astral projection. Her spirit had gone out astral traveling and looking for their new home—even though they didn't know they were moving yet. Astral projection occurs quite regularly to everyone. The fact that she had visited that house so many times, over such a long period, is a strong indication that she was probably visiting a home from a past life.

I believe that Mrs. Butler didn't randomly stumble upon her dream house. Instead, she was visiting a place where she had a wonderful history. It's likely that one of her ancestors from that past life helped her find it. It may have been an ancestor she didn't remember in her dream. But spirit does love to travel with us!

We don't know if Mrs. Butler kept a journal, though it was very likely for the time. She did have a chance to tell her guests every detail every morning for a long time. But if you don't have a houseful of guests to hear the stories of your dreams at breakfast, you can write your experiences in your dream journal. Who knows? Your dreams may just take you to a place from your past and your future!

Mrs. Butler's story is also a marvelous example of how visual you can be in your dreams. Whether you are visual or conceptual, you may perceive a dream vision in great detail like Mrs. Butler had. Even when you experience it as partial or fleeting, the details are still there for you. This is also true with images in spirit communication. When you perceive an image from spirit, imagine it as you would in your dreams. That can be helpful—especially if you don't tend to be clairvoyant. Sometimes, when you put yourself in a dreamy mental state, it loosens you up, freeing the image to build upon itself and expand with greater details a little bit at a time. The dreamy mind process can take you to a lot of ancestral locales, too. Let's find out.

Livin' the Dream!

I always like to keep my eyes open for new ways to connect with my ancestors and get their messages, and sometimes inspiration comes in unexpected ways. Now let's go back to Ireland and another party there. Only this time, the topics of conversation were séances and seeing spirit!

It was a little over a hundred years ago, and there was great company in attendance—both in number and celebrity. The great poet and Spiritualist William Butler Yeats and his wife were there, as well as Oliver St. John Gogarty—poet, writer, satirist, and critic.

There were so many people at this country house party that several had gone to bed, a few were in the library, and two different séances were happening in separate rooms, with a bridge game in another. (Wow! Don't you wish we lived at that time? Wait a minute—we probably did! Only some of us were probably the maids who cleaned up afterward.)

Clearly there were a lot of fun and interesting things going on at that party. But of all the fascinating people there that night, it was Gogarty who had a life-altering breakthrough. (And it's Gogarty who makes it a teachable moment for us.)

Gogarty was over the moon! He was so excited because he had finally *felt, heard,* and *seen* a spirit for himself! At long last he didn't just have to believe it because he heard about it from a friend. He got to experience spirit firsthand.

"I believe in ghosts," he said. "That is, I know that there are times . . . when those who are sufficiently impressionable may perceive a dream projected as if to the dreamy mind: a waking dream."

I share this story with you because it is Gogarty who sheds some wonderful light on the perception of spirit. Gogarty wasn't dreaming when he had felt, heard, and seen spirit. He had simply made himself more impressionable by opening his dreamy mind.

What a perfect description! A dream (an imaging) is projected (sent by spirit) to the dreamy, imaginative mind. It's more than just a daydream. It's *a waking dream* because your experience is like a dream—somewhat hazy, misty, and a little indefinite, yet you are alert to every part of it. So give yourself over to every dreamlike expression that your ancestors send you. It may feel like a vague sensation coming out of the mist, but your *impressionable mind* will know it all.

Mrs. Butler found her favorite house in her dreams, but now in this process you'll be using the dreamy mind to see some ancestral locales. But you can also use this process anytime for any purpose. Simply change some of the command phrases to fit the discoveries you're seeking to make.

....

Traveling through the Dreamy Mind

Close your eyes, and relax. Say to yourself, I open my dreamy mind. *And you do—to all the ancestors around you.*

Now your spirit ancestors want to send to your dreamy mind a vision of an ancestral home or land. With a few deep breaths, say to yourself, I see the lands of my past. *Immediately, you start to have a waking dream of the place where they send you.*

It really does feel almost as if you were in a dream or in a sleepy state ready to nod off. It might be a little bit cloudy, yet there it is—one of your ancestral homes, towns, or lands. Whatever you get, it fills your mind, softly and easily.

Be in this place completely. It might seem a little blurry—just like a dream. But let the dream unfold now. Don't just watch it; be in it. And notice how you feel, too.

This dreamy experience seems to flow and open up with ease. You could be witnessing a great landscape. Or you could be stepping into an ancient building. There could be one house, and then it could change to another. Don't analyze or think about anything. Just feel everything you get in your dreamy mind.

Notice everything. What do you see or sense? Who is there? What's happening? Simply walk through this dream and notice it all.

After a few moments, ask spirit for one last thing. Declare to yourself, I open my dreamy mind. *And notice any last image, word, or symbol you get. When it's over, say thank you to these ancestors. Bring yourself back, and take some notes in your journal.*

. . . .

I love doing this little process. Though it works very easily with place experience, it's fantastic for any purpose—and for no purpose at all. That's really the way I do it most often. While I'm just sitting at my desk working, I close my eyes and say, *I open my dreamy mind.* Immediately, spirit is there and showing me something. I rarely have a very long experience. Sometimes I get a single image. Sometimes I just perceive the beginning of a dreamy scene.

When you do it, you may find that the opening scene of the *dream* can identify who is projecting the dream to you. When I find myself on a shore looking at a wooden sailboat on a calm, sunny day, I know that it's my husband—who built wooden sailboats— giving me the dreamy scene.

When you open your dreamy mind, you can get images about your work projects with your group or purpose ancestors. You can also get lovely, misty messages about relationships, your landcestral legacies, or your past lives.

So be sure to try it every way and any way. When you do this as a longer process, always put yourself in the dream and trust everything you get. When you do it as a quick command throughout your day, what you perceive may be short or in little hazy bits and pieces. I actually love getting things that way through my day. It's a moment of inspiration that can unfold for me. Sometimes, when I need some insight about a very specific task, I hold that thought for a moment. Then I close my eyes and say, *I open my dreamy mind.* And spirit's response—though it may be allegorical—is immediate. It's actually one of my favorite things to do with spirit—opening my dreamy mind!

An Ancient Ancestral Town on
the Euphrates River

For more than 20 years, Joan Kellogg, a Jungian specialist, investigated the implications of colors, shapes, and symbols from different cultures and societies around the world. Out of this investigation, Kellogg developed a psychological tool called the Mandala Assessment Research Instrument, or MARI. This system employs the universal applications of colors, shapes, and symbols to help you discover more about yourself, about the potential that lies within you, and about the opportunities that you can embrace.

After Kellogg's death, Michelle Takei, Ph.D., continued the work—further expanding and refining the MARI system. (You can find out more at MARICreativeResources.com.) Their collaborative effort has made this unique inner-discovery tool available to people through certified practitioners all over the world. But this global connection actually started thousands of years ago.

Many years after Kellogg had developed MARI, she discovered that there was once a city named Mari on the Euphrates River in ancient Mesopotamia. Sometime between 3000 and 2000 B.C.E., the Mesopotamians of Mari had made brightly colored mandalas themselves. Amid the vivid colors on these intricately designed circles of baked clay, a large star was placed at the center. These were called star murals, and they were found throughout the Royal Palace of Mari.

Now, you may think that the similarities between the mandalas used in MARI and the city of Mari with its mandala-like star murals might have been coincidence. And if so, it certainly was a remarkable one. But the events we call coincidences or synchronicity can often mask something so much more. The connection between present-day MARI and the ancient city of Mari very likely indicates a past-life legacy.

A Legacy from a Distant Shore

Though karmic legacies can include past-life patterns and karmic lessons, there are many legacies that spring forward from past lives that can be very beneficial and creative.

Kellogg's work with symbols and their meanings to develop her new psychological system, as well as naming that system MARI, are exceptional indicators of a karmic legacy at work. Even beyond her furtherance of the symbol system, it was a legacy for Takei, too. She had known that in a previous life she had worked in a temple with other women. And it is likely that she and Kellogg worked together in Mari in the palace temple near the statue of the goddess of flowing water.

The scribes in Mari were both male and female, a gender balance that was unusual in the ancient world. The writing and teaching that Kellogg and Takei have both done in this life are emblematic of their work as scribes in the Royal Palace of Mari. If you'd like to discover the towns and locations of your past-life legacies, go back to Chapter 16 and the process Talents from the Past. As you do the process again, ask your past-life guides to show you where you were when you developed those skills. And if you find yourself hopping from one place to another, remember—you were probably talented in a number of different past lives!

Well, we've looked at a lot of places from the past. Now it's time to look to the future!

CHAPTER 22

YOUR FUTURE
WITH YOUR
FORERUNNERS

Often do the spirits
Of great events stride on before the events,
And in today already walks tomorrow.

— FRIEDRICH SCHILLER

Tomorrow is born out of today. It comes from today's thoughts, today's decisions, and today's actions. And since tomorrow already walks in today, tomorrow can be seen today—especially with the help of those spirits who stride on before us.

In this chapter, you'll be looking at your future with your ancestors—in a lot of different ways and for many different reasons. Since you've already experienced a variety of different symbols, those will be a good start in getting messages about the future.

Using Time Commands with Intuitive Symbols

As you've seen, symbols can be used to give you insight about many specific areas of your life. Their imagery and action can reveal a story and exhibit myriad layers of information about relationships, work, home, and spiritual life. Seeing or sensing a symbol from spirit (as well as all the details that you notice about it) will indicate the situation as it is now.

After that, you can use a time command to place the symbol in the future. That will make the symbol change or grow or alter in some way, indicating the evolution of that situation over time.

The following mini-exercises will give you an idea, but you can also use any of the intuitive symbols that are shown on the lists in Chapters 19 or 20—or any other symbols you've seen in this book, or elsewhere.

Choose Your Time

Just think of a specific situation in your life about which you would like some guidance, and then ask spirit to share an appropriate symbol. Take a few minutes to sense everything about that symbol, and then direct yourself to see or sense that symbol as it would be in two months, then in four months, then even later.

Let yourself choose the time frame that would be most helpful to you. Whenever you change the time, the symbol or scene will be different in some way. Notice those differences and everything else you sense; they will tell you about the situation at that time.

In these next little exercises, some of the symbols will be familiar to you. Let the symbol change whenever the time element is changed. If anything occurs in the imaging that seems to be a challenge, know that you have the time to create your life in your way.

. . . .

Stairway of Tomorrow

Close your eyes, and take a deep breath. Say to yourself, I call the ancestors who stride on before me. *Immediately, you see and sense them all around you. As you do, take a moment to feel their loving embrace.*

Now think of your work, career, or any special project about which you'd like some insight. As soon as you decide, your ancestors show you the symbol of a staircase that represents your progress in this endeavor. Sense it and notice everything completely—the size, shape, structure, and colors, and how they feel to you. Do you see yourself on the stairs? Where? Take a few moments to experience it all.

After you finish that, say to yourself, I see this symbol in two months. *And instantly the staircase changes. Take a few moments to sense everything it shows you about this endeavor. Notice how it all feels to you. Do you see or sense yourself on the stairs? If so, where?*

After a few minutes, start to shift your focus. Say to yourself, I see this symbol in four months. *And the staircase changes in that moment. Take a minute to notice everything this staircase shows you. What's happening with this endeavor in four months? Notice every little thing—and where you might see yourself upon the staircase then. Be in the scene and perceive it all, including how you feel.*

Take a moment or two to wrap that up. Then start to bring yourself back. Say thank you to these loving ancestors, and take some notes when you're finished.

. . . .

. . . .

A Rose in Time

Take a deep breath, and close your eyes. Say to yourself, My ancestors who walk before me are here. *Instantly, you feel them around you, bringing their loving embrace.*

Think of a particular relationship in your life about which you'd like some insight. As soon as that relationship comes to mind, spirit shares a symbol of a rose to represent that relationship. Remember, if you get something else, let that happen, too.

Take a moment to notice the size, colors, texture, how much it has bloomed, and anything else that stands out for you. Also notice how it feels.

After a moment, say to yourself, I see this symbol in four months. *Immediately, it changes in some way. Whatever you see or sense, it reflects this relationship in four months' time. Take a few minutes to notice every little detail and how those details feel to you.*

When you're done with that, say to yourself, I sense this symbol in eight months. *Instantly, you see or sense a rose that represents this relationship at that time. Perhaps there are a number of roses or different flowers. Let whatever happens happen, and notice it all.*

Now take a deep breath, and say thank you to your ancestors. After you bring yourself back, take some notes in your journal.

· ·

· ·

Set the Timer on the Stove

Spirit is now going to give you the symbol of a stove top with pots and pans on it to reflect all the projects you have. They could be tasks for work, or things to do for your family or home. Or they could be creative projects. Don't think about your list of things to do. Just hold the idea "my projects" in your mind.

Now close your eyes, and with a deep breath say to yourself, My ancestors who walk before me are here. *And they are! Feel their loving presence for a moment.*

Then they show you the symbol of a stove top, and on the burners are the pots and pans that reflect the different projects you have. Some may be large, some small. Some are on the back burners, and some are on the front. Some may be simmering, and some may be at a rolling boil. There may be some pots sitting on the counter waiting to go on the stove.

Take a look at everything. Don't think about anything. Just see, sense, and feel it all. Also notice if there are any projects you want to be cooking that don't seem to be there at all.

After a few minutes, say to yourself, I see this symbol in two months. Immediately, you notice that the stovetop has changed. Perhaps there are more pots and pans—or less. Perhaps the stove has more burners— or less. Notice everything. What's cooking? What needs your attention? How are things different? How do your projects feel in two months?

Now thank your ancestors as you bring yourself back. Get ready to take some notes in your journal—and especially note what you might want to do to address the projects that are at hand.

Of course, you can ask to see any time element, with any symbol, but I don't like to go too far into the future because there are so many variables. Free will is a capricious thing, and when you bring together the free will of many people, future events can be very tentative, indeed. In truth, the real reason I look forward a few months is so I can get a lead on how the trends are unfolding. If you do that, it will help you shift directions, take stronger action, and develop alternatives where new opportunities may exist.

Also, as you work with symbols and use time commands to "move" them forward in time, begin to notice where *your* time lines are. Be aware of how you sense time. Notice how you perceive two months away, four months away, six months away, one year away, and even two years away. You'll find a reliable trend in sensing time that can inform all your perceptions. Once you know how to tell time intuitively, your ancestors in spirit will show it to you—even before you ask about it!

In the Service of Spirit

Spirit works in service all the time. They bring their assistance to you when you ask—and even when you're not aware of it at all. But there are a lot of times when spirit would like your help, too.

In his book *Mosses from an Old Manse*, Nathaniel Hawthorne, the author of many books including *The Scarlet Letter* and *The*

House of the Seven Gables, describes the years he spent in Concord, Massachusetts, during the 1840s. He had rented a home that recently—and frequently—had been a parsonage. He often sensed the spirit of the vicar who lived there before him. Hawthorne could hear the swish of a minister's robes and the rustling of the papers of his sermons.

Of course there were many other spirits, too. Hawthorne shared tales of other spectral happenings there. He believed spirits were so typical in houses of antiquity in New England that they were hardly worth mentioning.

Nathaniel loved what he found stored in the garret. There were hundreds of old books, manuscripts, and folios written by generations of literary and religious authors going back to the Puritan days. Hawthorne found a chest of the vicar's manuscripts in the garret. He felt that perhaps the parson would have liked him to edit and publish a selection of some of his pieces. Alas, Hawthorne was very busy with his own writing at that time. And that's a good thing—because Hawthorne wrote the *Old Manse* during his years there, sharing many wonderful stories—including those about the vicar.

Though Hawthorne couldn't bring his editorial assistance to the parson, his outreach and service to spirit was considerable. Wherever he went, he would seek others of like mind for discussions about the afterlife and to have little meetings with spirit. During the time they spent in Italy, his family would have séances with the Brownings—Elizabeth Barrett and Robert—every Friday evening. Like Yeats, Conan Doyle, Poe, Dickinson, and so many others of their time, their interest in the ancestral world wasn't just a curiosity. It was an active pursuit—a pursuit that spirit appreciated then and still appreciates today.

Perhaps that may be one of the most important ways that we all can serve our ancestors. They make so much of an effort to lift our awareness of them. What a service it is for us to reach back to them—and help others reach out to them, too. And that brings us to another opportunity for service to spirit, if you'd like to do it—connecting to the ancestral realms for your friends, family, and other people.

Double-Duty Service: Introducing Others to Their Ancestors

Once you start connecting with your own ancestors, don't be surprised if others ask you to do it for them. Many people are interested in the world beyond. And some of your friends and family will probably want you to connect with their ancestors, too. So if you're interested, let yourself give it a little try.

Start with someone you know well. See it as an opportunity to practice the different sensings you've been learning. Sometimes, you may already know the ancestors of your friends. So it may cause you to have some doubt—thinking that you're only remembering your best friend's grandmother instead of perceiving her. But you certainly already know your own relatives in spirit, and you can still talk with them. So of course you can talk with others you know in spirit, too. All you have to do is trust!

There's another challenge that can happen when you connect with spirit for a friend—or for anybody. You could get a name or other perception that your friend doesn't recognize. When that happens, don't back down. Trust everything absolutely. Just tell your friend to look into it and write it down. It might apply to something yet to come.

I recall a student of mine named Elsa whose best friend, Carol, asked her to reach out to her ancestors. Elsa kept getting the name George, but she thought she was wrong because Carol couldn't recognize it. Later, Carol found out from her grandmother that George was her grandmother's uncle, and he had never moved from England to the U.S. with the rest of the family.

Carol was very excited to start meeting George and her other British ancestors. She and Elsa were planning a trip to England, and Elsa helped Carol learn the techniques to connect with spirit for herself. She met George and her other ancestors in England, and they were there for her when she got home, too.

It's really very simple. Once you open the door to spirit, it becomes a part of your energy—like every other part of your history and your interests. Your friends and family will naturally want you to make a connection and do a reading for them. Then you really would be doing double-duty service. You'll be serving both your friends as well as their ancestors by building a bridge that brings them together.

So, if you feel called to link with their ancestors for your friends, give it a try. It's a service to everyone involved—including you, because it gives you the chance to practice your techniques and also to make more friends in the ancestral world.

Don't be concerned if your friends want to ask questions about future trends and opportunities. You've had lots of experience with sensing symbols—from yes and no to extended and gestalt symbols. The ancestral world will never let you down. Just ask for an image. Remind your friend that the symbol you get is not about the outcome but about the process. Then share the image with your friend and ask how it might apply. However it happens for you, let yourself be lifted in the light and the joy of knowing spirit.

Guidelines for Getting Ancestral Insight for Others

Here are some guidelines to help you make the ancestral connection for other people.

- Remember that there is always free will—for you, for spirit, for the people with whom you share ancestral messages. Tell your friends that—regardless of a symbol or its interpretation—there are always options and freedom of choice.

- If there's something you don't understand, ask questions and seek clarity from spirit. Notice the little things. Even if you don't know what they mean, tell your friends about them.

- Walk your talk. The greatest message there can be is that of the indwelling spirit. To make it real for others, make it real in your life and in your relationships. Let the *presence* of your spirit be the message of your life.

- Spirit doesn't want to tell you or your friends what to do. They just want you to know about all your options. Share all of the interpretations of a symbol, but most of all, share the image. Then let your friends draw their own conclusions.

- Support your friends in making their own decisions. Even after learning about their options from their many different ancestors, *it is their own spirit—the one who has gone before eternally—who should guide them most.*

- Help your friends learn to speak with their own ancestors. Share ideas and techniques that have worked for you. Consider having a meditation group where you can all work together with the ancestral realms.

- Remind your friends that the world of spirit is one of Divine light and love. During any kind of ancestral connection or any kind of reading—whether getting one or giving one—if any information surfaces that is tainted with jealousy, anger, hate, judgment, or fear, it is not the voice of spirit. (The following guidelines for recognizing good information will help you when giving guidance to your family and friends—and when you're getting a reading from a professional medium, too.)

Standards for Good Information

It's important, when sharing spirit's messages with others, to maintain the same standards in *giving* information that you would in *receiving* information. The standards for good information are:

- **Is the information verifiable?** Spirit can share the strongest tendencies, trends, and options that are likely to come. But, since they are in the future, it may not be possible to verify them—yet. So if some things can't be verified, tell your friends to stay open to those coming possibilities. Time will tell the story.

- **Does the information help you to experience and express love?** Even challenges and difficult situations can lead to growth and greater compassion for the self and others. Let every insight lift the love in your life and that of your friends.

- **Does the information give hopeful and helpful alternatives?** There is never only one way, and spirit can see many avenues at once. So share those options—in choices and actions—that bring greater power, light, well-being, and grace to you and your friends. To engage your Higher Self is to live your best life.

Become a World Server

Of course, you don't have to do readings for other people to be of service to others or to spirit. The ways that you could serve are boundless. So many people and places in the world are beset with troubles. From the droughts of Africa to the battles of Eastern Europe, from the conflicts caused by bigotry and hate to the starving families who live in poverty—the planet itself and humanity are greatly in need of healing.

It can be quite overwhelming when you think about it all. Though there are always things you—and everyone—can do. Whether the ways to help are little or big you can get some guidance on how to serve.

. . . .

Ready to Serve

Take a deep breath, and close your eyes. Say to yourself, The ancestors who serve with me are here. *And suddenly you notice them around you—those who serve, from your family, your landcestors, your groups and purpose ancestors are with you.*

They, who have served in so many places, ways, and times, are there to support you. And your Higher Self, your first and foremost forerunner, directs you now to look down at your hands. Notice that you are holding a serving tray. And upon that tray is a symbol that gives you an idea of how you can serve.

What is that symbol? Notice its size and colors and how you feel about it. Does it tell you what your service can be? What do you feel you want to do?

Now take one last look at your serving tray, and see that spirit has put a little something else on it. What is it? Notice everything about it. How does it feel? After a moment with this second symbol, say thank you to your wonderful ancestors. Bring yourself back, and take some notes in your journal.

. . . .

I have led this process in a few of my classes, and one time a student had a puppy on her tray. She started to volunteer a little time each week at her local Animal Protective League. Another student saw her checkbook on her tray, and she started to donate to some charities that she liked. Yet, even though everyone may not be able to donate or volunteer, everyone absolutely can be a World Server!

You can spend some time in your meditations sending light and love to those in need—and to the planet itself. You can hold a special healing purpose during your prayers, and you can send powerful words and energy to any people or place. If you belong to a meditation group, your group could do these, too—independently and together. With any of these steps—even when done in small ways—you become a world server.

We are now entering the Age of Aquarius, the age of the collective. Those of us who find ourselves on a path of spiritual discovery can do these little things every day. Of course, each individual will bring assistance. But when many thousands, or hundreds of thousands, of people take action with the purpose of global healing, the energy will increase exponentially, and a much more significant impact can be made.

Know that all those in the ancestral realms work with you on this, too. And they thank you. The grateful hearts of a thousand generations send their love to you.

Live More Closely with Your Ancestors

Whether they are forerunners whom you never knew, or family ancestors who had troubles in life, or Ascended Masters of purpose who wish to work with you, you have a chance to create a greater relationship with them now. Together you can build a future of deeper love, wisdom, opportunity, joy, and discovery every day. You have opened the door, and you have the chance to keep it open.

Eleanor Roosevelt and her father, Elliott, adored each other. They were both open-minded, curious, and very intelligent. He, more than any other person in her life, gave her the support to believe in herself and go for her dreams.

Sadly, as much as Elliott was an extraordinary thinker, he was also an extraordinary drinker. His drinking became more and more severe every year. Eleanor was quite young when he was sent off to Abingdon, Virginia, to a place where he could be safe, but where he continued to drink exceedingly. He went home for short visits occasionally, but his communication with Eleanor took place mostly through an abundance of letters.

Then, in 1894, Elliott died. He had made an attempt at suicide by jumping out a window, but it was unsuccessful. He died of a seizure a few days later. Eleanor was 10, and in that year, she lost her mother and one of her brothers, too. Eleanor felt abandoned, and she was sent to live with relatives.

For Eleanor, after Elliott passed into spirit, things changed significantly in their relationship but not in the way you think! She said that after her father's death, she *lived more closely with him* than when he was alive. She had opened a new door.

We can live *more closely* with any of our ancestors in spirit, too! Now, they are in spirit, like Elliott. They are not away in some distant place; they are not held back. They are here, and they *are free*—more than ever before! And now we have learned to sense them, to talk with them. We are free to live *more closely* with them!

So let's do this process now and open up to the ancestors that you knew, landcestors from bygone days, group and purpose forerunners, and your higher guides and Ascended Masters. This is an easy process to help you get in the habit of being with your ancestors and living more closely with them. So let your ancestors join you and just be there with you. Have a little conversation and feel them close by.

Remember to give yourself over to everything you sense. You are a Divine soul, and so is every ancestor who approaches. Feel how good it feels to let them draw near.

. . . .

Living More Closely

Take a deep breath, and close your eyes. With each breath, you relax more deeply and feel the radiant light and love within you. Now say to yourself, My ancestors draw close. *Immediately, you start to sense and see some around you.*

First, notice one or two ancestors from your life who may have been distant to you—either emotionally or actually. You notice as they draw near that they are shining brightly. They are free from any of their old heaviness or difficulties that had troubled them. And they're now in their Divine light.

Take a moment simply to be with them. They may give you a word, a symbol, a feeling, or just a hug. However it happens, let yourself draw near to them, and feel the closeness you can have with each other.

After a few minutes, let them take a little step back. Say again, My ancestors draw close. *And this time a few of your group and purpose ancestors, and your higher guides come near. Feel their embrace, and let them share some images and ideas about your group histories and your present purposes. Be easy together, just as if you were having coffee and a little chat. Let yourself get any scene, symbol, or word. Have an effortless conversation with them as you spend these moments together.*

After a few moments, start to wrap that up. Just think of the mutually supportive and happy relationships you can have simply by sitting down and having an easy conversation with any of your ancestors regularly throughout your week.

> *Say thank you, and make a commitment to live more closely with your ancestors. Even as you walk through your day, stop for a moment and say to yourself,* I live more closely with my ancestors every day. *Then simply notice who's with you in that moment, and share an embrace.*

. . . .

Legacy, Service, and Purpose— a Future of Meaning

Though they are not quite the same, legacy, service, and purpose are connected. They are the fuel that moves you toward your future.

You have received a great legacy in every endeavor, from thousands of ancestors, across the centuries. But your legacy is not just something you receive from your different ancestors. It's something you give. Once you've received your legacy of talents, energy, and gifts, think about how you can give. What does your legacy ask you to do? What purpose fills your heart? When you can answer that— when you can do that, you will leave your legacy to the world.

Sometimes you might want a little help in answering those important questions. How can you give? How do you live your purpose? What's the next step? Your ancestors, of course, can help you discover those answers.

This brings to mind a documentary I watched on PBS called *My Grandparents' War.* The actress Helena Bonham Carter was investigating the great contributions her grandparents on both sides had made during World War II. It was clear, though they were two generations past, Helena felt these ancestors were never really gone. She said, "Whenever you're lonely . . . or you don't really know what you're doing, or have a loss of a sense of direction, you just have to listen very hard—because they [your ancestors] are just but a degree away, and they can show you the next step." I love this quote for a number of reasons. Bonham Carter indicates that your ancestors can help give you direction when you've lost your way. But she says first to listen for them whenever you're lonely. Your ancestors love you. So let yourself just be with them, and feel their embrace. You are never alone!

I also love that she says they *are just but a degree away.* That was powerful for me because in astrology that describes a conjunction, an aspect of planets that are so close to each other in a chart that they influence each other. One degree is a very close conjunction, indeed, and it shows a condition of unity. You and your ancestors are close at every level. You are unified in your purpose; you work together in unison, sometimes operating simultaneously. Just a degree away is one of the purest aspects in astrology, and it's the purest truth with your ancestors.

Finally, I really appreciate that Bonham Carter tells you that your ancestors will show you the next step. Working with spirit is a collaborative effort, and they sometimes can see things when your own vision is cloudy. So here's a chance for you to get some clarity now. Your ancestors are here to show you the next step!

. . . .

The Next Step

Close your eyes, and with a deep breath, say to yourself, My ancestors are here. *And there they are— just but a degree away! They are all around you—to help, to love, to show you the way.*

Now, you may feel a little uncertain about something you're doing, or about a direction you want to take. Your ancestors are here for you.

Say to yourself, My ancestors show me the next step. *And there it is—an image, a symbol, a word— something that reflects your next step. It is your next action. It may be a very little step, but notice what it is that you feel like doing.*

See yourself taking this step—doing this little thing that helps you move forward. And ask your ancestors any question you may have. When you do, you immediately get a response from them. It's easy to see and sense. Simply notice what happens.

Take a moment to finish that up, and say thank you to these loving folk. Bring yourself back and take a few notes about the next step that you perceived from your ancestral guides.

. . . .

Your ancestors are always there to show you the next step, and the next. They move with you in your life, your purpose, and your joy. You are never alone.

**Together with your ancestors,
you recover your past and uncover your future.
With your ancestors, you share your legacies
with the world and touch tomorrow today.**

Appendix of Symbols

There are some symbols with almost universal meanings. But no symbol can ever mean the same thing for everybody all the time. Symbols are more personal than that. When you speak with your ancestors, each image that you get must be considered within the context of your experience of it. What are the other images around it? What is the general framework of the whole scene? How does it feel to you? Are there any other smaller components that give more meaning to the message? How does that symbol apply to the situation in question or to your life in general? If you're not sure about the meaning of any symbols, write about them in your journal, so you can watch for a pattern.

The following is an alphabetical list of many symbols that your ancestors may use in their communications with you. Of course, there are many others, too. Keep notes of all the symbols you get in your journal.

babies: Pregnancy or babies coming, new life, rebirth, enthusiasm; birth of new projects, careers, or purposes.

battles (war): Personal conflicts in life, at work, or in relationships; internal emotional or psychological battles; possible past-life experiences.

birds

 in flight: Flight, travel by flight, freedom.

 nesting: Creating a family or home. (Broken wings, caged birds, etc., indicate dispiritedness, heaviness, being trapped, and feeling like there are no choices.)

blanket: How well you are embraced, covered, warmed, comforted, and assured (sometimes for insurance policies and business contracts, but often for relationships). The condition of the blanket indicates the condition of the relationship (e.g., brightly colored, torn, faded, worn, rough, soft, too small).

boats: Movement, travel (sometimes on or near water), past-life experiences on or near water. Occasionally, a move. Sometimes a relationship riding on the seas of emotion (the condition of the boat and specific details of the image will indicate the nature of the relationship).

books: Literary discovery, study; many books: possible college; few books: single classes or independent study; blank books: writing or sometimes journaling.

bookstores: Places where you can learn about yourself. In the image, always notice what part of the bookstore you visit and the books that stand out most for you.

bridges: A time of transition, a possible move.

candles (*see* **light beacons**)

cars and vehicles (*see* **roads**)

chains (also shackles): Restrictions, constraints, immobility (sometimes self-imposed), feeling trapped, a heavy workload. Can indicate karmic duty or lessons.

chess board in play: Strategic planning; interactions of many people drawn together, whether personally or at work; dealing with others' political maneuvering.

clouds

 dark and foreboding: Challenges or difficulties, stormy emotional experience.

 fluffy and light: Happiness, natural easiness, breezy situations and personalities.

 foggy (especially when seen around a person's head): Confusion, inability to see things clearly, lack of direction (often self-created).

coins (*see* **money**)

concrete (also stone or steel): An unchanging condition; a fixed and inflexible person, unlikely to be influenced.

cornucopias (*see* **fall fruits**)

crowns: Lofty or noble ideas, self-respect, satisfaction, a promotion at work, increased reputation and recognition, past-life experience as royalty or nobility.

 tarnishing of or loss of: Loss of one's self-respect, demotion or loss of a position at work, loss of an uplifting opportunity.

desk: Work, work projects, organization, representations of daily activities. (The condition of the desk and what's on it indicates the condition of the work and projects.)

directions

left/west: Past, past-life patterns, history, completion, yin, past relationships and endeavors.

up/north: Higher mind, spirit, rest, receptivity, yin, upliftment, elevated thought.

right/east: Future, goals and direction, creation, expression, yang, forward movement.

down/south: Emotions, physical world, activity, energy, yang, strategic power, foundational strength.

doors (*see* **keys**)

fall fruits (such as grapes, pumpkins): Harvest, abundance, sometimes the completion of a task, the autumn, cycles coming to fruition, reward, the return of your efforts.

farms: Opportunity to grow, expand, plant, connections to nature. (The season and other details seen in the image will indicate more about the message.)

fire or flames: The most yang of the four elements, symbolizing energy, heat, power, passion, activity, force, light, illumination, awareness.

flight: Freedom, ascension, mobility, travel, astral projection, gathering momentum, speed, the experience of spirit.

flowers: Different talents and opportunities blooming (dependent upon the color and kind of flower), joy, celebration; budding and flowering of creative projects, work endeavors, and relationships. Can also signify the time of year based on the season of the flower seen. (*also see* garden; lotus flower; roses)

fog (*see* **clouds, fog**)

games (*see* **chess board in play; monopoly board; poker game; sporting activities**)

garden: Life and growth of the seeds you plant. The condition and size of the garden will inform the message (e.g., barren, choked with weeds, full of new growth, patchy, bountiful).

grains (*see* **wheat**)

guns (*see* **weapons**)

halos: The auric body, enlightened mind, higher spiritual thoughts, the ascended masters, the angelic realms, accelerating one's frequency.

higher ground (hill tops, mountain peaks, etc.): Advantage, gain, opportunity, strength, ascension through hard work, success, movement to a higher perspective and/or position, effort to raise oneself.

hills (*see* **higher ground**)

horses: Strength, freedom, power.

ice skating rink or pond: Feeling strength under you, confidence or vulnerability (feeling like you're on thin ice).

> **with skaters:** Indicates interactions in relationships in your personal life or at work.

keys (also doors): Opportunities, openings to new situations and potentials. Number of keys or doors can indicate number of choices or diversification. Doors wide-open show ease of opportunity.

lanterns (*see* **light beacons**)

libraries (*see* **universities**)

light beacons (lanterns, candles, lighthouses, etc.) Illumination, direction, clarity, understanding, clearing the darkness, enlightenment.

lighthouse (*see* **light beacons**)

lightning: Power, suddenness, illumination, dramatic and sweeping change, discovery and use of the heavenly gifts.

lotus: Representing the spiritual evolution of the individual from the muddy waters of darkness or desire, the symbol of beauty, eternal wisdom, understanding, unfoldment.

monopoly board: Business, investments, real estate, finance. (Activity and things on the board will indicate the nature of the message.)

money (coins or paper): Endeavor, industry, career, finances, investments, security, income, job.

moon: Emotions, changes, intuition, cycles, receptivity, reflection, psychic energy, mothering, nurturing, meditation, calm, clairvoyance.

> **increscent moon (when points of the crescent are pointing left):** Time of increase in action and opportunity.

> **decrescent moon (when points of the crescent are pointing right):** Time of decrease and slowing down somewhat; let the natural cycles take their course.

mountain peaks (*see* **higher ground**)

oak trees and leaves: Sacred to the druids, symbol of strength, power, stability, sturdiness, authority. (*also see* trees)

path: One's direction in life, a course of action, one's sense of purpose and karmic directives. (The condition of the path, as well as the people and things on it, will inform the message.)

    path, obstructed: Inability to take action, loss of purpose or direction, hesitance to confront karmic lessons, outer or inner barriers impede your moving forward.

pens (*see* **writing utensils**)

pockets

    closed: Fearful about money, unsure about how to spend, stingy.

    deep: Bountiful opportunity, broad resources, accumulation, generosity, desire to share.

    empty: Financial loss, lack, sparsity, concerns.

    hands thrust deeply into: Determination not to take action, desire not to participate in a certain situation, withholding personal or creative expression, sometimes withholding financial support.

poker game (cards, chips, table): Getting in the game, taking a risk or a gamble. (In the image, the people playing, the size of the bet, the cards showing—if they can be seen—will all inform more of the message.)

pyramid: A place of mystical power, journeys of mystical and spiritual discovery, past lives in Egypt.

rabbits: Fertility, gentleness, family, serenity.

roads and vehicles: One's authority within one's career, projects, and life in general; the choices and actions regarding those. (The specifics within the image will indicate the nature of those choices, e.g., going backward; driving or being driven, traveling on a bumpy road; uphill or downhill.)

roller coaster: Many ups and downs in life, emotional inconsistencies. (Can indicate excitement, turbulence, or both—depending on the emotions you feel with it.)

roses

    pink: Caring, nurturing, gentleness, sometimes reciprocity in a relationship.

    red: Love, devotion, passion.

white: Purity, spirit, upliftment.

yellow: Creativity, thoughtfulness, joy.

scales of justice

evenly balanced: Keeping the different parts of your life in balance, justice, fairness, equitability (whether in relationships, agreements, or legal dealings).

hidden: Unknown and possibly deceitful legal dealings.

tipped: Injustice, victimization, imbalance (either legally, financially, or personally).

toppled: Severe and illegal misdeeds.

serving tray: Opportunities for service, past-life experiences in service.

snail: Slow action, deliberate movement, progress through small steps.

sporting activities: Developing personal strength, discipline, focus, joyful exertion. (Some sporting activities may indicate past-life experiences.)

competitive sports: Competition, group endeavors, team leadership, group strategies.

stairway: Ascent of career, individual projects, reputation, or talent. (The condition of the stairway or location of the person on it—if one is on it—will further inform the message.)

steel (*see* **concrete**)

stone (*see* **concrete**)

stove top: Projects that are active or inactive in your life now. (Which burners are filled, what's waiting on the side, what's on the back or front burners, and other details give you more insight.)

suit of clothing: Comfort with work activity, position at work, nature of a single project. (The fit, condition, and feel of the suit will inform the message about the project or the position and your comfort with it.)

suitcase: Travel; small case: short travel; large case: distant travel.

sun: The source of life, vitality, energy, authority, creativity, power, creation, work, career, how you shine.

swords (*see* **weapons**)

travel (*see* **boats; bridges; directions; roads and vehicles; trains and tracks; water, traveling upon or over**)

thrones: An individual's position or reputation lifting higher (often relating to career), a position of nobility or royalty in a past life.

trains and train tracks: Being on track with a career, a single project, or one's life in general.

treasure chest: A valuable opportunity at hand, richness, wishes, a dream come true.

tree: The condition of the tree will give the details of the situation (e.g., fruit-bearing, withered, strong, with fall leaves, spring-blossoming). (*also see* oak tree, tree of life)

tree of life: The Qabbalistic tree of life can symbolize life, family, relationships, work, or individual projects.

triangle: Most commonly, the human trinity of mind, body, and spirit. Mystical meanings include the hermetic symbol of fire, the theosophical symbol of the first three rays of power/will, love/wisdom, and intellect. For the Freemasons, the triangle reflected many things including the "shining delta" (the greek letter Δ) and the cosmic triad where the base line meant duration and the sides, light and darkness (Jules Boucher *The Masonic Symbols* pp. 86–94).

trumpets: Messages, awakening, a call to important information, angelic inspirations, spirit communication, spiritualism, an icon of the Archangel Gabriel.

two (of anything): Duality, alternatives, choices; a second, sometimes unknown, opportunity; occasionally, ambivalence or indecision.

universities (or libraries): Places of higher learning, opportunities for greater study; possible careers of teaching, lecturing, writing; possible past-life histories at such locations or in such activities.

vehicles (*see*** cars and roads)**

water

    calm: The most yin of the four elements, symbolizing receptivity, quiescence, meditation, peacefulness, ease; sometimes, a loving situation or relationship.

    pouring of: Sharing and expressing of one's emotions and/ or spirit; the integration of the emotional and the spiritual (when pouring into other water).

    traveling upon or over: A trip across or near water, initiating a monumental undertaking (as in crossing a large body of water), broadening one's horizons and moving into new territory, moving one's home.

turbulent: Upheaval in one's own emotional body, difficult emotions or conflict in a situation or relationship.

war (*see* **battles, weapons**)

weapons (swords, guns, etc.): Potential battles at work or in personal relationships, possible past-life experiences in the military or in countries torn by war. (*also see* battles)

weather systems: Emotions; situations or relationships that are cloudy or clear, stormy or sunny, turbulent or peaceful (*also see* clouds, lightning).

wheat (and other grains): Fertility, richness, abundance, fullness, harvest.

wings: Flight, exhilaration, freedom, ascension.

broken: Debilitation, feeling earthbound, restricted, captive.

writing utensils (pens, typewriters, etc.): Writing, publishing, editing; authorship of any sort; past-life experiences in any of these endeavors.

Acknowledgments

It would be impossible to thank all of those who have lent their support to me in creating this book, because this book is an aggregate of learnings that have evolved over time. There have been so many people through my life who have shared their path of spiritual discovery. Little flashes of light that have helped me become who I am today have also made this book what it is today. There is no measure of gratitude that could effectively thank the extraordinary people who have brought me so much understanding, help, insight, peace, and perspective in so many ways.

This would, of course, include my wonderful families of life and love, and all my colleagues and friends. You have my deepest appreciation forever. I stand in the inspiration, strength, and happiness of your close and ever-present embrace.

And to everyone who brings so much light and joy to me wherever I teach around the world—my students, clients, group members, and audiences everywhere—you have all meant so much to me. You will never know how deeply you have touched my life. You are all my teachers, and I thank you!

ABOUT THE AUTHOR

Sharon Anne Klingler is a best-selling author, a medium, and an inspiring speaker. *The Huffington Post* declared her book *Power Words*, "My kind of book, as it gives us all extraordinary superpower tools to help uncover our highest selves." And author Denise Linn described it as "perhaps the most profound, transformative book ever written on the influence that . . . language has on our lives." Sharon's other works include the best-selling *The Akashic Tarot; Intuition & Beyond; Secrets of Success* with her sister, *New York Times* best-selling author Sandra Anne Taylor; *Life with Spirit;* and many other titles.

One of the world's leading intuitives, Sharon has worked with television news anchors; film writers and producers; Emmy, Tony, Oscar, and Grammy winners; the FBI; members of Congress; and high-profile clients around the world. Sharon has lectured regularly on Ministerial faculties in the U.S. and Canada, at Georgetown University, St. James's Church London, and around the U.S., England, New Zealand, and Australia. She has been featured on BBC and ITV London; BBC Scotland; the Oprah Winfrey Network; CNN; the Discovery Channel; NBC, ABC, and CBS; and on major outlets across the globe. She has also been featured in *The London Daily Express, TV Guide, Nexus Magazine,* and in many other newspapers and magazines worldwide.

Sharon is a Registered Medium at the Lily Dale Assembly and an ordained Spiritualist minister. For more informaiton, go to www.SharonKlingler.com or www.StarbringerAssociates.com.

Hay House Titles of Related Interest

YOU CAN HEAL YOUR LIFE, the movie, starring Louise Hay & Friends
(available as an online streaming video)
www.hayhouse.com/louise-movie

THE SHIFT, the movie,
starring Dr. Wayne W. Dyer
(available as an online streaming video)
www.hayhouse.com/the-shift-movie

The Akashic Records Made Easy: Unlock the Infinite Power, Wisdom and Energy of the Universe by Sandra Anne Taylor

Letters to a Starseed: Messages and Activations for Remembering Who You Are and Why You Came Here by Rebecca Campbell

Manifesting Your Magical Life: A Practical Guide to Everyday Magic with the Angels by Radleigh Valentine

Trust Your Vibes: Live an Extraordinary Life by Using Your Intuitive Intelligence by Sonia Choquette

You Are the Medicine: 13 Moons of Indigenous Wisdom, Ancestral Connection, and Animal Spirit Guidance by Asha Frost

All of the above are available at your local bookstore,
or may be ordered by contacting Hay House (see next page).

We hope you enjoyed this Hay House book. If you'd like to receive our online catalog featuring additional information on Hay House books and products, or if you'd like to find out more about the Hay Foundation, please contact:

Hay House, Inc., P.O. Box 5100, Carlsbad, CA 92018-5100
(760) 431-7695 or (800) 654-5126
(760) 431-6948 (fax) or (800) 650-5115 (fax)
www.hayhouse.com® • www.hayfoundation.org

———

Published in Australia by: Hay House Australia Pty. Ltd.,
18/36 Ralph St., Alexandria NSW 2015
Phone: 612-9669-4299 • *Fax:* 612-9669-4144
www.hayhouse.com.au

Published in the United Kingdom by: Hay House UK, Ltd.,
The Sixth Floor, Watson House, 54 Baker Street, London W1U 7BU
Phone: +44 (0)20 3927 7290 • *Fax:* +44 (0)20 3927 7291
www.hayhouse.co.uk

Published in India by: Hay House Publishers India,
Muskaan Complex, Plot No. 3, B-2, Vasant Kunj, New Delhi 110 070
Phone: 91-11-4176-1620 • *Fax:* 91-11-4176-1630
www.hayhouse.co.in

———

Access New Knowledge.
Anytime. Anywhere.

Learn and evolve at your own pace
with the world's leading experts.

www.hayhouseU.com

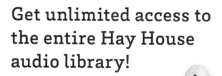